Insightful player

FOOTBALL PROS LEAD
A BOLD MOVEMENT OF HOPE

Including stories from Roger Staubach,

Jerricho Cotchery, Rashied Davis, Heath Evans,

Antonio Garay, Jarvis Green, Reggie Kelly,

Devin McCourty, Jason McCourty, Montell Owens,

Tony Richardson, Usama Young and many others

Chrissy Carew

Rick Horrow
The **Sports Professor**

An Imprint of Morgan James Publishing • NEW YORK

Insightful
player

ISBN: 978-1-61448-054-9 (Paperback)
978-1-61448-055-6 (eBook)
Library of Congress Control Number: 2011934384

Published by:

Rick Horrow
The Sports Professor

An Imprint of Morgan James Publishing
1225 Franklin Ave Ste 32
Garden City, NY 11530-1693
Toll Free 800-485-4943
www.MorganJamesPublishing.com

Cover/Interior Design by:
Rachel Lopez
rachel@r2cdesign.com

To my loving parents, the late Walter R. Carew Senior and Catherine Carew, for giving me a rich spiritual foundation that blessed me with an insatiable thirst to align my life with God's purpose. To my precious sister, Mary, who has always been my earth angel. And to my beautiful husband, Kip, who is my greatest gift from God.

TABLE OF CONTENTS

PRAISE FOR
INSIGHTFUL PLAYER

Insightful Player™ *shows us that good news in sports can be compelling, interesting and important. Chrissy Carew has gathered the stories of top athletes who live the right way, and we're fortunate to have them gathered all in one valuable piece of work. The players she writes about don't just mouth the old bromides; they live them. I know many of these players, and I know when Heath Evans formerly of the Saints says, "Live your values even when times are tough," it's true—because I know this is the way Evans has lived his life, in and out of athletics. This is a terrific addition to the bookshelves of people who live their lives right, or want to.* —**Peter King, Senior Writer, *Sports Illustrated***

The stories contained in Insightful Player™ *fill your heart with joy and put your mind to work. Revealing moments, life changing decisions and captivating athletes take the reader on a wonderful journey as they unveil their reshaped lives. The landscape of your life can't help but be inspired by these stories. They will give you hope and perhaps provide a new compass to follow in your journey.* —**Kevin Harlan, CBS Sports, TNT Sports**

Too much attention is paid to the misdeeds of athletes today when the REAL truth is that some of the most incredible stories are of those who are not just playing but are changing the world. Insightful Player™ *shines a long overdue light on those real winners in sports. Thanks from all of us who need inspiration!* —**Don Yaeger, *New York Times* Best-Selling Author (www.donyaeger.com)**

I love the NFL and Insightful Player™ *brings out the best in the league through these great stories about exceptional role models. For those who get down on how much they make,* Insightful Player™ *will show how much heart they have and the positive difference they are making in the world. Read this book and be inspired and share it with your kids.* **—Ken Blanchard, Co-Author of *New York Times* best-seller, *The One Minute Manager* with Spencer Johnson and Co-Author of *Everyone's a Coach* with Don Shula**

With Insightful Player™, *Chrissy Carew has assembled a dream team of NFL role-models who share their knowledge and inspiration with the rest of us. You don't need to be a sports fan to love this book—just a fan of life. It's a real gift.* **—Steve Farber, Author of *The Radical Leap Re-Energized, Greater Than Yourself***

These stories are a reminder that professional athletes are powerful role models, and the ones who embrace that responsibility and project the lessons they have learned to help others have an immense capacity to do good. We used to do an annual Good Guys issue in our magazine, and these are the types of players we would salute. Readers love getting the rare chance to hear positive off-field stories and Insightful Player™ *does a great job of identifying the athletes who make a difference.* **—Dan Graf, Former Managing Editor, *Sporting News Magazine***

Insightful Player™ *offers their stories to inspire others. Chrissy Carew is inspired to see that the good gets as much publicity if not more than the bad. One might think the current bad-boy image NFL players are developing might cause many to flock to her cause.* **—Tom King, Sports Writer, *Nashua Telegraph***

Insightful Player™ *is a crucial tool that refutes the stereotype of men, and athletes, as less than good and heroic role models. These are in fact men who have done amazing things with their lives, often against all odds. We can all take heart in their stories and the wisdom our young people can glean from reading them.* **—Tom Matlack, Founder of The Good Men Project**

With Insightful Player™, *Chrissy Carew has unlocked a treasure trove full of inspirational stories of NFL players and managed to bring them to the forefront of a media landscape that is all too often inundated with negative and exploitative headlines about professional athletes. What makes this initiative even more special is Chrissy's passion and success in using these powerful stories and lessons to bring guidance to today's youth in character building, as well as give them a roadmap on how to best achieve future success.* **—Matthew Allinson, Esq., Founder & CEO of Access Athletes, LLC (www.AccessAthletes.com)**

In a word, INSPIRING. With Insightful Player™, *Chrissy Carew shares remarkable and inspirational stories we never knew of football players and legends who we know very well. This is a must read for everyone from the young student-athlete to the senior executive. It will not only inspire us all, it will create a significant change in our mindset and approach to life.* **—Mark Beal, Managing Partner, Taylor**

Chrissy Carew's Insightful Player™—*serves the world that has been starving for the positively brilliant human and inspired side of professional sports' super heroes. Carew's book scores the super-bowl-win-of-the-human-spirit through the play book of sharing untold inspirational stories of players who have transformed overwhelming and life-threatening odds into triumphant lives of meaning, purpose and mastery. She shares how each featured player is now giving back by sharing their valor, experience, wisdom and time to be America's (indeed the world's) positive role model. If you are a fan of LIFE—buy this stand-up-and-cheer book for yourself and everyone you care about.* **—Peter J. Reding, Founder of The Foundation for Inspired Learning, Author of *Positively Brilliant Self-Mastery, Reclaim Your Authentic Self Now***

Insightful Player™ *is filled with amazing stories that are dramatic testimonials of how people can overcome great obstacles with hard work and a belief in oneself. All the Insightful Players are magnificent roles models who share intimate details of their lives to offer inspiration and hope. A must read for anyone struggling to survive life's challenges or those in search of a deeper meaning of life. Parents, teachers and coaches should get these stories in the hands of kids right away.* **—Joan Herrmann, Publisher and Radio Producer & Host of "Change Your Attitude, Change Your Life," New York's AM970, The Apple**

Chrissy Carew's ingenuity behind Insightful Player™ *is a testament to her passion to incite positive change among today's youth. She has created a timeless fusion between sports and admirers by sharing remarkable life experiences of NFL players—allowing them to learn the true meaning of integrity, faith, patience, hard work, and generosity.* Insightful Player™ *is a must read for all who want to be inspired to be the best they can be, inside and out.* **—Monica Davis, Founder of *Exceptional People Magazine***

Insightful Player™ *offers us all hope. It provides an opportunity to gain insights and wisdom from elite NFL players who have overcome amazing odds to stay in the game. It is an examination into the depths of their inner lives, to understand how each persevered to become a great player, while building character along the way. Chrissy takes us on a journey through childhood and into maturity, revealing secrets and insights about these athletes that are seldom told. She has combed through numerous players in the NFL, and uncovered the amazing stories of players who share their painful admissions, their motivations, and their passions, for the game we ALL love so much. These are life stories, told through sports, and a great read for everyone. I am in grateful for the opportunity to partner with* Insightful Player™ *and for Chrissy Carew's commitment in supporting the Kids in the Game™ with goals of increasing access and improving the quality of programs that inspire and engage young athletes.* —**John Ballantine, Founder of Trusted Sports Foundation (www.trustedsports.org)**

In Insightful Player™, *Chrissy has shown us the richness of very talented individuals that have a lot more to offer than is shown in their work in sports. The gold nuggets of brilliance, compassion, contribution, heart and values that these stories illustrate are deeply inspirational. These players have lived through and overcome many of the challenges that young people face. They are models of possibilities, endurance and spirit. And spirit not only in the sense we think of in sports, but in the deep connection with the soul and God force that inspires us all. This work is a gift. Share it with everyone that is important to you… and with anyone that could use a boost.* —**Pamela Richarde, Executive Coach, Past President, International Coach Federation**

Chrissy Carew captured moving stories about athletes who are great human beings and magnificent role models. The world needs more of this, especially for our kids and especially now. Insightful Player™ *is a wonderful book filled with inspiration and practical tools that will empower kids and adults to create a great life. Read this book now, get inspired and spread the word.* —**Patrick Williams, Ed.D., Master Certified Coach, Co-Author, *Becoming a Professional Life Coach***

Insightful Player™ *is on stride to change the world for the better. Kids, teachers, parents and coaches need this book and they need it now. These inspiring stories should be integrated into our school's curriculum. What a great idea to showcase these incredible role models on the worldwide stage. Insightful Player™ is just in time because we are desperate for role models. Coach Carew's unwavering dedication and riveting passion to make this world a better place is remarkable. This book will evoke the very best in everyone who reads it. Buy this book for everyone you care about.* —**Sandy Vilas, Master Certified Coach, CEO, CoachInc.com**

The power and vision of the "Insightful Player" Coach Chrissy Carew's book and teaching message can truly change the world for millions of kids and adults everywhere. With her own exceptional grace, talent and insight "Coach Carew" has interviewed football's most inspiring, exceptional players and together they show us all greater options and a new pathway for negotiating life, living on purpose and setting and winning worthy goals.

Read this book, share it with family and friends and enjoy the power and effects of true inspiration! **—Judy Krings, Ph.D., Professional Certified Coach, Author, Photo Adventures in Cuba: Unlock Your Power of Positivity**

Carew's extraordinary Insightful Player opens locker room doors to reveal dramatic, passionate real-deal character strengths stories. Admired and respected NFL players generate tell-it-like-it-is, power-packed lasting learning legacies. Positivity perspectives with gridiron grit and gratitude for challenging life lessons learned. Big men do cry, and these men aren't afraid for you to see it. Princes of pathos and pluck, they model how to survive and thrive, no matter how many times they (or you!) drop the ball. A motivational masterpiece, this books scores. What a perfect gift! **—Dianne Legro, Certified Action Coach**

The Insightful Player model shows us that prominence and success come not from shallow conformity or adhering to a group of accepted, previously set out guidelines, but instead from always staying true to the deepest, most central parts of our own consciences, and from never, ever, giving up faith. **—David Dean, Founder and Executive Director of Unity Hoops Basketball (www.unityhoopsbasketball.org)**

FOREWORD

By James Brown, *network sportscaster, correspondent and three-time Emmy award winning studio host of "The NFL Today" on CBS and "Inside the NFL" on Showtime, Sports Illustrated's "Best Studio Host of the Decade", and author, Role of a Lifetime: Reflections of Faith, Family, and Significant Living.*

I n my many years as a host of CBS's "The NFL Today" and other sports shows, I've met thousands of professional athletes, a substantial number of whom have been football players. Many NFL players have inspired me with their insights, humility, sense of spirituality, and their altruism. Others were more focused on superficial pursuits.

I often ask the question—what's the difference between these two kinds of players? Why do some men in the NFL recognize their potential for not just playing a great game, or even winning a Super Bowl ring, but using their global platform to inspire their many fans, especially the youngest, on to personal greatness? Showing kids that hard work and constant practice can turn you into a fine linebacker is a good thing. Demonstrating that a strong set of ethics and values, along with character and a healthy dose of humility, will pave the way to a meaningful life is undeniably even more important.

Deep within the folds of the NFL, buried far below the player stats, Super Bowl appearances and razor endorsements, is a secret: the league is full of fantastic role models who have so much to teach kids, if fans only knew more about their stories. The aberrant behavior of a few players dominates the news, whereas those who do volunteer work, mentor children, bring visibility to charitable causes, and essentially help to make stronger communities, so often go unheralded.

Why doesn't the public hear more about these remarkable men? Why are we not looking to them as the fine role models they are for our children, for grownups struggling to find their place in a difficult world—and examples who can inspire all of us to even greater heights?

Chrissy Carew has hit upon a problem that adults everywhere sense: The world is in a spiritual crisis. But while many wring their hands, Chrissy found a way to approach a solution. As if she was designing an offense, she formed her Insightful Player™ team and is trailblazing a path to inspire others to be a part of the solution… primarily for the sake of our kids. The Insightful Player™ campaign and its bold movement of hope are helping to fill a huge void in our world—that of spreading positive news and values to our youth.

Insightful Player™ team members are current and former NFL players who are role models of integrity, personally committed to teaching today's youth through their own examples. They want to help young people believe in themselves, commit to the very best within, and relentlessly pursue their dreams.

The Insightful Player™ team members are men who used these same tools—self-motivation, passion and laser-focus—to pursue their dreams, which resulted in a career in the National Football League. They overcame great obstacles and hardships to become not just fine athletes, but also extraordinary individuals who serve as an inspiration to us all.

Each of the 32 football players on the Insightful Player™ team shares how he not only overcame adversity, but the guiding principles that enabled them to weather the storms and become stronger for it! They all developed the wisdom to know that trials and tribulations in one's life can serve to prepare them for bigger challenges.

These players are much more than athletes. They are remarkable human beings and magnificent role models. Their stories will give you an inside look at what each player is most passionate about, lessons learned from mistakes they made, and wisdom gained from obstacles they have overcome. Each account demonstrates the ways in which their commitment to their values and the insight they received from their experiences help shape them into the people they are.

These touching stories are meant to be shared with others. Read them with your kids, who will learn that no matter what their circumstances, they are not alone; others have fought the same battles and won. Share them with family and friends. Give them as gifts. Begin discussion groups. But most of all, share them with every young person you know! By exposing these inspirational stories that reflect the immense power of the human spirit to as many readers as possible, especially our youth, Chrissy Carew is giving all of us a means with which to evoke the very best within all of us to make this world a much better and more loving place.

James Brown
June 1, 2011

James Brown, known to NFL fans everywhere as J.B., is a three-time Emmy Award winner for Outstanding Studio Host as well as Sports Illustrated's "Best Studio Host of the Decade." He has also contributed to "60 Minutes."

After graduating from Harvard, where he received a degree in American Government and received All-Ivy League honors in his last three seasons on the basketball court, Brown was named one of the 100 most influential student athletes by the NCAA.

In September 2009, Brown released Role of a Lifetime: Reflections of Faith, Family, and Significant Living. In this acclaimed memoir, Brown relates how he came to the role in life he was meant to play, and teaches readers how to discover life's purpose for themselves.

He and his wife Dorothy reside in Maryland.

PREFACE

For as long as I can remember, my father has had a very big impact on me. To me and to many who knew him, my father was bigger than life. He was a high school English teacher and the head football and baseball coach. Between the two sports, football was his biggest love. It would have been impossible to grow up in my family and not love the game, like he did.

My family lived in Concord, Massachusetts, a historical and very small town. When I was a kid, Concord was my whole world and my father was my idol. I remember attending my very first high school football game when I was around five. My father was the head football coach and I was so excited to watch him coach. It was a very exciting day. Concord won the game in the last few seconds, and to my amazement, the players carried my father off the field. I was star-struck! I was in awe! At the time, it didn't make sense to me that he wasn't president of the United States.

In addition to being a very gifted athlete, my father was a man of integrity, a devout Catholic, a dedicated U.S. Army veteran and devoted family man. My parents had a beautiful 53-year marriage.

I grew up one of six kids with four super-jock brothers and one sister who was beautiful, very feminine and very sweet, just like my mother. I was an extreme tomboy and very competitive in sports. I was always pushing myself to beat out all the boys, and succeeded most of the time—they hated that.

One of my very first memories was when my father taught me to think *Yes I can,* when I was certain I *could not.* We were taking a walk around the neighborhood and I just could not keep up with him. Always the competitor and always pushing himself, my father was walking at a very, very fast clip. I couldn't have been any older than four or five. "Slow down," I pleaded, "I can't keep up with you!" I was huffing and puffing and running as fast as I could to keep up with him. He turned to me while actually stepping up his pace and said, "Yes you can!"

And so I did. That was one of many important lessons I learned from my father. In that moment, I developed a deep-rooted belief that I still hold onto today… nothing is impossible, absolutely nothing! I have been doubly blessed because my mother had many empowering lessons of her own.

My life took on a particular purpose that continues to define it today when, at the age of 23, I was watching the evening news when a report of a horrific car crash flashed onto the screen. The reporter gestured to the badly mangled car behind him, its body crushed like an accordion, and announced that although there were fatalities, he could not say the victims' names because their families hadn't yet been notified. I watched, incredulous. Suppose those same families who had not yet been notified—or who perhaps had just minutes ago heard about the deaths of their loved ones—were watching this same newscast?

It was a chilling thought to me, one that kept me from falling asleep that night. At 4 a.m., I got out of bed and called the station manager to ask how the network could have done something so unconscionable as to run that footage. The network representative at the other end of the phone told me he understood my perspective that the event represented someone's personal tragedy, but that this kind of footage is why people turn on the local news. Horror sells.

His answer touched off a surge of soul-searching for me. Could he be right? Was the media so insensitive to the families of those people killed in the accident simply because it's what people want to see when they turn on the news? Why couldn't the news feature more positive stories—stories that would inspire people and encourage them that the world is at times a good and uplifting place? Wouldn't that sell, too?

I undertook a personal campaign back then, asking everyone whose paths crossed mine whether they agreed that viewers wanted the media to cover horrible stories. I asked them whether they would watch news broadcasts that featured upbeat accounts rather than horrific events. Most of them admitted they didn't know whether those stories would capture their attention in the same way. I felt crushed at this evidence of society's overall sense of inhumanity. Believing there was nothing I could do to change such a prevalent sentiment, I tried to bury my discouragement. But in doing so, I only created a restlessness that took many years to resolve.

About six years ago, I reached a point in my career where I felt compelled to pause and reassess. At that time, I had worked successfully as a personal coach for ten years. I loved the work. But it still seemed something was missing. In my job, I could reach out and help one person at a time, but given what a vast place the world is and how damaging it can be to so many people, that didn't seem sufficient. I wanted to touch the masses.

And yet the negative voice inside my head kept pushing me back, telling me I was an idiot for thinking I could have any kind of lasting effect on society. My heart, speaking with the pure and simple voice of my soul, said I needed to do it; my head, resounding with self-inflicted negativity, said there was no way I was capable or even worthy of making such an effort.

All my life, I've been an NFL fan, just as my father and brothers were. NFL games were a constant backdrop throughout my upbringing. And I couldn't stop thinking about the idea of using NFL players as role models. By that point, I was firmly convinced that children growing up today have a daunting lack of role models to look to as good examples of how to live a life governed by ethics and values. The forces kids have to struggle against today scare the wits out of me. I believe that we adults need to embrace and comfort our children. We need to coach them and let them see for themselves how important they are. We need to help them find their passion. We need to create opportunities for our children to recognize, experience, respect and honor their talents. We need to instill in our kids the importance of serving others. Only if we do this can we expect them to follow a compelling vision of what's possible. To fail in this mission, as I see it, could mean the end of humankind.

So I pushed past my fears and self-doubts. I traveled to NFL corporate headquarters to share my vision with officials there.

And the NFL leaders listened. They heard my vision and they agreed in its merit. They suggested I approach each of the NFL's 32 teams individually and talk to their player development directors. Easy, I thought. With a 2" binder in which I'd created a sheet for each of the 32 teams, I began calling. All I had to do was communicate my excitement about using my personal coaching skills to evoke from the players their ability to be magnificent role models on and off the field.

And then I ran into a roadblock. It wasn't that the player development directors hated my idea; it was just that they didn't buy into it with the passion I believed was needed in order for me to see it through. Though some were marginally interested in what I was proposing, as a body they were committed to sticking with the NFL's internal programs, which emphasize personal growth and development against a backdrop of professional football. They didn't think their players had time alongside that program to help me with what I wanted to do.

I felt as if my glorious vision had been quashed. It was discouraging. I questioned God, asking Him why He would give me this inspiration and then deny me the ability to see it through. I indulged in some self-pity and a sense of defeat.

But then I stopped feeling sorry for myself and took a more positive tack. Brainstorming with a colleague, I decided to itemize the points I'd distilled thus far from the project, and together we came up with this list:

1. There are a lot of magnificent role models in the NFL, but few know about their successes.

2. The NFL may have the biggest stage in the world.

3. If these wonderful players were on that stage, they could make this world a better place, especially for kids.

4. This is the work that has been waiting for me all along: to get these wonderful players on their worldwide stage. Focus on being the catalyst and the coaching will follow.

Taking a step back from that initial wave of idealistic passion, reorganizing my thoughts and marshalling my energy gave the project the boost it needed to get finally under way. This is how Insightful Player™ was born. I reached out to all the teams again, but this time I went through their public relations departments. I proposed writing feature stories about their high-integrity players for the sole purpose of lifting the spirit of their worldwide audience, especially kids. A lot of teams were excited by this vision. A few insisted I have placement for these stories before they would allow me access to their players. And a few teams never responded to my attempts at contact.

At this point, I've profiled 32 players as part of the Insightful Player™ campaign. Each of those men is a remarkable human being and a magnificent role model. Many of them believe firmly in the value of telling their stories, especially those that involve overcoming hardships, in hopes of helping today's youth see their way to a clearer path to success. Several of them are now using the same skills of perseverance and commitment that they developed as football players to commit their lives to a greater purpose by starting a charitable foundation or community outreach program.

Already, I myself have learned so much from these players. The farther I get into the Insightful Player™ campaign, the more I believe that my original vision has tremendous potential: to get this message to a much wider audience. It is that belief that carries me onward as I promote what I now believe to be my life's work. I still think back to that night 34 years ago when I watched the evening news and thought that surely we can prosper as a society from being exposed to more positive messages, and this is how I hope to make that happen.

Chrissy Carew
April 2011

INTRODUCTION

Insightful Player™ is a bold movement of hope committed to lifting the spirit of the human race, starting with our kids. Grandiose, I know. I passionately believe we all need to do our part to help make our world a better place. This is the route I chose and it has been even more fulfilling than I ever imagined.

If we want the human race to continue, we need to start with kids. We need to help shape our kids into high integrity leaders now. We all need to really step it up and give our youth an abundance of love and support. The Insightful Players are all wholeheartedly committed to doing whatever it takes to reach further and deeper to inspire kids and adults too. This is why Insightful Player™ was born.

You will find a special collection of inspiring stories about some first-rate human beings. I look at these 32 wonderful players as the standard-bearers in the sports industry for integrity, courage, kindness, generosity, humility, perseverance, gumption and grace. I have tremendous respect and affection for each one of them.

Each Insightful Player™ team member cares about you and wants you to believe in yourself, commit to the very best within yourself, and relentlessly pursue your most far-reaching dreams. The Insightful Player™ stories will give you an inside look at what each player is most passionate about, lessons learned from mistakes they made, and wisdom gained from obstacles they have overcome. Each story demonstrates the ways in which their values and their experiences help shape them into the extraordinary people they are.

The players share their stories and show you how they not only overcame adversity but learned to respect it and became grateful for how it helped them leap forward. They became fascinated with adversity because they discovered it gave them:

- profound inner strength and resilience

- immense courage

- genuine self-respect

- deep-rooted confidence

- tremendous hope and a positive attitude

- honest-to-goodness humility

- an insatiable desire to be all they can be

- a generous spirit fueled by serving others

They all developed the wisdom to realize that enhancing their relationship with adversity produced astounding results. These players are much more than athletes. They are remarkable human beings and magnificent role models.

Each Insightful Player™ story shows solid evidence of the immense power of the human spirit. We all need to be reminded of this, especially kids and especially now!

Here are some of the highlights:

- A player's father was murdered when he was eight; he had to duck for cover in his home because bullets were flying on his street...

- Another player saw shootings at the age of five and often saw dead bodies on his street...

- A Hall of Fame player never had a winter coat, winter boots or food to eat...

- A player was put in classes for the mentally disabled, his father "beat the tar" out of him, his coaches said he had no talent...

- Another player lost his arm, part of his shoulder and several ribs to cancer. He was told he would never be able to participate in sports. Two months after his surgery he was a strong competitor on a racquetball team. He is now an avid runner and golfer

Young people today look up to professional athletes for their power, grace and ability on the field or the court. Sometimes sports figures are also heralded by young people for their high-flying lifestyles, with material assets and high-profile friends. This project elicits a different side of those who excel at professional sports: the inner drive, faith and motivation that made them the success stories they are. It is my hope that by drawing out these very important stories, I can inspire today's youth to follow this example: not an example of expensive possessions and celebrity lifestyle, but an example of embodying your values and deepest moral beliefs in everything you do as you strive to reach your own successes.

CHAPTER 1

HALL OF FAMER AND
FORMER DALLAS COWBOYS QUARTERBACK

ROGER STAUBACH

In a League of His Own As the Ultimate Role Model and the First Insightful Player™ Team Member

Roger Staubach is the epitome of an Insightful Player™ team member because he has always shaped his life around his values. He is devoted to his Christian faith, his wife of more than 45 years, his five grown children, and his many grandchildren. He has an unwavering commitment to his friends, employees, and co-workers. All these combine to make him the perfect man with which to begin the Insightful Player™ stories.

Roger has led a soul-centered life both on and off the field. He is recognized for giving birth to the "Hail Mary Pass" in a 1975 wild card playoff game against the highly favored Vikings. With only seconds left on the clock, and just before throwing the game-winning, 50-yard touchdown, he said a Hail Mary.

His faith was nurtured in his modest home in Cincinnati. Growing up as an only child with his parents and grandmother, Roger feels tremendous gratitude for having the loving and hard-working role models that his parents were. One of his primary guiding principles is to put yourself in other people's shoes. "Respect and think of someone other than yourself," Roger often says. Many, many times there is a bigger agenda than our own, he believes, which we have to adhere to and support—that's what teamwork is all about.

As an example, Roger didn't play quarterback until his senior year in high school. At first, he didn't want to play quarterback and asked his coach why he was being asked to make the switch from defensive back and receiver to quarterback. "Coach McCarthy wanted me to play quarterback because the guys listened to me. This was a big change in my life." he learned. Being open to a bigger perspective that involved his teammates brought forth his NFL Hall of Fame talent as a quarterback, and his leadership skills skyrocketed.

Roger looked at football as a way to go to college. He recognized that his parents worked very hard and gave him a very good life, but thought it would have been tough on them to send him to college. He also knew they would have found a way to make it happen. His determination to maximize his athletic talent so he could go to college without strapping his parents financially paid off. He was offered a football scholarship from a number of schools and he chose the Naval Academy.

Roger made a commitment to serve his country for four years upon graduation. When he was drafted by the NFL, his commitment to his country didn't waiver. To a 23-year-old, four years seemed like an eternity and he didn't think he would have the opportunity to play professional football. During his four years of military service, Roger kept in great shape and was able to play some football on base. In his fourth year in the service, he was able to participate in a Cowboys training camp during a two-week leave. It was during that training camp that he knew playing in the NFL was still a possibility for him.

Roger was a tremendous leader who persistently worked to show his teammates he could be a winning quarterback. He had tremendous respect and confidence in his teammates and he made it abundantly clear he couldn't do it without them. Similarly, he would later in his life show tremendous respect for all employees at The Staubach Company, an innovative real estate firm. Roger brought in the very best broker talent by offering them a significant stake in the company and giving them the autonomy to excel. He sold the company to Jones Lang LaSalle Americas, Inc., in 2008 for $613 million. At the time of the sale, 88% of the stock was owned by employees. Roger has steadfast respect for his talented and high-integrity employees. He was passionate about rewarding them because they played a major role in building his company.

Another of Roger's guiding principles can best be summed up in his words as "Don't be afraid to fail; do the best you can and appreciate the chance." When Roger was playing in a tournament basketball game as a high school sophomore, he missed a free throw in the final seconds and cost his team the game. He was devastated, blew in and out of the locker room without taking a shower, and went home. He sat up in his room in pain and feeling very discouraged.

According to Roger, "This was a defining moment in my life. When you fail, you want to give up. That day, I made a very important decision not to give up even though I was in a lot of pain. I wanted to be in that position again with the game on the line because I knew I could have success.

"Since then, I have not been afraid to fail. I have been in many situations when things didn't work out, and many situations that worked out very well. I got into many critical situations as an athlete and in business. I knew I would do the best I could based on what I believed and what got me into those circumstances. I began to really appreciate the fact that I had a chance, and with my genuine respect for having a chance, I no longer was afraid to fail."

Spiritual faith has always given a sense of permanence to his life. Roger was heartbroken watching his mother suffer and eventually die from cancer. He couldn't understand why God would allow that to happen to someone who was always doing good for others. He didn't have an answer for this, so he let his faith kick in. He wholeheartedly believes there is a permanence to our lives. His permanence is his Christian faith, but he has a great deal of respect for other faiths and beliefs. "If we live our lives properly here, that permanence, which is our salvation, is going to be there for us," he said.

Roger believes we can find the best within ourselves and the best in others when things are tough. "Adversity reveals genius and prosperity conceals it," he commented. "You must persevere. Don't give up on your faith, or sacrifice your values. You've got to fight through adversity and you are going to be better for it."

His faith has helped him in tough times. It helps him tap into a healthy sense of perspective by reminding him to look at the bigger picture. When facing a challenge, he developed a habit of asking himself, "How does this relate to the bigger picture and to the commitments I've made spiritually?

"Start each day asking yourself, 'What impact am I going to have on someone in a positive way?'" If you use this approach, you are going to enjoy your life while helping others enjoy theirs. What a good feeling you get when you help someone else! You do have to keep a balance, however, so you don't give what you don't have to give, or become tempted to sacrifice your values."

Roger knows firsthand how important a role a mentor can play. "Some mentors play a direct role and others influence us indirectly. An example of indirect mentors can be the people you spend your time with. It is important to be with people who are doing the right thing. We need to be responsible to ourselves, no matter who we are or what circumstance we are in.

"Sometimes kids don't have parents who are good role models. Don't use that as an excuse. Find mentors to support you. When you look at anyone's success, you'll also find someone who has influenced them in a positive way.

"I was very fortunate to have loving parents who were exceptional role models. I also had mentors outside my family, people who also believed in me and recognized my leadership qualities. They all had one thing in common, and that was how they set the example of living an integrity-based life.

"My personal mentors were: Jim McCarthy, my high school football coach; the late Tom Landry, my Dallas Cowboys coach; and Henry S. Miller, owner of the Henry S. Miller real estate firm in Texas. Henry started off as my off-season employer who helped me build a very successful real estate career after I retired from the NFL."

Establishing one's priorities effectively is of paramount importance, Roger believes. He was a husband and father first, and a quarterback second. He was confident in his ability to play football but never knew if he would get hurt. If he did get hurt, he was prepared to do something else to provide for his family. He worked in real estate off season because he wanted to get business experience and felt fully responsible for making sure he would always be able to provide for his family. He worked extremely hard as a husband and a dad, as well as a quarterback, and teammate.

Roger Staubach is an accomplished, wise, and kindhearted man who is committed to being the best man he can possibly be, while inspiring and nurturing those same qualities in those around him. He shows perseverance, is highly respectful of others and is steadfast in having his values, including his deep Christian faith, navigate his life.

He has always been competitive with himself rather than being competitive with others. He passionately believes that if we all respected someone other than ourselves, it would be a sure way to rid the world of the terrible disease of discrimination.

Roger is the kind of role model we need in our world: the kind we want our young people to emulate and aspire to, and one we can use as a guide for our own lives. Because the sole purpose of the Insightful Player™ series is to lift your spirits to awe-inspiring heights, I cannot think of an NFL player better suited to open the book.

INSTANT REPLAY OF ROGER'S *GUIDING PRINCIPLES*

1. Put yourself in other people's shoes. Respect and think of someone other than yourself.

2. Many, many times there is a bigger agenda than our own, which we have to adhere to and support—that's what teamwork is all about.

3. Don't be afraid to fail. Do the very best you can and have a genuine appreciation for having a chance.

4. Ground your life with spiritual faith.

5. Adversity reveals genius and prosperity conceals it. You must persevere, don't give up on your faith or sacrifice your values.

6. Start each day asking yourself what impact am I going to have on someone in a positive way. You will really enjoy your life while helping others enjoy theirs.

7. Having a mentor is a must have for everybody. Find mentors to support you and spend time with people who are doing the right thing.

8. Make sure you have your priorities right. Put your family first and take responsibility for the people who are counting on you.

These principles continue to guide Roger's life every day. Today, he is Executive Chairman—Americas, an active member on the board of Jones Lang LaSalle Americas, Inc., and is working to show the company is the best real estate company in the world.

CHAPTER 2

THE NEW ENGLAND PATRIOTS'

KYLE ARRINGTON

Profoundly Grateful That Sports Taught Him to Control His Temper and God Taught Him to Trust His Plan

Kyle Arrington's mother feared that her son's explosive temper would be his undoing. Whether he was playing kickball with his friends or video games with his three siblings, anything less than a perfect performance drove him into a tailspin. Fighting with classmates got him twice suspended from middle school, and his parents were afraid he would one day lash out too far—and end up in jail.

A burgeoning interest in sports turned out to be the antidote to his bad temper, though: both football and Tai Kwan Do. In football, he learned to pour his energy into making the best plays on the field rather than lashing out at people who antagonized him. And from Tai Kwan Do, he developed focus, concentration and self-discipline, honing his skills so rapidly that he earned his black belt by his early teens.

Kyle was 12 years old before he began playing organized sports. Raised in suburban Maryland in a happy, secure two-parent household, he was by his parents' account an active and physical child from the time he could walk, but like the children around him, he spent his free time playing pick-up games with his siblings and other kids. Then one day he noticed that no one seemed to be around to play with, so he called a friend and learned that his peers had just joined a Pop Warner football league. He decided to sign up as well, motivated simply by the wish to be with his friends.

And he was a strong player from the outset. "My defensive coach noticed that I was all over the field," he said. "Whether it was tackling the quarterback or the running back or the receiver, I was there. I was all over the place. I said, I can get into this! It was fun."

Joining the football league turned out to be a move that would profoundly affect his future. As soon as he started playing football, Kyle discovered a passion for other sports as well: basketball, soccer, martial arts. The pursuits provided more than just an outlet for his physical energy, though: they also taught him an alternative to letting his temper get the best of him.

"My Tai Kwan Do instructor was all about having fun, but also about respecting your peers, and even more so, having respect for yourself and being obedient to your parents. But I think mainly what I took from it was to treat others how you want to be treated. It was definitely a transformation I could feel within myself. From the first week, I could feel myself calming down and nothing really ever seemed as big as I would make it. Man, I don't know where I'd be today if I didn't partake in that at such a young age. It probably saved my life, really. So I can't thank my parents enough for getting me involved with Tai Kwan Do and the other sports."

Despite his talents, the ascension to pro football player was a very gradual one. Even in high school, Kyle didn't yet see football as a future career path. "I watch kids nowadays and they get involved so early, whether it's basketball, football, you name it. To me it was more of a hobby. I never really got serious about football until college. So, it's not like I had big schools looking at me. In high school, I played junior varsity for two years. In my junior year, I finally made it to varsity and ended up dislocating my shoulder a couple of times during the season. I sat out the whole year, so in terms of playing time I went into college as an underdog. I played only one full year of varsity football in high school."

A spiritual person who learned from his parents' example to put his faith in God and believe that God would set him on the necessary course, Kyle considered it an enormous blessing that Hofstra gave him a full football scholarship—an eventuality he had essentially lost hope in after his high school injury. It was at that point that his lifelong religious faith dwindled somewhat. "I'm thinking to myself, why me?" Kyle remembers now. "It really put me in kind of a dark place. I'm thinking, all right, I'm going to miss this whole year. I'm really going to have to do something to wow these scouts and recruiters next season. And more so, will I even be ready for next year? What if it happens again? Injuries when you're that young kind of make you gun-shy as a kid and it can still your career."

Gradually, though, he reconnected with his sense of faith. "Senior year in high school, I was past the shoulder injury and said to myself that I was going to work out, get bigger and stronger and have a mentally tough attitude. I reminded myself that whatever happened, it was definitely God's plan and it was already written for me. I decided that if football wasn't meant to be, I'd accept that, and I'd be happy with whatever God has in store for me, because what matters is health, faith and family. Football is just a game."

With this mindset, Kyle went on to play a successful senior year, and was thrilled with the acceptance and scholarship from Hofstra, even though he knew it wasn't exactly a straight shot from there into a pro career. "Coming into to the NFL from a Division 1-AA program is not unheard of but it's not as common as these big schools where it's like clockwork with their guys going into the NFL. So it was definitely an uphill battle."

It was a battle he was willing to fight hard to win, though. Fear of re-injuring himself in high school, as well as a natural inclination to be more of a runner than a tackler, had caused him to earn something of a "soft" reputation, and he saw college as a chance to change that. "I went to Hofstra my freshman year thinking that as soon as training camp starts, this is a fresh start. These guys, these upperclassmen don't know what I bring to the table. I know I'm a good athlete. I know I can pick the ball off, intercept the ball. I also know I can tackle."

Fueled by this positive mindset, his college career went well, and he graduated from Hofstra determined to find his place in the NFL. Once again, his resolve to make it as a football player was tested. "I ended up a free agent invited to the Eagles' training camp, and that was a great experience. My eyes were really opened to how important it was to wow everyone, every possible chance I got." But it turned out not to be enough. Hard as he tried, "I just couldn't awe them when the bullets went live," he said of his inability to make the team.

"During the 2008 preseason, it didn't come together for me like it did throughout the training camp. They put me in the practice squad and a week later, released me."

Disappointingly, the pattern would repeat itself. "Tampa picked me up for their practice squad, and I was on the practice for the rest of the remaining season," he said of the year following his college graduation. "Then I came back to wow 'em again, but this time I had a so-so training camp experience. It was a little mediocre, below average for me, but pre-season I thought I did a pretty good job. There were only one or two passes caught on me during pre-season." Because he knew how hard he had tried, Kyle was able to be philosophical about the events that followed. "Tampa put me on the practice squad, then they activated me a couple of days after that for the first game of the season. After I didn't make any tackles the first game,

I got that call again, and they released me again, but this time they didn't put me back on the practice squad. They just kicked me out."

This lack of initial professional success was a harsh taste of reality for someone who had previously been viewed as a star athlete.

"It's just a feeling I wasn't used to, being not wanted," Kyle recalls. "Growing up in a small town in Maryland as a pretty good athlete, I could pretty much count on being 'the man' on any team I was a part of. But now here I was, getting called to come up to training camp and work out, and then after that I impressed them only enough to be put on the practice squad."

And then, finally, his luck changed. "Six or seven weeks after that, I got a call from the Patriots. They activated me and gave me my shot. I went down to the Miami game with them and made two tackles. The rest is pretty much history from there. I eventually had the opportunity to start 14 games on special teams and score a couple of touchdowns."

Now, Kyle is a starting cornerback with the New England Patriots, having joined their active roster full-time in 2009. His intensity over the past two seasons has earned him special notice from Patriots coach Bill Belichick, not normally one to lavish his players with public praise.

"Kyle's a guy that works hard," Belichick told a reporter from the Providence Journal during the 2010/11 season. "He did a good job for us last year. On special teams, he led the team in tackles. He was very productive, had a good training camp. He's got good speed. He's tough, he tackles well. He's aggressive. When he's had an opportunity, he's done a good job at taking advantage of it."

If there's one thing his football career thus far has taught Kyle, it's that success is never a certainty. "I started off okay for a special teams guy who had played defense since college. Then I had a rough patch and then got hot again and then finished the season kind of average. It was definitely a learning experience."

After all, said Kyle, every player who makes it through a college football program is athletically gifted. What sets apart the ones who go on to professional ranking is often mental attitude. "I'm a firm believer that hard work will get you there, but you have to work even harder just to stay there," he says now as he reflects on his experiences. It's definitely not a given."

Because of this mindset, Kyle never rests on his laurels. During the off-season, he admits he dislikes talking about football with friends and family, but it's not because he isn't thinking about it. "When I come home off-season, I just stretch out and relax as much as I can, but I'm also seriously working on my craft. Not only am I training but I also commit myself to watching films of myself and my opponents. I believe in training not only to be great physically but equally if not more so mentally."

Looking back, Kyle said he wouldn't change anything at all: not the trouble he had making it onto a pro team, not even the shoulder injury in high school. "That injury was like a new beginning for me as far as where I was physically, emotionally, and mentally. I was sitting there asking, why me? I've always considered myself a decent God-fearing human being. I never really got into any serious trouble, so I questioned the Lord a couple of times during that period, like, why me? That's when you need faith the most. In a lot of cases, God is not going to give you everything because you're not ready for it. Who knows, if I was a big recruit coming out and I went to Miami or Ohio State, I might never even have made it past college as a football player. Or I might have gotten kicked out of college just because I thought I was some big shot. That's what I think about sometimes. I embrace everything that much more because I know nothing is given in this world. You have to go out there and take it. You have to commit yourself to going after what you really want in life. Ever since high school, I thought football would be the route. I've tried to make every sacrifice that I thought was necessary in order to pursue that career."

And in retrospect, he sometimes wishes he had made academics more of a priority along with sports. "If I could do it again, I definitely would try harder in school. That opens a lot of doors, more so than athletics could ever do. If you have good grades in school, that means you can go to a prestigious college. And that opens up a lot of opportunities for you to do whatever you want. You don't just have that one outlet which is sports."

Already, Kyle is thinking about where life will lead him once his pro career is over. He'll soon marry Vashonda, a woman he has known since high school; and he hopes to someday pursue a career in filmmaking and videography, just as his father did. But whatever does or does not work out, Kyle has learned enough to believe he can succeed. "No matter whether you're into sports or you name it, life is filled with disappointments and heartbreaks. That's life and you have to experience those kinds of things to make you appreciate what you do have and the opportunities you do get that much more. I've always said that nothing was ever given to me, and it makes me appreciate what I have that much more. I take nothing for granted. I just live for the moment because all that I am now doing still seems like a dream come true to me."

With his sense of self-determination and boundless resolve combined with faith and spirituality, Kyle reflects the fundamental values of an extraordinary Insightful Player™ team member.

INSTANT REPLAY OF KYLE'S *GUIDING PRINCIPLES*

1. Never stop pushing yourself. You will always need to strive for what you want; there is no point at which it will be handed to you for keeps.

2. Believe in God. Even when things don't go the way you hope, have faith that God has a meaningful and vital plan for you.

3. Show loyalty to your friends, family, superiors and teammates. Have the humility that comes from being part of a group.

4. Remember that mental resolve is even more important than physical ability when it comes to getting what you want—even if what you want is to be a professional athlete.

5. Follow the examples of those you admire.

6. Learn from your own mistakes. Look for the positive message to be found in every setback.

7. Appreciate what you've been given. It could be taken away at any time.

8. Treat other people with respect and kindness, in accordance with how you would want them to treat you.

9. No matter how strong an athlete you are, make academics your highest priority, because academic success ultimately has more potential for your future than athletic success.

CHAPTER 3

NFL FREE AGENT

ROCKY BOIMAN

Finds Lasting Success
on the Other Side of Failure

For NFL linebacker **Rocky Boiman,** self-motivation starts first thing in the morning—literally. On his bathroom mirror are dozens of Post-its with messages he's scribbled down to keep himself striving for improvement. "Life is not a dress rehearsal." "My finest moment is yet to come." "I am grateful for: my family's health, my health, the football talent and career the Lord has blessed me with, the love of my family, the opportunity and responsibility to help those around me." Others are shorter: "Believe." And "Focus."

Rocky said there are a lot of factors that keep him always reaching forever more personal success and fulfillment. First and foremost, there are his parents. He was raised in a close-knit, middle-class family of four on the west side of Cincinnati, Ohio. His parents pushed him hard, but with tremendous love and kindness.

"I was blessed with great parents, and I know not everyone is lucky enough to have this," he said. "It was a very disciplined household. My dad was strict with me, and I think it helped shape me. Every day while I was growing up—and even still today—I worked hard for my parents' approval. Whether it's in football or in life's endeavors, I want my mom and dad to be proud of me. That's an important feeling for a kid. Strong families are the backbone of this country right now."

But there's a problem with leadership, as Rocky sees it. "There are so many followers and the people that do claim to be leaders aren't really leaders. They're just kind of going along with the machine," he said. "Our country right now needs leaders, and there are not many of them out there."

As he sees it, part of the problem is an emerging trend of celebrities who gain fame for no apparent reason. "When I was growing up, and probably before that too, guys that people looked up to were great sports heroes, or war heroes," he said. "Now the 'heroes' that people look up to are reality television stars and people the likes of Paris Hilton, so-called celebrities who are in essence famous for being famous. I want to encourage kids to find people to admire who have worked hard, have talked the talk, have walked the walk, and have accomplished great things, whether it's in business, in the community, as a teacher or on the athletic field, something that has substance."

Even as a boy, he knew that the key to realizing his full potential was perseverance. Rocky started playing football at the age of seven and decided right then that he wanted to someday play for Notre Dame and then the NFL. It was a dream he would see come true, for which he gives ample credit to the solid foundation of family values that his parents instilled. "I had a positive outlook and a great supporting cast behind me," he says of his personal successes. It wouldn't have been even close to being possible without them."

While acknowledging how fortunate he was to have a solid nuclear family with two loving parents, he believes that children less blessed can find substitutes. "Not having good parental role models is going to make it tougher on you, no question about it. Life is not fair sometimes. But your job, as hard as it is, is to find positive figures in your life. Whether it's a grandmother, a grandfather, an uncle, a teacher, find these people, and not just the people that are going to pat you on the back all the time. The ones that are going to challenge you and allow you to fail, so you learn your weaknesses and you learn from them. Associate yourself with great people."

Believing in your own potential is important, but he also makes the point that there's little value in adults who artificially inflate children's sense of self-importance. "I think the education system wants everybody to feel good and feel positive about everything and have lots of self-esteem, which is great, but there is a point where it's too much," he said. "You should feel special about yourself, but you have to do something with that, accomplish something with that too, not just believe you're special because you're living here and breathing oxygen. Do something with those qualities. Better yourself every day."

Personal experience has led him to believe that one key to this kind of betterment is using adversity to your advantage by learning from it. His own football career has been a lesson in how what seems like bad luck can turn into something good. "When I signed with Dallas, I thought everything was great. I'd signed a contract with this team, a long contract, and then I got released instead. All of a sudden I was a thousand miles away from home asking myself, 'What am I going to do now? I don't even know if I want to do this anymore.' I called my parents and told them I was coming home. They would have supported me either way, but my dad talked me out of it. He knew that deep down, that's not the kind of kid I was, and that I was going to get through this. It was hard, and it was also a really defining moment in my career and in my life, because there I was, feeling like getting released meant that I'd been declared a failure. But you know, you pick yourself back up when that happens. You learn over time to say look, these things happen and it's not what happens to you, it's how you respond. Kids, whether they've been cut from a high school team or failed a class or whatever, can relate to that."

It was a lesson he himself learned from his parents. "The whole time I was growing up, my dad and mom allowed me to go out there and fail. They didn't coddle me or hold my hand though everything. If I didn't do as well as I wanted to in school, they told me to study harder. They certainly didn't run up to the teacher and say, 'Hey, how come you're not giving my kid a good grade, what's the deal?' I'm not a parent myself, and I can imagine that it must be so hard to sit there and watch your son or your daughter fail at something, but that's the best way for them to learn."

And sometimes, he discovered as a boy, what matters most is simply refusing to give up—a lesson as relevant to his NFL career as it was the time he and his father spent hours moving an air compressor into their cellar. It's a story he looks back on frequently as an adult. "My dad always had big ideas and worked very hard," he recounts. When I was maybe 12 or 14 years old, we moved into this new house and we were trying to get this huge piece of machinery, an air compressor, down the basement stairs. The thing weighed a thousand pounds and it was just my dad and me with a dolly trying to get it down the stairs and it was not going. An hour went by, we couldn't position it, we couldn't get it down, we were clearly going to hurt ourselves, and he just kept going. And finally I just stood there and said, 'I give up. This isn't working. It's not going down the stairs.' And my dad didn't pay any attention to me. He just kept working at it. I said again, 'Dad, look, it's not going down there.'

He dropped what he was doing and he said, 'Rock, all I can tell you is the damn thing isn't going to sit at the top of the stairs here. It's got to get downstairs. So I don't know what I have to tell you and I don't know what you have to do, but leaving it here at the top of the stairs is not an option. It's got to get downstairs so we'll figure it out.' And so, sure enough, after some time and some thought, we got it down there."

Rocky never forgot that astonishing display of determination. "He just had it so clearly in his mind that failure was not an option and that what we had to do was find the way that would make us succeed at our goal. That's a defining story in my life and something I think about when times are down. To this day, it's clear and vivid."

It was obvious enough to Rocky when to apply that lesson to his own life. Like most NFL players, he has had his share of injuries. "When you're injured, you have to fight through it. You learn to tell yourself, 'This isn't how it's going to end. It's going to have a good ending, but somehow I have to get to that point.' Just like my dad knew the ending with the air compressor had to be getting it into the basement, however we did that. Sometimes on the football field, you have to put aside all possibilities that it's going to end negatively, just get that out of your head and eliminate it. You can't dwell on the negatives or the possibility of an unfortunate outcome. If you do, you won't find the resolve to get back in the game, just as if my dad had given up like I wanted to, we couldn't have gotten the compressor down the stairs."

What happened to Rocky with the Dallas Cowboys turned out to be the best example he could wish for as far as turning around adversity. Signed to a three-year contract in March 2006, he was subsequently released six months later. It felt to him like a death knell on his career. "I've always thought of myself as a very resilient person, but I had never been cut from a team before."

The very next day, the phone rang. It was Tony Dungy of the Indianapolis Colts. "He's in his kitchen and I can hear his kids and the dog in the background and we're talking. Here I am, feeling the lowest of the low, and he says, 'Hey, you're a guy who in the past we've had an interest in, and I think you'd be a great fit for this team. Here's what we expect out of you and we'd really like you to come out for it.'" Not only did Rocky sign with the Colts; he went on to with a Super Bowl with that team. He also played for the Titans, the Eagles, the Chiefs and the Stealers before becoming a free agent in 2010.

"Now, when I talk to groups of kids, I say look, I've probably been fired more times than I've been hired, but each time I learned something for myself. Look at your own situation. You may not be the starter on your team right now; you may not be the smartest kid in your class; you may not pass a class. But the important thing to remember is that a person who has had it easy has probably never learned how to bounce back and is going to be more apt to give up. Adversity teaches you to take that negative and turn it into something that's going to be a real asset. Maybe you had a rough upbringing or had a rough experience in your life, or maybe your parents disciplined you pretty hard or you had to do without a lot of things some of your friends had, but all of those challenges result in more tools in your tool belt for when other, bigger complications come up in life."

And it is Tony Dungy to whom he attributes one of his leading moral values. "When the chips are down and everything is against you, the only thing you really have in life, besides your loved ones, is your character and how you live your life. Tony Dungy would always say that character and integrity are non-negotiable, 24/7 obligations. You can't practice them one day and then put them aside another day. When times are tough, that's when you really have to stick to those character issues, as hard as it may be. There may be an easier way out of a situation, but you have to say nope, I'm going to stick to my guns here. I'm going to do it the right way. I believe you'll be rewarded in the future."

Even without such a powerful moral compass, Rocky could make an impression on others just for his football skills. Back in high school in Cincinnati, his honors included Southwest Ohio Player of the Year, GCL Player of the Year, All City Player of the Year, and All State Player of the Year runner-up. At the University of Notre Dame, he was a three-year starter, team captain in his senior year, and was Pre-Season All American in 2001. As a pro player, he played in over 100 NFL games with over 30 starts. He holds the Oilers/Titans single season franchise record for special teams tackles with 28, and was named AFC Defensive Player of the Week.

But he has a profound spiritual belief that he is meant to do more with his life than set an example by playing a sport. Recently he launched the Rocky Boiman WIN Foundation. The primary function of the Foundation is to provide scholarship opportunities for Cincinnati youth to attend private schools, where they are given an opportunity to further their development. "WIN stands for 'What's Important Now,'" he explains. "Our mission is to create opportunities for young men and women to be further educated on the principles and responsibilities of leadership and to cultivate leadership qualities in any or all areas of life including family, business, athletics, and civic duty."

As he sees it, his work through the foundation is simply his fair payment back to the world that has given him so much—including the success as a pro football player that he first dreamed of as a seven-year old. "When I was just a kid saying my prayers at night, I'd say 'Lord, grant me the strength and the fortitude and the perseverance to hang in there and accomplish this goal, and I promise I will give back here one day,'" he said. "Running this foundation feels like the right way for me to hold up my end of the bargain. I've been blessed with many great opportunities and many great accomplishments and this is a way of fulfilling my commitments."

Applying all the tough lessons he has learned throughout his career as a linebacker to a future in which he hopes to improve the world, Rocky Boiman shows the spirit and intensity of a true Insightful Player™ team member.

INSTANT REPLAY OF ROCKY'S *GUIDING PRINCIPLES*

1. Believe that every setback carries a lesson for you, and seek to determine what that lesson is.

2. Follow role models who embody strong principles by "walking the walk and talking the talk," rather than those who are celebrities but lack substance.

3. Acknowledge that facing adversity builds strength. Embrace the opportunities that adversity brings.

4. Hold yourself to a high standard in how you behave toward your family, your community, your team.

5. The more you are given, the more you owe. Give something back to the world in whatever way you can.

6. Take responsibility for your actions, your attitude, and your decisions.

7. Seek out and emulate people who challenge you and who reflect the values you admire.

8. Regardless of whether or not you attend a church or belong to an organized religion, let your sense of spirituality and your relationship with God be your guide.

9. Refute the temptation to take the path of least resistance. Work hard and follow what you know to be the right course.

10. Make the best of your circumstances, even if they are less than ideal.

CHAPTER 4

THE SAINT LOUIS RAMS'

JASON BROWN

A Champion Who Surrenders to His Faith and Evokes the Same in Others, On and Off the Field

When **Jason Brown** was in high school in Henderson, North Carolina, he spent a lot of time on the football field, giving his best to his team. When he got home, tired and hungry, it was sometimes as late as 8:00 p.m. By the time he showered and sat down to eat his dinner he could barely keep his eyes open. But there was still homework to do. Jason knew that he could not focus on homework when he was falling asleep at the table. But he knew schoolwork was important.

His grandfather, Jasper Brown, had led the charge for integrating schools in the small town of Yanceyville, North Carolina, back in 1956. He fought tremendous opposition so that his four children and other black children in town could attend the same schools as white children. It was just like the famous Brown vs. Board of Education case, and eventually Jasper won.

So Jason wasn't about to let his grandfather down.

When he went to bed each night at nine, he made sure he set his alarm—for three o'clock in the morning.

Then, he would wake up quietly in the dark and study his books by lamplight, so as not to disturb the rest of the family. Sometimes, if he were lucky, he would finish his homework by 5:00 or 5:30 and doze off for a brief half hour before getting right back up at 6:00 a.m. to start his day.

It was Jason's willingness to make this kind of sacrifice that helped get him to the NFL.

Growing up, Jason's parents had a solid and loving relationship. They lived their lives with a strong sense of determination and belief in themselves. His father ran a successful landscaping business. While raising Jason and his brother and sister, his mother ran for, and was elected to, the school board. Later, she wrote a book about Jasper Brown and his fight for desegregation. Jason saw how his parents' work ethic and courage to take a stand had brought them success.

By the time Jason was in elementary school, he had started to develop his own methods of motivating himself. When he got home from school, like many kids, he didn't always feel like doing his homework. But he knew he should do it. So he came up with his own little reward system. He would make a peanut butter and jelly sandwich and cut it into four squares. After finishing his math homework, he would eat the first square, after finishing his English, he would eat the second square, and so on. Sometimes if he had a whole lot of math problems he would do them with a bag of Skittles, eating a single piece of candy after each completed problem. Before he knew it, his homework was done, and it hadn't felt like a chore.

Jason also attended church every week, no matter what. Although at first he fidgeted in the pew just like all kids do, he eventually began to listen to the preacher's message each week. Later, he would remember that God could be a source of comfort and guidance to turn to when he felt overwhelmed and troubled.

Although Jason was a good student, and athletic, he wasn't always popular in school. For many years, his classmates called him "Fat Boy" and other hurtful names. By the time he was in middle school, it was clear that Jason Brown was going to be big. Eventually, his size would prove to be an advantage on the football field. But it's hard to be big in middle school. Some kids teased him incessantly, shouting "Sherman, Sherman, Sherman" in reference to Eddie Murphy's character from *The Nutty Professor*, which had just come out in theaters.

Although he had been called names before, middle school felt harder, because Jason, like so many kids his age, was becoming more and more aware of the social world developing around him. Just like everyone else, he wanted to be popular and accepted by his classmates. But he was also able to see how sometimes other kids acted cruel—like the way they would tease him—in their quest to be popular.

Their taunts stung Jason, but he did not let them define him. Instead, he developed a thick skin and a spirit of perseverance. Perhaps he remembered the lessons he had learned from church and from his parents, and knew that he would get through this difficult time.

When Jason got to high school, he knew he wanted to play football. But he knew he needed to train his body to get it in the kind of shape that would serve him on the field. Although the school offered a weight training class, as a freshman he was not allowed to sign up. But he was determined to figure out a way. The taunting he endured in middle school had motivated him to work on his body, to make it strong, not just big. And before long, he had found a solution. A solution that required sacrifice.

During his lunch hour, Jason ate as quickly as he could, then headed off to the weight room where he would spend the remaining time lifting weights.

"Jason, you're stupid!" his friends would say. "Why are you doing that? You could be out here chillin' and having fun with us!"

And when he got to science class, which was right after lunch, he would usually be sweaty, because there wasn't enough time for him to shower after lifting weights. Sometimes the pretty girl sitting near him would crinkle her nose. "What's that smell?" she would say to her friend, and the two of them would whisper and laugh. "Move away from us, Jason!" they would say. "You stink!"

It took everything he had for Jason to get through the class and concentrate on his work. He knew he was making the right decisions—even if no one else in his class understood. There were many other times when he resisted peer pressure from his friends and classmates. Sometimes it was a very lonely path that he chose to walk. It wasn't easy, but at least he had the support of his family at the end of the day.

Eventually Jason's sacrifices began to pay off. As an upperclassman in high school, Jason became a football star. Pretty soon he was winning games, getting his name in the paper and earning a scholarship to the University of North Carolina at Chapel Hill. Maybe this was why he ended up being crowned homecoming king and prom king, even though he had never sought out popularity. But he realized even then, even when it felt good to be recognized and admired, that most people didn't understand the kind of sacrifices that it took to get there. But he knew that those sacrifices had made all the difference.

Jason was still basking in the glow of his high school achievements when he started at Chapel Hill. But it wasn't long before he realized that his high school experience was kind of like being a big fish in a small pond. Although he still felt like a big fish, now he had been thrown out into the ocean. And he was finding it hard to swim.

The peer pressures he experienced in high school only escalated in college. And now he was away from home, away from his mother and father who had been so supportive. Sure, he could always call them, but it wasn't the same.

Suddenly he was being tempted by things that he knew could lead to trouble: drugs and alcohol. And then there were all those pretty girls. Sometimes he felt like he was in a cartoon, with the Devil whispering in one ear, and an Angel pleading with him in the other ear.

"Oh yeah, go ahead man, you can do it," the Devil would say. "Be selfish and don't worry about the consequences. Don't worry about what might happen later, just listen to your friends and do what you want to do."

But then the Angel would say, "Guess what, you're better than this. You already know the right answer. You need to make the right choice. You need to make the decision. Not only do you need to think about the short-term consequences, but you need to think about the long-term consequences."

"No one will ever know!" the Devil interrupted. "Everyone's doing it!"

But the Angel told him, "You are a smart, beautiful person. You know it's always better to do what's right even if no one ever finds out about it."

Jason knew that the voice of the Angel was really the voice of God, whose message he remembered from all those years in church. He knew he had to turn to God when he felt tempted, when he felt alone. He knew that God's message of wisdom and love would lead him to make good decisions, even when it was very challenging.

It was this voice of love that had helped motivate Jason to make all those sacrifices when he was younger. He knew that if he won a football scholarship, he could ease the burden of paying for four years of college from his parents. Originally, his goal was to get a scholarship to North Carolina State and get a degree in landscape architecture so he could take over the family business. He imagined himself working outdoors, like his dad.

But having chosen football as a path to college, he had to revamp his plans when his sport led him to Chapel Hill, which didn't offer a landscape architecture degree. Perhaps this was part of why Jason started to feel a little lost, a big fish at sea.

By turning to God for comfort and guidance, by falling back on the good work habits he had developed in high school, Jason was able to overcome the temptations. He found a new purpose to help motivate him when he chose Communications as a major. Knowing that he loved to talk, he thought the degree could help prepare him to speak about his journey and inspire others. He especially hoped to inspire kids, because he knew from experience how tough it could be when your classmates don't understand and support you.

When it came to his schoolwork, and his efforts on the field, he remembered his father's advice: work smarter, not harder. One day when he and his brother were younger, they were helping their father out on a landscaping job. Jason and his brother Lunsford were both big, strong kids, although not as strong as their dad. When a landscaping trailer slipped off the tongue of the truck, the two brothers tried to lift it back on. But it was heavy. They huffed and puffed, but could not make it budge. Their dad watched them for a while before he asked, "Are you two finished?"

"It's impossible," cried Lunsford.

"We need a jack, but we don't have one," Jason insisted.

"I want you both to move out of the way and learn a lesson," their father replied.

The boys watched as their father grabbed a four-by-four piece of wood and a cinder block and created a simple lever—just like they had learned about in science class. With this simple machine he used the wood to lift the trailer back on the tongue with very little effort.

"Work smarter, not harder," said his father. And Jason never forgot that lesson.

Thinking about that day with his brother is hard now, because Lunsford was killed in Iraq on September 20, 2003. But knowing the sacrifice that he made and the legacy that he left behind means a lot to Jason. It made him realize how short and precious life is. And it helps Jason keep things in perspective whenever he feels challenged by life.

Jason succeeded in college—both on the field and in the classroom—and was eventually drafted by the NFL. He has enjoyed the benefits and glories of success, but he also knows that life needs to hold more meaning beyond success.

Jason got married when he was still in college, and now he and his wife Tay have a son, JW Jason Brown, Jr. and a daughter named Naomi. Jason calls his children "the most beautiful and precious gifts that God has ever given me and my wife."

But when he sees how much his children look up to him, he knows that this precious gift has come with tremendous responsibility. He knows he has to be a good example for them, just as his dad was for him.

He also feels a certain obligation to pass on the wisdom he learned from his parents, not only to his children, but to all kids, especially those who look up to athletes for inspiration. He knows that many kids face even more peer pressure than he did. He also fears that many do not understand the kind of personal sacrifice that it can take to reach their dreams, whether it be making the NFL, getting to college, or landing a good job.

Sometimes Jason finds himself very frustrated, when he sees other people who have tremendous potential but waste it away. He reminds them of the parable of the ant and the grasshopper. The ant spends the summer working hard, preparing for winter, while the grasshopper plays all summer, making fun of the ant. But when winter comes, the ant has everything he needs while the grasshopper has nothing and goes hungry. Many kids who spend their teen years succumbing to peer pressure get to adulthood and find themselves hit hard by the real world, like grasshoppers in winter. He hopes to inspire more kids to act like ants, rather than grasshoppers.

Jason doesn't always understand why so many people continue to make bad decisions even after they realize there will be negative consequences. He knows he could lecture them all day, but he also remembers that his own journey was very difficult. And he had something extremely important that maybe others don't have. He had the loving support of family, along with a strong faith in God that helped him get through the hard times.

So he tries to send kids the message that he got from his father, from his mother and from the voice of the angel on his shoulder: "You are a smart, beautiful person. You are way better than this. You already know that right answer. You need to make the right choice."

In an effort to further disseminate his beliefs, in 2008 Jason founded a Church Ministry Wisdom for Life (www.wisdom4life.org). The Church's main mission is to share wisdom with youth so they will have a more blessed, righteous, and purpose driven life.

Jason Brown is an Insightful Player™ team member and an exceptional role model who invites others to tune into God's coaching to help them make the best choices to lead a glorious life.

INSTANT REPLAY OF JASON'S *GUIDING PRINCIPLES*

1. Be willing to make the sacrifices to reach your dreams. This will help you develop perseverance and build character.

2. Discover the best way to motivate yourself and stick to it no matter what.

3. Create a relationship with God to empower you and encourage you to make the right choices.

4. Be a leader who sets an example regardless of what others think. This will help you develop self-respect and earn the respect of others.

5. Expand your perspective and change your strategy when things don't work out. When one door closes, another door always opens.

6. Work smarter, not harder. Let your wisdom guide you.

7. When you lose someone you love dearly, let that inspire you to keep things in perspective. Make them proud.

8. Develop a strong work ethic to maximize your talents and ensure success.

CHAPTER 5

THE NEW ORLEANS SAINTS'

DANNY CLARK

#55

Leaves a Positive Legacy
Every Time He Leaves a Room!

Every morning when **Danny Clark** wakes up, he decides to be happy regardless of what happened the day before. He has developed the habit of mentally setting an internal reset button when things go astray. He passionately believes that happiness is there for all of us, as long as we consciously choose to be happy every day.

Danny takes the idea of leaving a positive legacy very seriously and he is driven to leave this world a much better place than he found it. He is so committed to leading a life of significance that he sets out each day with the intention to leave a positive legacy every time he leaves a room!

He passionately believes his calling is to inspire others, especially kids, to take the road less traveled and be all they can be and help others to do the same. Danny said, "It is never too early to introduce this to children." He constantly encourages kids to honor their talents and to make mentoring other kids standard operating procedure. Danny noticed that kids who follow this advice skyrocket their skills, raise their self-esteem and empower those around them.

Danny grew up in Country Club Hills, Illinois. He is one of five boys, raised by his dad. He said, "My Dad did a great job of being the disciplinarian, but he was also the nurturer, the mother, too." His father was a great influence on him growing up. Danny discovered his passion for football at the age of eight. His father respected that passion and leveraged it to inspire Danny to hit the books. He always told his son that football would be null and void if his grades were not his number one priority. C's were not acceptable in his household; Danny had to be great in school in order to play football.

"My Dad was always so supportive. When I was really young, playing in Pop Warner football, he would always be there. He would come to watch me practice and play games after getting out of work. He would even rub my feet or rub my back when I got injured. I played five years of Pop Warner football before high school. I had my share of nicks and scrapes, and Dad was always there.

"My father always encouraged me when I got knocked down both on and off the field. He inspired me to get right back up and fight stronger and longer. That is what propels me today. Dad laid the foundation for helping me do really well in life and for always helping others."

Danny's father also taught him the importance of humility and respect. And to this day, Danny said, "My father's words permeate through me as a parent. My father is a great role model, and at a very young age I began to emulate him." Danny's father was always the gentleman. His manners were so polished that he was consistently polite to others even in situations where most people would lose their temper. "His example of treating people with respect, no matter what, rubbed off on me at a very young age," Danny said. "This also stirred something inside me that gave me an insatiable thirst to help others. I love my father to death."

Danny is grateful for everything about his life. His road wasn't as easy as you might imagine. He was a great student in high school and an all-conference quarterback and linebacker at Hillcrest High, in his hometown. He was ecstatic when he received a football scholarship to the University of Illinois. However, his dream of going to college and playing football with hopes of making it into the NFL almost came to a screeching halt. He thought he might have to give up his scholarship because at the young age of 19 he fathered a beautiful baby girl.

Danny realized that becoming a father at 19 wasn't the smartest move he ever made. Danny's father helped him gain perspective and realize that his daughter was his priority, certainly much bigger than football and college. Danny became committed to making sure his precious baby girl had the best life possible. His faith played a huge role, because Danny always believed that God doesn't give anyone more than they can handle. This gave him comfort and the confidence to figure out a way, with the help of the baby's mother, to do it all—put his baby first, go to school and play football.

Danny credits his daughter, Dasia, for his becoming a professional athlete. She inspired him to work his tail off both in the classroom and on the football field. He took her to study hall and integrated her into all the activities with the football team. Dasia was the driving force that pushed Danny over the top. He said, "She was such a blessing and I love her to death!"

"I want kids to know that adversity always brings you something great. At first I never thought it was possible to juggle college, football and a baby. What initially felt like a setback ended up having a profound impact on the rest of my life. It helped me build a rock-solid foundation and develop a powerful work ethic. It also made me more sensitive to others, helped me develop resilience to persevere and dramatically expanded my perspective of what's possible."

Danny believes that we should always look for the silver lining in every situation. He said, "Adversity builds character and always bears gifts if you are willing to look for them. Building character is one of the greatest gifts we get from adversity. We can never create a successful life without solid character."

A lesson he learned on the football field is that when things are going great, don't get too high; when things are tough, don't get too low. He has worked out a way to keep things in perspective as a professional football player—he gives himself 24 hours to celebrate a win and 24 hours to mourn a loss. He mounted a Staples 'easy button' on his locker while playing for the Giants to remind him to keep his attitude in check after a loss.

A coach and mentor who had a huge impact on Danny was the late Frank Gansz Sr., Danny's special teams coach after he was drafted by the Jaguars in 2000. (He also spent time with Oakland, New Orleans and Houston before joining the Giants in 2008.)

Danny refers to Coach Gansz as someone who will always be one of his favorite people in the football world and his life as a whole. Danny said, "He was a great man, he was a fantastic coach. He led by example and he taught me so much. One thing that stands out is how he always said, 'What you keep, you lose, and what you give will grow.' Coach Gansz recognized my desire to help others and he reinforced my belief that was exactly God's plan and why He sent me here."

When Danny talks about helping others, and in particular underprivileged children, his enthusiasm is so contagious that he could probably persuade Scrooge to get involved. His enthusiasm is real; he goes as far as saying that if he didn't share what was in his heart it would be sinful.

Danny has tremendous respect for the NFL platform and recognizes the opportunities available to him to inspire his fans. He has tremendous passion for empowering kids and encourages them to bust through obstacles and tackle their dreams.

He created the "Danny Clark 55 Foundation," inspired by his son Daniel Clark V (Nicky), who was born in March 2002. Three months premature and weighing just 1lb., 13 oz., Nicky was given a 35%-40% chance of living. Danny went through three grueling months not knowing if his child would live. He wasn't able to hold Nicky until two weeks after the baby was born. He prayed hard that Nicky would grow and be healthy without complications. Those prayers were answered. Today, Nicky is a healthy little boy.

Danny was impressed with the level of care his son got at the hospital neonatal intensive care unit. He also noticed that more support was needed for the newborns' families, and so he started the foundation to help families affected by premature births. With Danny's burning passion to help underprivileged children, he broadened the foundation's services to serve them. He runs several events a year, including mind, body and soul retreats, a comprehensive program designed for kids in seventh grade up to high school seniors. During the time he played for the New York Giants, Danny's foundation and that team also ran an annual fundraiser for the Ronald McDonald House of New York.

In addition, he enlists his teammates to support the foundation. Every Monday night during football season, he holds a fundraiser where teammates and the public come and watch Monday Night Football together. His teammates also support his annual "Shop with a Jock.' At Christmas time, they take kids from group homes to Wal-Mart to select gifts. What Danny finds astounding is that some of the kids get gifts for family members rather than themselves.

Danny Clark is a powerful Insightful Player™ team member who is filled with love and gives of himself freely. He intentionally chooses happiness every day. He is a magnificent role model who starts each day with the intention of making this world a better place. His commitment to leave a legacy every time he leaves a room is astounding and endearing. He certainly walks on the road less travelled and invites us all to join him.

INSTANT REPLAY OF DANNY'S *GUIDING PRINCIPLES*

1. Choose happiness every day, regardless of what happened the day before

2. Inject your greatest passions into all your responsibilities in life and strive to be your very best.

3. Treat everyone with respect, always.

4. Commit to looking for the blessings inside adversity. There is always a silver lining inside every obstacle.

5. Gain wisdom from mistakes to build character.

6. Grow your talents and mentor others to do the same. Begin doing this in preschool and never stop. Danny always remembers what Coach Gansz told him "What you keep, you lose, and what you give will grow."

7. Dramatically expand your perspective of what's possible—let your passion guide you here. Your passion sends you messages from your soul. Trust it always.

CHAPTER 6

THE PITTSBURGH STEELERS'

JERRICHO COTCHERY

Gives It All He's Got,
Becoming the Man God Created Him to Be

aised as the second-youngest of 13 children in a two-parent household in Birmingham, Alabama, **Jerricho Cotchery** did a fair amount of learning by example—both good and bad—early on. "I did a lot of observing," he now says. "I just watched everything going on around me. I still made my fair share of mistakes. But, I was able to learn from those mistakes at a young age and I'm very thankful for that. Seeing the outcome of the decisions guys around me made allowed me to get to where I am now."

Although the surroundings may have sometimes been tough for a young child, the love he witnessed between his parents embedded in Jerricho early lessons about commitment and devotion. "I have absolutely great parents. My dad struggled with alcoholism, but as a child I was able to witness the way that he grew past his problems. And I saw my mom praying for him constantly, ignoring those who said she should leave him, instead constantly praying for her husband and seeing God answer that prayer for her. To see them staying together to this day is an inspiration to me." Even more important than witnessing his parents' devotion to each other was seeing their spiritual commitment. Although when he was a child, he so dreaded going to church that he would hide under the bed until his mother dragged him out on Sunday mornings, he now says that "the most important thing my parents did for me was show me the way to the Lord. That's the best thing you can do for your kids."

Jerricho grew up motivated to create in himself a positive role model for children in circumstances similar to those of his childhood. "Even when I was still young, I wanted to help youth," he said. "The guys I grew up with, myself, my siblings: we all looked for help. The environment and the community that we grew up in didn't offer much help, so I always said that if I'm blessed enough to be able to make it out of this situation, I want to come back and inspire the youth to be whomever they want to be. I grew up in some of the worst situations and I feel blessed to have been able to get out of those situations. Now, I want to share some of that knowledge, understanding and wisdom with kids and try to inspire them as well."

Seeing himself as a positive role model didn't come easily to the Jets wide receiver, though. For that transformation, he credits his wife, Mercedes. "Before I met her, I lacked the inspiration to be the overall man and husband and father that I need to be, full circle. She's definitely an inspiration to me and I'm blessed to be able to have her as my wife."

Jerricho made big mistakes early on, as he tells it—mostly notably by becoming a gang member at the age of 12. Now he speaks openly about it in hopes of preventing other boys from following that same path. "I want to share everything that I've been through so that everyone can see that it's not as if didn't make any mistakes. I want them to see that I made the mistakes and I had to learn from those mistakes, and then they can say 'Hey, now he's in the NFL.' Joining a gang when I was young was a bad decision. Rivalry with different neighborhoods and different gangs: that's not the way to live, watching your back every day, going out different times of the night partying and all those things I shouldn't have been doing at a young age.

"When I was young, I was a guy that would get into a lot of fights," he now recounts. "I don't know the reason. If I saw that a situation wasn't right, I stepped in and I tried to do something about it. I got into a lot of fights trying to stand up for someone else." And from there, it escalated, he said. "Once you have that reputation, guys want to fight you. I guess a lot of guys just saw that I didn't back down from anybody, so they wanted to be around me and ended up sucking me into the gang."

Then, when Jerricho was 16, his friend Brian was killed in a car accident. The two of them along with some other friends were driving home from a sports practice when a tire blew out and the car rolled over. After that, everything changed. "That was the moment where everything came to light, I guess you could say that's when the light bulb went off," Jerricho said. "I lost a friend in that accident and I could have lost my own life as well as two more friends that were in the car with me as well. I had to think about Brian, my friend that died in the accident, and the type of guy that he was, the way he inspired so many people such a young age. I wasn't around him every day but I remember playing basketball and football against him when we were in high school. We were playing on the same team on the AAU circuit. He was a humble guy with a strong work ethic, always willing to help others."

Not only did the accident yank him off a path of self-destruction; it also put him on the road to a new relationship with a higher power. "Thinking about those things, I began to believe that God was speaking to me," he said. "After that I was more able to focus on what I needed to be in life, but I still had a ways to go."

A burgeoning talent for football helped him to straighten himself out. "I think the blessing for me was that I was very involved in football and basketball. The kids that don't have sports to preoccupy them the way I did are worse off, and they're the ones who end up in gangs and stay there. It doesn't matter whether it's sports or a professional goal, like wanting to be a doctor or a lawyer. You need to find something to pursue in life to get out of that situation. That's what I now tell kids that are involved in a gang. You're good at something. You have something that you're very talented at. You have to find that and pursue it."

Some of his friends didn't make it out of the dangerous life as easily as he did. Some are now in prison as a result; others met with even worse consequences. "I had a friend that got killed. Last time I remember talking to him, he was asking me to get him a Jets jersey. I said, 'Sure, man, give me your phone number.' I didn't save his number and so I never had it and I never had a chance to give him that jersey that I promised him. And he had five kids and one on the way. The reality is that my friends are still struggling. It's still happening."

Stronger and wiser after the car accident, gang-free and at the beginning of a new path toward spirituality, Jerricho began to see his star rise as a high school football player. He went on to North Carolina State University, where he was a two-time All-Atlantic Coast Conference selection and broke school records with 200 career receptions and 15 career 100-yard receiving games. In 2004 the Jets drafted him out of North Carolina State, and he has played for that team ever since.

Being willing to question God's methods has been an important theme ever since the accident, Jerricho said. "At the time, as a young kid, you can't understand how a guy 16 could not be able to live out a full life. Well, at that time, thinking he has so much life to live, I just kept wanting to ask, how could he be gone this soon? But God has reasons. Now, looking back at it, thinking about the type of guy that Brian was, I see that maybe he did live a full life, because he was here and he had a purpose for that time on this earth: he impacted my life and he impacted everyone else around him."

Later, after meeting and marrying Mercedes, Jerricho again found himself questioning the ways of God when he and his wife were unable to have biological children and their first attempt at adoption fell through. Again, he pondered the mysteries of God's ways: not only because of the heartbreak of losing the first adoption but in the way his outlook changed at that point. "I was totally against adopting beforehand and God changed my heart in a matter of one night. In your weakest moments, when you can't find strength within yourself, you have to get it from God. I couldn't understand why our first adoption fell through, why God allowed that to happen."

Mercedes had already met and held the infant, a boy, when the birth mother changed her mind. "I just needed an answer. God gave me the answer thirteen days later, with the birth of another child. Because in the beginning, in the process, I always said I wanted a daughter. He gave me the answer when he gave me the little girl that I said that I always wanted. That experience helped my relationship with God even more. Since then, that bond has been constantly growing and I'm trying to keep it that way."

The couple eventually welcomed a second addition to their family as well. As he and his wife raise their children, Jerricho continues with a successful career with the Jets and contributes to his community in numerous ways. He has crusaded against childhood obesity, become involved in a charter school called the Pride Academy, helped a Bayside, NY high school start a football team, and most importantly started the Cotchery Foundation (www. cotcheryfoundation.com), a not-for-profit organization established to benefit underprivileged youth, with a mission to inspire children to conceive and achieve goals through programs and services designed to enhance their futures.

But his highest priorities continue to be his wife, children and relationship with God. "With everything that's going on now, where I'm trying to be active in the community, I'm trying to help kids, when you're so focused on helping in so many ways, you can lose sight of the husband that you need to be at home. I have a wonderful wife and I don't want anything to hurt my relationship with her, to take time away from her, because she deserves every ounce of me. If she says I'm a great husband, that brings a smile to my face. That's what I want to be. I want to be the great father that I need to be in my kids' eyes and in God's eyes. And with that said, I have a lot of family members that haven't even experienced the relationship that I have with God, so that's something that weighs heavily on my heart every day. It weighs heavily on my heart that I'm not doing quite enough to help them in their lives, to be able to show them the man that I've become, the man that I'm striving to be, so they can see what it's all about."

Even having gained fame through the NFL and attention through his charitable work, Jerricho continues to wish he could do more to influence his extended family. "That's definitely the impact that I want to have first and foremost: an impact on my family. I have a lot of work to do in that aspect, though, because I have a very huge family, a lot of nieces and nephews. You just have to press forward and keep working at it."

Even as he tries to be a good husband and father, a community leader and an inspiring role model, he also keeps his sights on the importance of doing well at his profession. "I've been blessed with this talent to play football. I have to strive to do this to the best of my ability. It would be a shame for me to waste the opportunity I've been given. I worked my entire life to get to this point, to make it to the NFL. It's something I watched while I was growing up. Now, to be where I am in the NFL and get complacent and let it go to waste and not become the best player that I can possibly be... that would be a shame if I let that happen. So, that's what drives me every day. I've heard a number of stories, in which people say, 'That dude could have been a great player if he had just put his mind to it.' I just want to make sure I don't get complacent and let it go to waste."

This sense of drive goes beyond an obligation to his teammates, coaches and fans. "God has blessed me with this talent. I don't want to go to Judgment Day and hear God say, 'Why didn't you use your talent to the best of your ability?' What God has placed in me, he's placed upon my heart. Without God, I would have had no chance. He saved me and gave me a chance in life and so now I want to make the best of it and live a life that's pleasing to him."

Jerricho is a magnificent role model who has an unswerving commitment to serve underprivileged children. He helps them identify their dreams and empowers them to uncover their ideal path to realize them. His admirable character and steadfast dedication to community service has not gone unnoticed. He has received several awards for his admirable leadership, his generous spirit and his significant contribution to others.

With his sights always set on keeping to the right path and applying the life lessons he has learned, Jerricho Cotchery walks the walk and talks the talk of an Insightful Player™ team member.

INSTANT REPLAY OF JERRICHO'S *GUIDING PRINCIPLES*

1. Live in such a way that people who know you well could say after you are gone that you were the man or woman that God intended for you to be.

2. Be a source of comfort and emotional sustenance to your family.

3. Hold yourself up as a role model to young people in your community and in your family.

4. Recognize that everyone makes bad decisions; your success comes not from making only good decisions but from learning what you did wrong.

5. Believe sincerely that you can reach any goal you set for yourself, if it is truly a priority for you.

6. Observe the choices made by those around you. Learn how good choices and bad choices alike shape people's futures and cause specific outcomes.

7. Maintain a lifelong commitment to strengthening your relationship with your God.

8. Identify your skills, passions and talents, for they are what will save you and keep you on course.

9. Look to God for help and strength whenever you feel you need it. What you cannot handle in your life, God can.

CHAPTER 7

THE DETROIT LIONS'

RASHIED DAVIS

RASHIED DAVIS *with his wife, Dianna, and his daughter, Alanna.*

Exemplifies the Immense Power of the Human Spirit

Rashied Davis had to hit the floor to dodge bullets in his own home in South Central Los Angeles. His father was murdered by gang members at a McDonald's when Rashied was eight; he grew up around drugs, violence and poverty. Older family members belonged to gangs. He was bused out of his dangerous inner city neighborhood to attend school in the suburbs.

One of nine children raised by his mom and aunt, Rashied believes his background shaped him into the man he is. From a heartbreaking childhood, where he heard gunshots every night, he created a great life. He is a remarkable human being who epitomizes the power of the human spirit.

When Rashied was growing up, he thought South Central L.A. was the whole world. "When I was a kid, all my idols were gang members. They sold drugs; they had everything that I thought I wanted. But I am here today because I turned away from that stuff. I am here today because somewhere along the line I got some hope from somewhere and that hope, I feel, came from God," he said.

From the seventh grade through high school he was bused to school in the San Fernando Valley. At first, he begged his mother to let him go to school in the neighborhood, but she wouldn't budge. This turned out to be one of the biggest blessings of his life.

"I will always be very grateful to mom for knowing what was best for me. I was bused from poverty to an upper- and upper-middle class community. This experience really helped me see that the world where I grew up wasn't the entire world. It was also great to see kids who had more than I did as well as kids going through some of the same things I was going through. I had lots of friends and they were of all colors. I got a great education and going to school in the San Fernando Valley kept me out of trouble."

The turning point for Rashied came when he was 18. He had graduated from high school, he hadn't gone to college and didn't have a job. He was living with his cousin but wasn't contributing to the household because he didn't have any income. He got depressed wondering where his life was going. One day, he was driving home with his cousin and a friend in the car. He was so frustrated he started speeding. He drove so fast that he frightened his passengers.

When he got home he ran up the stairs into his bathroom, slammed the door shut and started crying. He said, "At that moment I started praying to God, and told Him 'I don't know what I am supposed to be doing but it isn't this; just help me find out where I'm supposed to be.' And at that moment, things started to change. I had to move back home, which I didn't want to do. I had a lot of anger inside; the neighborhood wasn't safe, I was angry with the local police, angry at my family. As I look back on it, I know God was moving things around in my life. He was saying, 'You need to be back at home.'"

Rashied knew that he had to take charge of his life. He said, "My life is my responsibility. It's no one else's. Not my mom's, not my father's if he was alive, no one else's. If kids grow up like I did or they grow up with a silver spoon, it's the same for all of us. I have learned over the years the difference between a man and a boy is, a man learns how to play a bad hand well. No matter what cards I have been dealt, I have figured out how to play a bad hand well. Every kid can learn to do this regardless of their environment."

Rashied wants kids to know that their lives mean much more than they think, much more than they could possibly imagine. He knows how hard it is to make the right decisions and to do it by yourself. He wants to encourage kids to lean on God because He is always there and when you lean on God, you are never alone. Leaning on God was what set him on the right track.

He talks about how important it is for kids to push forward and take full responsibility for creating the kind of life they want.

"Find out what it is you really want to do with your life. Do what's best for your future and continue to try hard and push forward. Never give up. Never listen to people who knock you down and tell you, you can't. You matter, everybody matters. Your life means something. If it doesn't mean something to you, it means something to somebody else," he said.

"I started noticing God's helping hand through my cousin. He had mentioned that we should sign up and play football at West Los Angeles Junior College. Shortly after I moved home, my cousin called me and said, 'We are going to check into the school and see if we can play football,'" Rashied said.

Rashied had some reservations about trying out for football. He didn't play in high school because he weighed only 140 pounds. But he signed up to play and also ran track to show the coaches he was serious. He worked out every day in the weight room. If he couldn't get a ride, he took the bus. He ended up starting in his freshman year. He has always had an amazing work ethic and turned out to be a great student and athlete.

Rashied felt like he was living a dream. He was astounded when he started getting letters from colleges stating they were interested in him. This helped Rashied develop a deep sense of pride. He began to realize that he could get a scholarship to a four-year university if he was good enough. Rashied said, "Thank God I wound up being good enough. So that one weak moment in my cousin's bathroom was instrumental in bringing me to where I am today."

Things began to shift for Rashied. He started learning a lot about himself, how much he could handle and how much he was capable of. He said, "It took me a long while to get to this point in my life. It still isn't easy and things have never been easy in my life, never, ever. I am very blessed to be able to come to Chicago."

He was admitted to San Jose State University after two years at junior college. A wide receiver with an average of 19.6 yards per catch, he was moved to defense to play cornerback in his senior year. The Arena Football League took notice because of his ability to play both offense and defense and the semester before graduating, Rashied signed with the San Jose SaberCats.

Rashied spent almost four years with the SaberCats. He broke franchise records as a return specialist, wide receiver and cornerback. His best years were in 2004 and 2005, and he was voted the team's most valuable player and the offensive player of the year in 2005. As hard as he worked during football season, he worked equally hard off-season. He worked at Best Buy and continued to take classes toward his degree.

Before the 2005 NFL season, the Chicago Bears signed Rashied as a cornerback, but he was converted to wide receiver before the 2006 season. Rashied is very grateful to be playing in the NFL, but as much as he loves football, it does not define who he is. He says, "Football is what I do, it's not who I am."

He has an enormous drive to help underprivileged children succeed. He and his beloved wife, Dianna, recently started a charitable organization called Rashied Davis Charities (www.RashiedDavisCharities.org). He said, "We focus on literacy and character education and we provide field trips for children in third and fourth grades. Our mission statement is to teach children how to overcome obstacles to success through inspiration, preparation and discipline."

Rashied has a genuine passion for supporting underprivileged children. He said, "I want to show and give these kids hope and say, 'I know you live in this area, but there's a whole other world outside of here. These are your current circumstances, but you don't have to live in those circumstances your whole life. You can pull yourself through with a lot of hard work, a lot of determination and a lot of faith.'" He wants to show these kids that he comes from where they live, that he is the same person they are.

Rashied Davis Charities is creating Saturday Place, where children learn to see beyond their existing circumstances, acquire the knowledge and academic skills necessary for success and understand their obligation to self and others. The Saturday Place is a tutoring program that focuses on enrichment, literacy and character education for third and fourth graders.

Rashied is married to Dianna, his college sweetheart. They have a beautiful marriage and a precious daughter, Alanna, as well as a son, Eli.

Rashied Davis is an exemplary role model and an Insightful Player™ team member who will leave his imprint on this world for many generations to come. If everyone in the world adopted Rashied's attitude, then we would have peace on earth.

INSTANT REPLAY OF RASHIED'S *GUIDING PRINCIPLES*

1. Push forward and take full responsibility for creating the kind of life you want.

2. Make it a priority to find out what you really want to do in life.

3. Learn how to play every bad hand well regardless of your situation.

4. Never give up. Never listen to people who knock you down and tell you, you can't. You matter, everybody matters.

5. Don't let your activities or profession define who you are. Football is what I do, it's not who I am.

6. Lean on God because He is always there, and when you lean on God, you are never alone.

CHAPTER 8

NFL FREE AGENT

JAMES DEARTH

A Gentle Giant Living a Purpose-Driven Life

Before he became a Christian, **James Dearth** was like a Mack truck plowing through a red light—nothing was going to stop him from reaching his goal of winning football games.

Today, the 6-foot-4 inch, 265-pound long snapper and tight end is one of the most gentle and down-to-earth people you could meet. Armed with 13 years of NFL experience, his strong faith in Christ and a good heart, James does more than play pro football. He is an inspiration, not just to teammates, but to everyone he encounters.

But it wasn't an easy road to travel.

James remembers the moment he realized he wanted to be a professional football player. He was five.

He and his dad were watching Sunday afternoon football and James was glued to the TV. James remembers telling his dad, "I'm going to play that when I grow up.

"I was very clear that my goal was to play in the NFL. From that afternoon on, football became my everything."

James excelled in every sport he played. Basketball, baseball or football, James was a star who played with determination, focus and prowess. He was such a gifted baseball player; he believes that he could have played pro baseball right out of high school in Scurry, Texas. But he always stayed true to his first love, football.

But James will be the first to admit that his love grew into an obsession. In high school, James was a talented quarterback who was consumed with winning. He was so intense that it was impossible to be around him before a game. James said, "If my team lost, my family knew they couldn't talk to me because I would flip out. They all knew that I would snap at them. I was the guy who didn't see anything else but winning football games. Nobody wanted to look at me; nobody wanted to talk to me."

The only exception was a new kid in school, a devout Christian named Scott, who went out of his way to befriend James in his senior year, despite James's resistance.

"I gave Scott no reason to want to be my friend. I didn't know anything about God, but Scott kept talking to me about Christ and shared His messages with me. I tried to disprove him and disprove God because I did NOT want to change the way I was living."

Another pivotal person entered James's life that year in the person of a new coach, Willie Bailey.

"He taught me so much about being a man and about being a leader on the field. I used to gripe at teammates when they made a mistake, and Coach Bailey would not tolerate my negative behavior," James said.

"During half-time at a game we were losing, Coach Bailey jumped all over me in front of the entire team. He told me I was the leader of the team and I needed to build these guys up rather than tear them down. I needed to be positive. He taught me that if you say one negative thing to someone it takes at least ten positive things to make up for it. This hit me like a ton of bricks and this created a huge shift in my life. "

This made James realize that he had a large void in his heart. He felt this chronic sense of restlessness, like nothing was ever good enough and there was always more to be had. He was never happy.

The restlessness, combined with his obsession with football, reached a climax that same year when he suffered 11 injuries that could have maimed him for life. "I broke fingers, I tore my lower abs, I pulled both of my groin muscles, I strained my quads, I separated cartilage from my rib cage and I had a broken back." James is the first to admit he didn't care about himself, and nothing was more important than football because he "loved it more than life itself." Football was his god and no injury was going to stop him from getting what he wanted. He didn't care if he hurt people on or off the field. He was a charging bull, and if he had to hurt someone to get ahead, he would. He thought it was everyone's job to stay clear of him.

The almost fatal obsession James had for football left him with many questions he couldn't answer. He later realized that the easiest way for him to numb his mind against these doubts was to keep playing harder and harder. Like many of us, it usually takes someone else to point out our mistakes and move us in the right direction. In his case the key was the combination of Coach Bailey's guidance, his injuries and his friend Scott.

Scott realized that James was someone who needed help. Scott also saw a lot of goodness underneath James's tough-guy exterior. He never gave up, despite James's resistance.

Scott's persistence, unconditional love and support opened James's eyes to becoming a Christian. He still loved football but realized that, "Football will never love you back . . . Sports will never love you back. But your family, they'll love you back, your friends will love you back and God will never stop loving you. That's what you invest your time in. I mean, obviously you want to do well, and you put your time in training and you put your time in studying the sport you're playing, but never to the extent of losing people that are dear to you."

James began to realize that nothing is more important than the relationships you maintain with your family and loved ones. In a society that seems to do its best to pull families apart, James began to understand the true meaning of relationships and has done his best to maintain them. All through college and up to today, James has been known as a person who values his family and friends above all else.

James may have made a great transformation, but he believes there is a lot of room for improvement. He believes that we are who we are not just by learning but by emulating the role models in our lives. James had many role models: Mike Singletary, Walter Peyton, Reggie White. These great players had the skills and attitudes that James admired. He was pleasantly surprised to find that they also shared the same interests and faith as he did.

James is driven by his love of God and love of others. His football skills are a gift and a blessing and he passionately believes that God gave him this gift to help others on and off the field. He came to realize that playing football is what he does, not who he is. He is a loving husband, father, friend, teammate, son and most of all, a child of God. He wants people to learn from his mistakes. He especially wants to teach kids not to let an ambition become an obsession.

James wants all kids to know that the same qualities they admire in others, they have within themselves. The key is to grab onto these qualities and let them help you grow and build character.

James is a strong leader who always strives to do the right thing. He recognizes that nobody achieves success on their own. An important lesson he learned from his beloved high school coach, Willie Bailey, was the power of staying positive at all times.

He also learned from his former Jets coach, Eric Mangini, "Never sacrifice what you want most in life for what you want now."

James is both a role model and a teacher. His life has been an example of how sports should be. Sports are meant to inspire and not be an object of worship. His mission now extends beyond the NFL and he has a loyal business partner beside him as he takes on a new challenge in his life.

James and former Jets teammate Derrick Blaylock have established Crossover Sports Training, a franchise of Athletic Republic. Far from being just another money-making venture, Crossover Sports Training not only aims to help children realize their dreams by being proficient in sports but it also teaches them values. He sees this as an important mission to ensure that children learn the true meaning of sports and how to properly harness their potential.

In teaching kids how to play sports properly and how to live life properly, James will be doing what he does best. He will show kids how to play well and be what a player ought to be; someone who is fit physically, mentally, emotionally and spiritually. James knows that this is the first step in revolutionizing the sports industry and he is committed to training and mentoring athletes to be masters at the game and at life itself.

At Crossover Sports Training, James will share the lessons he learned and the wisdom he gained from his past mistakes. He has been reborn in spirit and deeds.

Another wonderful lesson we can learn from James is the importance of family. He is head over heels in love with his high school sweetheart and beautiful wife, Laurie. He treasures their three wonderful children: Kaitlyn, Kendall and Kolton. James knows the true essence of parenting and how important parents are to a child's life. He said that "Mom and Dad are given to us by God for a reason because they have life experience and wisdom. They're there for us and to teach us and to help us not make the same mistakes they made in life."

One of James's greatest qualities is his ability to see the goodness in everyone and bring out their best. He said, "I just think that the people need to see the goodness in others. If we all look hard enough, we'll see it, because it is within everyone."

There isn't a person who would not be touched or blessed by the wisdom and inspiration James has to offer. He is a big man with an even bigger heart. James is an Insightful Player™ team member who is groomed to bring out the very best in others, one very special person at a time.

Even if he had to live his life again, James would never stray from the path he has taken. It has shaped his character and inspired him to grow spirituality. We see the true person he is, and it is truly admirable how he was able to turn an obsession which could have cost him his health and life into something wonderful that is set to mold the character of America's youth for generations to come.

INSTANT REPLAY OF JAMES'S *GUIDING PRINCIPLES*

1. Remember that sports will never love you back, but your family and friends will love you back and God will never stop loving you. Realize that nothing is more important than the relationships you maintain with your family, loved ones and God.

2. Be a strong leader who always strives to do the right thing and recognize that nobody attains success on their own.

3. See the goodness in everyone and bring out their very best. People need to see the goodness in others. If we all look hard enough, we'll see it, because it is within everyone. It is important to look for the goodness within yourself too.

4. Sports are meant to inspire and be a part of life, not all of life.

5. Never let an obsession take over your life. Instead, use it as an inspiration to achieve all your goals.

6. Strive to be fit, physically, mentally, emotionally and spiritually.

7. Respect and honor your parents. God sent them to us to share their wisdom and help us to avoid repeating their mistakes.

CHAPTER 9

NFL FREE AGENT

CHRIS DRAFT

Astounding Dedication to Strengthen Others Improves the World around Him

O ther NFL players arrive at training camp in the summer presumably well-rested and ready to start the long, arduous process of getting in shape for a new football season. For **Chris Draft**, one wonders whether training camp marks the beginning of his yearly downtime. The 13-season linebacker who has played for seven NFL teams maintains such an astonishingly busy schedule of philanthropic work, charity, community outreach and personal development during the off-season that it's easy to imagine him welcoming the relative ease of physical training by contrast.

In 2006, he founded the Chris Draft Family Foundation, focusing on the overarching themes of education, healthy lifestyles, character development, personal responsibility, self-discipline and physical fitness. But his work running the foundation is only the tip of the iceberg. During the 2007 season, he received proclamations from the city of St. Louis and the Mecklenburg County, North Carolina Commissioners for service to the community. His community work in St. Louis also won him an AT&T National Sportsmanship Award. Chris was nominated by his St. Louis Rams teammates for a JB Award, an honor bestowed on only a handful of active NFL players, for his commitment to achieve excellence off the field through building better communities and stronger families.

In January 2008 he received the NFL Alumni Spirit Award, presented annually to "an individual who has shown a commitment to community service" consistent with the NFL Alumni mission of *Caring for Kids*. That same year, Chris was formally recognized on the floor of the Georgia General Assembly for outstanding contributions to young people, Georgia communities and the state.

He is the 2009 National Ambassador for the National Parent Teacher Association and has just written a children's book, *Do You Want to Play Catch?* All proceeds go to his foundation to support national programs and initiatives. The message of the book is the importance of reading and exercising with your children and how those practices serve as vehicles to build relationships with your children. He runs "Project Blind Side," a community service endeavor in which he meets with young people for a screening of the movie "The Blind Side," after which the youths engage in an interactive panel discussion. Each then writes a short essay, and the writer of the best essay has dinner with Chris and special guests.

Chris credits his philanthropic spirit and his fundamental belief in giving back to the community to his mother, a social worker, and his father, a salesman. Both his parents were youth coaches. He describes a typical scenario from his childhood. "We'd be walking down the street and see some trash on the side of the road. My parents would tell me to pick it up. I'd say, 'But it wasn't mine.' 'Did I ask you that?' they would ask. 'You walk by it, it's your responsibility.' So that's what was instilled in my brother and me. If you're there and you can do something about it, then you do something about it."

As a role model, he hopes to see other NFL players following his example. "At the end of the day, the real key message is that you don't have to wait for a leader. One aspect of football is that on the field, everyone is a leader. It's true that a team has captains, but at any time, anybody can make the play. So one of my goals is empowering everyone individually as leaders so that they're able first to identify a problem and then go on to be the solution to that problem."

Raised in a two-parent household with one brother, Chris learned early on about teamwork and commitment. His parents were both college athletes who played football with their sons and tennis with each other. When a youth coach commented to Chris and his teammates that girls couldn't play ball, his mother promptly picked up the ball and threw it, demonstrating her credo that your limitations are only as real as you believe they are and not as real as other people say they are. Her proactive approach to all elements of life not only manifested in this "can-do" attitude, teaching kids not to listen to naysayers or to discouraging messages, but also, in this case, put her in the role of assistant coach.

Chris remembers the look his mother gave him the first time he bought a pair of Nike sneakers. "I knew what she was going to say: 'They had better last, because you could have bought a couple of pairs of shoes for that amount. They might not be as stylish and they might not have the Nike logo on them, but what is it that you're getting the shoes for? Moving around and running around, or just so they look good?' It's a matter of pursuing your priorities and values, and recognizing the opportunities to express those priorities in the choices you make. I knew too my mother was telling me that everything should be functional, and I still believe that."

Chris's first sport was soccer. He was only four years old when his father began coaching his older brother's team and asked for a special dispensation to allow his younger son to play. But Chris let him down. "I didn't want to run around the field when my dad said to. Basically I ended up acting like a little baby, until my dad just told me to sit over by my mom. I tell kids this story now and explain how my mom didn't try to be all comforting. Instead, she said 'Either get out there and practice with your teammates or you're not going to play for the rest of the year.' I use that as an example, because from the beginning, my parents made it very clear that you don't pick and choose what you want to do. If you're in, you're in, and that doesn't matter how good you are or how bad you are; the question is, are you going to be on that team, are you going to be a part of that group? If you are, you go all in."

Young Chris got the message, and so when he first took to the football field as a ten-year-old, it was a different story. "At the first practice, I was committed to showing them that I was a running back, because I'm fast, I'm agile and I can do it. They didn't believe I could play that position. So, in my efforts to show them how wrong their decision was not to have me play running back, I gave everything I had, and man, I was so sore the next day. After that first football practice, my dad said 'I know you're a little sore, but you're going to go back out there and you're going to work right through that soreness because you've made a commitment.' When you start it, you finish it."

Growing up as an African-American in Orange County, California presented its own challenges. He discovered early on that certain stereotypes about young black men caused people to make assumptions about him, such as that he was a poor student and was likely to get into fights. When he was accepted by Stanford, one of the most academically competitive universities in the country, he discovered there were people around him who did not realize he had taken honors classes throughout high school. "Everyone, regardless of their racial makeup or other circumstances, faces the assumptions and expectations people have about them. Even if they lack external encouragement, kids need to find inner resources with which they can find their strengths, accept their limitations and make the best of themselves regardless of what people might say or think."

His parents constantly reminded him that performance trumped stereotype; he would have to change people's assumptions by proving himself in the classroom and on the playing field. "They always stood tall with this kind of militant attitude," Chris recalls. "Once I came to see early on that I was doing well in the classroom and also good at sports, I acknowledge that I could break down some of these stereotypes." But not all young people have such influential parents or such a compelling inner compass, Chris notes. So when he speaks with young people now, he emphasizes to them his own high expectations of them. "I try to help them find their game plan and let them know that I expect greatness from them," he said.

At the same time, he makes it clear to the young people he counsels in his role as a spokesperson that their messages of affirmation have to come from within and not just from outside, and this is true regardless of a person's race, creed or economic status. The cold reality, as he explains it, is that young, poor black males like those he often meets with cannot expect to meet with large reserves of encouragement. "I was out in L.A. recently talking to some kids, and I said, 'Don't think there are going to be a whole bunch of people cheering for you. You guys are from the projects, you know that the expectations of what you are going to do is not going to be that high. So what you're going to do is make it up in your mind that regardless of what they say, you're going to make it.'"

Self-determination is key, he said, and he considers it a paramount priority to communicate this to young teens. "If you're willing to fight and you want to get out of the situation you're in, you've got to ask yourself, what is it that you're willing to do? What type of person do you want to be? What is in your character?"

It is Chris's hope that he presents a living example of how to enact the right values; through his deeds, he tries to show young people what his priorities are. Much of his outreach work is dedicated to the subject of asthma, a problem he has suffered from himself since college, and it taught him much of what he knows about perseverance. "I thought I was going to be done playing my junior year in college because it got to the point where I couldn't breathe," he said.

"Football is about pushing yourself. When you feel like you don't have any more, you push a little bit more and you find something that you didn't think you had. But at that point, I was feeling like if I pushed this thing anymore, I was going to kill myself. My parents were saying I had to find out what was wrong and I knew I had to do that too, because one of the things that's so important to me is being an advocate for myself. The trainers were trying to tell me I was faking it or it was in my mind, but since I was at Stanford, which has one of the best hospitals in the world, I could go get tested for all kinds of things. But it made me realize, what if I were not a football player and what if I were not at Stanford? How would I advocate for my health needs then?"

Being a long-time asthma sufferer reinforces for him time and again the importance of holding on to a sense of resilience. "With the asthma, it's a daily mindset. I just have to keep rolling and always be listening to my body. As an athlete, I have to feel my body out every day and say, 'Is what I'm doing working for me?'"

But in a way, the omnipresent health concerns just reinforce the transience of life as a professional athlete. "It's the nature of the NFL that you could be gone tomorrow, meaning done as a pro player, but the nature of my asthma means that I could be gone tomorrow for good. And so I ask myself all the time, 'If this were my last day, could I say I worked hard? Did I do my best and give everything today? Regardless of what people perceive of my level of talent, did I throw myself into my work today?'"

His relationship with God encourages constant self-improvement as well. "I am a Christian. What that means to me is what I learned about it from my mom: it's who you are. It's the person that you are. And it's what God gave us. He gave me purpose and He gave me opportunity. I've experienced the blessings of attending Stanford, of having football skills, and of my parents keeping me focused and insisting that I not waste my talents. I've been blessed to be in this game for 13 years. But when younger guys are surprised at my longevity in the game, I tell them it's one year at a time."

"People that are fortunate enough to be 'gifted' tend to be gifted in one area," commented Chris's old friend Alec Coughlin, former VP of Marketing for the Saint Louis Rams. "To say Chris Draft is gifted is a massive understatement, because there really isn't an area he *isn't* gifted in. Perhaps the most remarkable gift is his relentless pursuit to apply his enormously rare abilities towards the improvement of society as a whole and his ability to inspire others to do the same. Chris is the ultimate NFL role model."

With his tireless commitment to helping those who look up to him, advocating on behalf of communities and their members, and being the best man and football player he can be, Chris Draft sets a high benchmark in defining the goals and possibilities to which one man can climb as an Insightful Player™ team member.

INSTANT REPLAY OF CHRIS'S *GUIDING PRINCIPLES*

1. Embody your ideals. Live out the rules you set, so that no one can accuse you of insincerity.

2. Don't wait for someone else to step forward as a leader. Empower yourself to fix any problem you see or lead any effort in which you believe in.

3. Emphasize priorities and values over flair. Whether it's about a pair of sneakers or your performance on the football field, be sure that there is substance and quality beneath the exterior.

4. When you choose to make a commitment to something, see it through. As part of a team, it doesn't matter as much how well you play as whether or not you stand with your team on the field.

5. Finish what you start. Don't let physical or mental obstacles keep you from seeing your efforts to completion.

6. Take responsibility for the people and the environment around you. Be an agent of positive change.

7. Allow the quality of your work to speak for your character. If people assume the worst about you, let your actions and deeds prove them wrong.

8. Don't rely on "cheerleaders" to convince you of your worth. Be your own best cheerleader.

9. Give 100% effort to whatever you undertake. Stay until the job is done.

10. Look for the opportunity to change someone's life.

CHAPTER 10

NFL FREE AGENT

HEATH EVANS

A Champion for His Wife, His Teammates, and Children All Over the World

Heath Evans was raised in Florida by parents who were determined to protect him from the dangers and pitfalls of life. They instilled in him strong Christian values, warning him to beware of the consequences of the choices he made in his life. His father, an ex-Marine, had made choices in his life that he regretted, and wanted to pass on the lessons he had learned to his son. At first glance Heath's father may have appeared intimidating, but he is a man who knows how to love, touch and build up his children. Heath always knew that his father loved him and would be there when Heath needed him. His mother was always loving and nurturing, and both of his parents strove to provide a positive example for Heath and his sister.

Heath's father was extremely open with his son. He told Heath about some of the big mistakes that he had made as a young man in the Marine Corps. He didn't hide his past, but used it as a way to point his son in a different direction. And Heath took his father's advice to heart.

At a very young age, Heath expressed a strong desire to be a good Christian. One day when he was about four years old, he came out of Sunday School and ran to his mother. He had just learned about Heaven and Hell and how Jesus died for his sins. "I told her I was a sinner because I tell lies and I'm disobedient and I wanted to go to Heaven with Jesus and she led me in a prayer right then, repenting of all my few sins at four years of age!" As he grew up, Heath continued to strive to do right by his parents and the teachings of his church. But it wasn't until he went off to college, on his own for the first time and facing challenges, that he sought out a deeper personal connection with God.

Heath attended a challenging private high school. He suffered from several learning disabilities, including attention deficit hyperactivity disorder (ADHD) and dyslexia. His parents did everything they could to help him, eventually hiring professional tutors. They also adjusted their expectations, knowing that while A's were sometimes possible for Heath, there were other times when getting a C in a difficult class was considered a big success.

Although neither one of Heath's parents was a big athlete, they encouraged their children— Heath and his sister—to follow their dreams. On the other hand, they did not try to push them to do anything they didn't want to do. While Heath sought out a more public life by playing for the NFL, his sister, who had an amazing voice, chose to stay out of the limelight. His parents understood and supported them both.

Although high school was extremely tough, when Heath finally made it through he found that the work in college seemed easy by comparison. But being away from home, at Auburn University in Alabama, presented other challenges for Heath. With his father's warnings embedded firmly in his head, he was able to resist many of the usual temptations of youth, such as drugs and alcohol. When it came to women, he found the temptation much harder to resist. But Heath was determined to stay a virgin, and save himself for marriage.

He met a pretty girl on the very first day of college, and before long they had connected on many levels. Both were from Florida and a little homesick. She taught him many things, helped him study, and provided comfort when he needed it. But before long he was tempted to go farther with her sexually than he wanted. This made him feel very guilty. He had tried so hard to have high moral standards. And he believed he had failed. He was just like everyone else. He didn't want his parents to know. Although he was disappointed in himself, he was also humbled. He turned to God and asked for forgiveness to help wash away his guilt and shame. He was extremely grateful to have his faith, because he realized now how comforting it could be. It was hard to be perfect all the time. It was good to know that it wasn't the end of the world to make a mistake once in a while, that he could have a second chance. After that, he was able to share his experiences with his parents, and to feel reconnected with them once again.

The relationship with the girl didn't last, but Heath was determined to do better next time. But he didn't realize that the next woman he would fall in love with would change his life forever and open up his heart and mind to a mission of helping suffering children.

When Heath met Beth Ann, he fell in love almost immediately. She was a beautiful woman who sparked something special in Heath. She reminded him of his mother—she had all the qualities he admired about his mom and really seemed to understand him. On their first date, he told her "Guess what? I'm going to marry you."

They quickly grew close. Heath had never met anyone who made him feel so happy. And he was pretty sure he made her happy too. But sometimes Beth Ann seemed sad and withdrawn, and Heath could not figure out why. One day she finally opened up and shared some painful memories that had haunted her since childhood. When she was in third grade, she had been repeatedly sexually abused by an older classmate. At first she told no one, and then finally got the nerve up to tell her parents when she was in sixth grade. Still, her parents didn't really know what to do and she hadn't gotten any treatment. The issue was swept under the rug. When Heath heard her story, he was filled with compassion, and also anger at her abuser. He was shocked that she had had to suffer in silence all these years. He knew her parents loved her, and realized that it was the culture of the times that had led to the secrecy that had made Beth Ann feel so alone for so many years.

Before long, Heath and Beth Ann married, and together they started The Heath Evans Foundation (www.heathevans.org). Their goals were to raise the curtain of secrecy on the subject of child sexual abuse and to provide financial assistance for therapy for victims.

Beth Ann encourages children who have suffered such abuse to contact the Foundation, which provides counseling and other services for victims. Beth Ann explains, "They can go to our website and we will do our best to help them. We are often able to coordinate transportation to and from counseling depending on where they live. I would also strongly encourage them to pray. God sees what is happening and He cares. Psalm 56:8 tells us that God keeps and records each tear, and He sees our sorrow."

Many of those who have contacted the Foundation have become close to Beth Ann during their treatment. It means a lot to them to know someone who understands their suffering. She shares what she has learned through her journey. "Realizing the truth is what helps me feel not so alone. The truth is I am not alone. God has promised never to leave nor forsake me. What happened to me has caused me to be able to help and identify with other hurting people. Also, counseling helps me to…share my pain in a safe environment and gain wisdom and strength for my life."

Beth Ann thanks Heath for being there for her at a time when she needed it most. "Heath's support means more to me than I could share. I have learned from Heath what unconditional love and forgiveness is all about. Without him being my biggest cheerleader I might still be stuck crying in a closet."

Heath wants to get a message to children that have been sexually abused all across the world, not just in America. "We want to bring hope and healing to the broken-hearted children of this world that are really being ravaged because no one will stand up and do anything about it," he explains. "One out of four young girls and one out of six young boys will be sexually abused before the age of eighteen." Heath is surprised by how little attention has been given to this issue, and he is determined to shine the light on the problem as much as possible.

Heath believes there are elements in American culture that contribute to the problem. He comes down hard on the pornography industry, especially since he has met sexual assault victims who have suffered directly from it. He hopes that by spreading awareness of the problem he will at least encourage people to turn away from such vices, knowing that they are more dangerous than they may seem.

Heath feels a strong need to protect his own children, like his parents did for him. He knows that sometimes this means telling them "No" even when it is hard. "In our home, we always say that both of our girls, every single day, need a healthy dose of vitamin N, vitamin No. So many kids grow up in this world today don't know how to tell themselves no."

Heath knows that he is not perfect—that he struggles with weakness and temptation as much as the next person. He finds that it helps a tremendous amount to have a trusted friend with whom he can share honestly.

"When we keep these little secrets in our life, we want to bury the stuff. People sometimes think, 'Oh, I can do this, my wife never knows.' Well that's not true. It's going to affect your marriage. It's going to affect your parenthood. It's going to affect everything about you."

"Our goal in our family is, if we screw up, let's get it out in the open, because most times if you get the little screw-ups out in the open, the big screw-ups never come."

New Orleans Saints coach Sean Payton sought out Heath for the team because he knew that in addition to his versatility on the field, Heath was able to bring leadership to the locker room and help motivate his teammates. In the 2009 season, Heath and his teammates won Super Bowl XLIV. Although a season-ending injury prevented him from playing, his coach asked him to stay involved by continuing to lead in the locker room. His teammates found him to be a great influence, and although they were almost as disappointed as he was about the injury, they were very happy to have him around for support.

Despite all of his accomplishments, Heath has fears and insecurities just like everybody else. Sometimes he fears being inadequate for his wife and children. Sometimes he fears the linebackers he goes up against. One of his long-term dreams is to write a book. Sometimes he thinks, "Who am I, who failed English three times in high school, to try and write a book?" But Heath also knows that he has been able to overcome fears and insecurities in the past, and that with support from those close to him he can overcome anything he puts his mind to. He remembers the struggles he had with his learning disabilities and how his parents' patience and acceptance helped show him that he would make it through.

A lot remains on Heath's plate. He spends time working on the Foundation, and on sharpening his leadership skills. He is also a talented motivational speaker, and has a steady speaking schedule. But each and every day, he asks himself: "Am I being there for Beth Ann and the girls? Am I picking up my kids, giving them hugs? Am I talking with my wife, encouraging her, lifting her spirits when she needs me?" He knows he needs to make his family a priority, no matter how much else he has going on in his life.

In the past, he worried about how his injury might affect his long-term career. But he turned to his Christian faith for guidance, and it helps him keep everything in perspective.

Any time he signs an autograph, he signs "Heath Evans 44," then underneath adds a Bible verse from Jeremiah which he find inspirational: *For I know the plans I have for you, declares the Lord. Plans to prosper you, not to harm you, but plans to give you a hope and a future.*

Heath explains further what this verse means to him personally: "Everyone has a tougher story than I do, or bigger heartaches than I do, but I've been through some tough stuff in life where I've had to sit back and go, 'Why God?' or 'Why this?' or 'Why now?' A broken ankle in college or my kneeinjury in 2009, or the struggle with Beth Ann when the sexual abuse stuff came to the forefront of our lives and we had to deal with the nitty gritty. You know, God's got a plan and I trust that plan. We live in a very human, natural world but I believe everything is sifted through the hands of God that enters my life. And I believe that he uses things to strengthen us and to build us up and that we suffer these things in life so that we can comfort others.

"Beth Ann's story is awesome because she has chosen to say, 'You know what? I walked through this nasty mess and now I'm going to get through it myself. I'm going to heal and prosper from it and then I'm going to use it to protect and bless other people.' And I think that's kind of why we're put here."

Every morning when Heath gets up he tells himself that this day is not about him, it's not about feeling sorry for himself. He'll ask himself if there is someone in the locker room he can encourage, or if he can help Beth Ann around the house. He aims to be a good Christian person not only when circumstances are blessed and prosperous, but also when things are tough and hard. His values are emblematic of an Insightful Player™ team member.

INSTANT REPLAY OF HEATH'S *GUIDING PRINCIPLES*

1. Listen to the lessons that others have to teach.

2. Don't be afraid to speak out.

3. Don't keep secrets.

4. Trust that God has a plan for you.

5. Live your values even when times are tough.

6. Love your family through tough times. Never quit or give up on them regardless of the situation.

7. Create and follow through on a plan to reach your goals. You can overcome your fears and insecurities by keeping focused on your goals.

8. Surround yourself with people that will help you reach your goals. Don't fall into the trap of doing it alone.

9. Find a confidant to share it all.

10. Ask yourself some hard questions every day to make sure you are honoring your priorities.

CHAPTER 11

THE SAN DIEGO CHARGERS'

ANTONIO GARAY

Nurtured by Lifelong Family Ties, He Uses Injury and Adversity as Motivation to Improve

Antonio Garay's extended family holds a New Jersey state record for the most state medals in wrestling: nine medals total among two generations of Garay men. But that's only the beginning of Antonio's legacy as an athlete. His father was both a wrestler and football player at Hofstra University before going on to an NFL career that included seasons with the Rams, Raiders, Patriots, and Jets. His mother was also a two-sport collegiate, playing tennis and softball. Like their father, his brother was both a football player and a wrestler at Hofstra, where his sister earned a full scholarship to play volleyball after a successful two-sport high school career. Two of his uncles were state-level wrestling competitors, one a state champion, and so were several cousins.

But it wasn't all about sports in their home. Just as important to his parents were fundamental values such as spirituality, ethical practices, academic pursuits and fairness. With so many positive influences shaping his upbringing, when the San Diego Chargers defensive tackle talks about his childhood, he is just as likely to convey a lesson learned from his parents being of different religions or his cousins urging him to be the best athlete he could be as a story about how he became an NFL player.

Antonio's hometown of Rahway, New Jersey, has always been a significant part of his life too, functioning almost as an extension of his family. "My community was a big influence in my upbringing and my fortunes," he said. "That's one of the reasons why every year during the off-season, I do some volunteer coaching at my old high school. My brother is the assistant football coach there. I help him and I work with the wrestling team."

Like his other family members, Antonio was always a good athlete, but he believes the success that led him eventually to the NFL, where he played for the Bears, the Browns and the Jets before taking up his current position with the San Diego Chargers, comes more from within him than from any level of physical prowess. "People find success in so many different ways," he said. "Everyone hits bumps in the road, it's just that for some people the bumps are a little more visible to the public."

For Antonio, these publicly visible pitfalls mostly had to do with injuries. Though he believes his long series of injuries was coincidental, that history marked him as a risky draft pick. But each time, sheer force of will drove him back into the game eventually. "I've been in situations throughout my career where some people doubted me," he said. "And there were definitely times when knowing that someone did not think I could do something was what motivated me most to do it. I've always felt driven to surpass people's expectations of me."

The biggest blow came in the form of a broken leg soon after he was signed with the Bears. For an athlete who had already suffered an unusually high number of serious injuries, this one could easily have crushed the hopes of a less determined spirit. But not Antonio. The awareness that a string of injuries like his could permanently dent the reputation of a rising sports star only made him determined to come back better than ever.

It wasn't solely a matter of impressing the doubters. He was equally motivated by wanting to live up to the high expectations that some of his supporters held for him. "I always feel that there's more that I could do. And the reason there's always more for me to do is that there are a lot of people in my corner. I don't want to let anybody down, because they're constantly behind me." Those thoughts compelled Antonio to work equally hard when he was in rehab or on a practice squad as he did during the seasons when he was a regularly playing team member. "Sometimes people close to me say, "If it ended today, if you don't go back next season, you've still had a great career." They support me no matter what, but at the same time, hearing that has sometimes driven me to work even harder. My dreams have always been to play NFL football. I play because I want to win."

As a young athlete, Antonio came to realize early on that while some forms of guidance and advice are more useful than others, there are always lessons to be learned from any input. "Sometimes people have great things to say about you and sometimes people have bad things to say about you, but the lesson is in how you deal with it. Not all criticism is correct or helpful, but it's worthwhile to have the mindset that any form of criticism has an effect on you and in some way helps to mold you into the person who you're going to be. As you grow up, you have to cross a lot of different roads. And it helps to remember that all the people, coaches and parents and teachers, who have guided you along the way influence the way you will decide to cross that road."

Even as a child, Antonio was aware of how fortunate he was to be raised in a two-parent household; now he is even more appreciative of the positive influence of both his parents. The unflagging love and support from his parents and siblings fortified his ability to get along well with the outside world—which is of paramount importance when you play on a team, Antonio said. "There are always some coaches you like better than other coaches, and the same thing with teammates, but at the end of the week when you have a high school football game, everyone's got to put their differences aside, because the ultimate goal is still to win that game."

It's a lesson that kids are wise to carry into adulthood, Antonio said, because the same can be true in the workplace. "You're not always going to have the same chemistry with every person you meet in life. You might not particularly like or mesh well with the people that you work with, but you still have to have a solid working relationship. You have to be able to put your differences aside and go after a common goal. Sometimes at an early age, it's not always easy for kids to see that, but it's something worthwhile that kids can learn from team sports."

Spirituality was a guiding force throughout his youth also. His parents came from different faiths: his mother was Jewish and his father Catholic. Together, they imparted to their children the value of both religions and cultures. "They didn't isolate their beliefs," Antonio said, and when he chose to attend Boston College, a Jesuit school, his mother was comfortable with the decision. As an adult, Antonio said that what shapes his thinking is more of a general belief in the power of spirituality and ethics than any one tradition.

"I owe all my success to my two parents," he said. "A lot of what they instilled in me had to do with both of their cultures and both of their religions and their backgrounds and their upbringing. I'm a very faithful person, but I've never gotten into a situation where I felt I had to choose, not between my parents and not between their beliefs. When I talk with my mother and my father, it's like talking to my best friend. Because there's always been so much communication, I have always had a high standard of morals and ethics."

In college, he suffered the first of a long line of injuries that would sideline him for weeks or months at a time. "A word that I got to know more about when I was in college was adversity. And that's something that I always try to overcome, no matter what level I am at, what's going on in my life, no matter how bad or how bleak things look, I am always very positive. I'm not out to judge what is the right or wrong way to do something, but I think the way that I have approached most things is simply to do something the best way that I know how."

Antonio estimates that he had 40 relatives living in his hometown while he was growing up, and knowing that he was seen as something of a role model to his young cousins as well as his younger brother and sister helped him to stay on track. "With so many people that are in my corner cheering for me, I always felt like I'd be letting them down if I wasn't self-motivated to continue my path, to continue my journey. As I see it, if all of a sudden my younger brother and sister and cousins saw me fall by the wayside because my mentality got weak and I couldn't push on, I wouldn't just be cheating myself, I'd be cheating everyone involved. And I know that there are people following my life and career, young people looking up to me, who I don't even know about, just as there are people who have touched me in my life and probably don't even know that."

With the awareness that he is serving as an example for so many, Antonio can't help holding himself to a high standard. "For me to not work hard or not really push myself to the limit so that I can obtain the goals that I set for myself would be contradicting everything I've ever said while talking to my brother, my sister, my younger cousins, any of the kids in my community. It is really important to me that I practice what I preach."

Pursuing more than one sport helped him to become a well-rounded athlete. Before he focused on football, he played soccer and was on the wrestling team, a sport that his father continues to coach. He gives his early soccer skills a great deal of credit for their influence on his football abilities. "In soccer, I played left wing, which required a lot of running up and down the field. That enabled me to develop my athleticism and my speed and not just be another big kid on the football field. Wrestling was important to me because it's a one-on-one competition even though you're part of a team. And in some ways, wrestling really influenced the way I see other sports too. In wrestling, it's you versus your opponent. There is no other person you can blame anything on if you don't do well. You can't go back and say, "Well, the match didn't go well because of this other teammate's mistakes.' Everything is on yourself."

This sense of self-reliance turned out to be paramount in recovering from various injuries throughout his career. Time and again, with help from family and supporters, he rallied his spirits to fight against the mental defeat that often plagues injured athletes. "I've had friends who have gotten hurt and it has ended their careers," he said. "But for me, if I was injured, I would immediately say 'All right, so I'm hurt; what do I have to do to heal and recover?' And then I'd spend the seven to nine months of recovery getting myself ready for when I came back. I think some athletes misremember their abilities when they're getting over an injury. They start to say, 'I did this so much better before I got hurt' or 'I was so much faster' or whatever. I always maintained the mentality that regardless of what I was good at or bad at, I'm going to make sure that when I come back to the game, I'm better than I was before."

Growing up, Antonio had older cousins around him as well, and from them he learned different but equally valuable lessons. "These days, people sometimes ask me who I looked up to when I was a kid. They expect me to name a big-time football player or some kind of professional athlete. The truth of the matter is, when I was younger, my world was small and revolved all around my family. So, when I saw my older cousins playing a sport, I wanted to compete against them. And even though they were bigger and stronger, playing against them made me realize I didn't know what my body could do yet. I had to learn. So now when I speak to kids or am trying to teach something, I'll hear them say "Oh, I don't think I can do that." And I tell them the lesson I learned from playing with my older cousins: "You're so young, you don't know *what* you can or can't do yet. There are some things that other people can do better than you, but it doesn't mean that you can't do it."

Urging kids to explore their physical limits is only part of the message Antonio imparts to the young people he meets with and helps to coach. He also ensures that they understand the importance of their studies. "Kids tell me 'Well, school is not for me, but I want to be a professional athlete.' I tell them, 'If you want to be a professional athlete, school is going to have to be a big part of it!' Not caring about school but wanting to have a career in sports is like saying you want to be a doctor or a vet without going to school."

Antonio believes that being unlucky when it came to injuries only served to fortify his faith and his inner drive. "I think what helped me get through a lot of my injuries was just that I was always so positive and always had faith that things were going to work out just as long as I continued to work for it. My belief really is things don't happen only because you *want* them to happen. You have to *need* them to happen. You have to want it that badly."

Inner drive is a principle Antonio embodies—all the more so due to all the time he's spent recovering from injuries. He describes a recent season when he maintained his workout schedule with the team even though it seemed obvious to many onlookers that he wouldn't be ready to play that year. "I think a lot of people were looking at me and thinking, 'The season's almost over, why don't you just stop working out?' I heard so many people say, 'Well, it was a good run, if your career is over, you did everything you could. You tried your best at it.' Then my father suggested I go back to Boston College while I was training and finish my master's degree in teaching. And that was kind of a turning point for me. I realized how much I did not want to forego my professional football career. I called up my advisor at Boston College and told her I'd been working very hard with my trainer and that I felt I'd be cheating myself if I didn't follow through with my ultimate goal to play for the NFL again. I knew that I just had to stay on this path and that things were going to work out."

In this case, Antonio was right about things working out. He was picked up by the San Diego Chargers and had a highly successful 2010 season.

And if (or when) his career is in fact over? Antonio already has a plan in place for following through on his desire to give something back to his community, especially its youth. He has recently started a foundation to assist the youth from his hometown and region to make wise choices and take advantage of positive opportunities.

With his pursuit of the highest principles, well-defined moral values, a belief in the importance of academics and an unshakeable family support system, Antonio Garay reflects the tenets at the heart of the Insightful Player™ campaign.

INSTANT REPLAY OF ANTONIO'S *GUIDING PRINCIPLES*

1. Realize that you can learn from criticism, even if you don't agree with it.

2. Recognize the importance of getting along with other people even if it's something that takes work: on a playing field, at a job, or anywhere.

3. Listen to what other people have to say. If you agree with them, let them inspire you; if you disagree, think about the perspective they are offering you.

4. Make family a priority. Spend time together, learn from each other, and build each other up.

5. Let adversity serve as a motivating force. Every bump in the road has the potential to be a launching point.

6. Nourish your inner drive. If your heart feels not just a desire but an insistence on reaching your goals, you will get there.

7. Hold yourself up as a role model to others. Remember that your choices and actions affect not just you but all those who are watching to see what you will do.

8. Cultivate your spiritual side, and have faith that it will lead you to make the right decisions.

9. Appreciate differences in people—cultural, religious, and philosophical—and look for ways to learn from them.

CHAPTER 12

THE HOUSTON TEXANS'

JARVIS GREEN

PHOTO COURTESY *of Dylan Cyr*

Determination to Learn from Adversity Fosters Deep-Rooted Resilience and Profound Growth

For his sense of self-discipline, **Jarvis Green** thanks his parents. For perseverance, he credits his high school coach, who called him back onto the field one day in seventh grade after Jarvis decided he wasn't cut out to be a football player. And for the physical endurance that has helped him to become a world-class professional athlete, he acknowledges the influence of his twin brother Jason. It's not that

Jason encouraged or inspired him to be a runner. It's that Jarvis learned to use running as a positive outlet for the negative energy he built up when he and his twin would fight as teens.

The boys had scuffled ever since they were small: they had great affection for each other but also frequently fell into physical skirmishes. And though this was typical for them, once they turned 16, his mother began to see it differently. For the first time, her sons were larger than she was, and she no longer felt able to separate the two of them once they started scuffling. "So that's when she said, 'You'll have to leave the house because I can't sit here and break you up, you're getting too big for me.' She didn't mean leave long-term; just to terminate the fight. Since I was a minute older, I was the one who got out of the house, and I just started walking around the lane in the neighborhood."

Jarvis quickly realized that walking off steam was a good way to handle the frequent altercations with his brother. "And then as the days went by, walking turned to jogging. I was jogging five miles a day. As a football player, I was never a superstar, I was just an average guy playing football. But I truly think one reason I reached the point I did in the pros is that I just started jogging to the point where my endurance level was so high, it showed on the football field. I remember running in thunderstorms, lightning storms, a lot of rain, hailstorms. I remember running by the levee along the Mississippi River and through the cane fields. Running through all kinds of conditions. And that ability kind of separated me from the other players on the football team. That's when I came into my own as a football player."

As a young boy, Jarvis was picked on at school. He fought back, and that caused trouble at home. When he was on the verge of being expelled from school for fighting, his parents held up the threat of being placed in a juvenile home. That scared him enough to swear off fighting for good—even though the other kids at school, knowing the pressure Jarvis was under to stay the course, deliberately tried to goad him into more fights. "We all face times when we have to make decisions. It doesn't matter if you're an adult or a little kid; we all have times when we have to look at what we know about right and wrong and make a decision. I was faced with a huge decision when I was in the third grade, knowing that if I got in another fight, I would have gotten expelled for the year.

"I was a great kid in school, always the teacher's pet. I was small then. And so I always got picked on. And then I'd get into serious fights for trying to defend myself." But when faced with his parents' ultimatum, Jarvis stopped fighting and learn to let the other kids' teasing roll off his back. "It was tough, but I was a kid that didn't really care what people said about me. I didn't care if people commented on my haircut or what I had on, and I kept moving. I went to school, I was happy and I was proud of what I had, what my parents had done for us and what they had given us."

Despite the scuffles with his brother, Jarvis said he grew up in a generally secure household. His mother, he said, "made us feel like we were worth a million dollars. What she instilled in us was to respect ourselves, to respect others and to treat people fair." Their hometown of Donaldsonville, Louisiana, was safe and welcoming for children: Jarvis and his twin, like their three elder siblings before them, played outside much of the day and ran interchangeably among the homes of neighbors, friends and relatives.

Until middle school, his mother kept him out of organized sports, although his older brothers were both playing high school football by that time. When he finally had the chance to take the field in seventh grade, the opportunity almost fell through his fingers. "I was out there doing a drill and I started complaining, saying the other guys hit too hard, this and that. I remember I was tackling the running back, who was my cousin. He was probably three times the size of me and he ran over me two times in a row. The third time, I said to the coach, 'I'm done with this, this isn't for me.' I took my helmet off and threw the helmet down and ran into the locker room. I said, 'I quit.' But my coach—Coach Ronnie Rabilis—rest his soul, he ran after me and said, 'I coached your brothers and I'm not going to let you off this easy,' and he got me back out there.

I went back out there and we went back to the same drill. He put the same guy in front of me and he said, 'Tackle him.' From that day on I was positive about the sport and just about a lot of things, about not giving up, because it was so easy to give up."

It helped Jarvis that his coach could empathize with the frustration. "He said, 'I understand. It's easier to walk off the field, nothing to it. How hard was it for you to stay there and get run over?' I said, 'That was very hard.' And then he said, 'Son, welcome to the real world. In life that's going to happen and you have to keep going, keep fighting and pressing on.' From that point on, I played sports and stayed out of trouble with the other kids. If it wasn't for him, I wouldn't be here today."

For much of Jarvis's childhood, his was a two-parent home. Then his parents divorced when he was in high school. His father told him about the breakup and impressed upon him the need to take care of his mother. "By that time, my older brothers and sister had gone through college and moved on with their lives, so it was just my mom and my twin brother Jason and me left at home. I remember times were tough, because we had been living on Social Security that my dad received as the result of a back injury, so when he moved out a lot of that was lost as income."

It was a big burden for a young man to carry. "My junior and senior year of high school, I was picking up jobs to keep the lights on and keep water running, helping my mom, and just being a man overnight. And having to do all those things plus playing football meant missing my senior prom and not doing a lot of things that a kid in high school would love to do. I remember leaving practice, going to work and working 20 to 25 hours a week trying to bring home $100. What I brought home, I would give to my mom to put toward the bills. I did that for my entire senior year."

His first years at Louisiana State University weren't much easier. As a major in construction engineering, he saw his grades occasionally dip dangerously low, only to rebound when classmates helped him understand complicated concepts or collaborate with him on group projects. He sustained serious back injuries in a car accident his freshman year but refused to give up football and played much of his college career with fractures in his back. "I don't know how I played. It was a stronger power, it wasn't just me. God was helping me through it. I went to different doctors and different surgeons. The head trainer at LSU was always there for me and helping me get through it all. It was tough going. I just had to get through it, play football, go to school, take care of my mom. All of those factors were in play throughout my college career."

Despite the emotional tumult that sometimes prevailed between his parents, they had always practiced deep religious values when Jarvis was growing up, and the influence of his Baptist upbringing gave him faith when times were difficult.

Now, when he speaks with young people, he reminds them that growing up in an unsettled household doesn't have to be seen as an entirely bad thing. "I tell kids, if you grew up in an abusive home and didn't have opportunities to do things the other kids in a better situation could do, you still have a chance to do what you want to do. You don't have to sit there and reenact the past. My approach was that I just wanted to have a good life. I wanted to be happy. All parents want their kids to live a better life than they do. My mom, she always told us that each generation should have a better life than the generation before."

And all the tough times taught him lessons, he now said. Through it all, he was learning tenacity and family loyalty. When the family needed more leadership than his father was providing, a cousin, Ronnie Garrison, stepped in to assist Jarvis's mother and to mentor the boys. When Jarvis's mother eventually lost her house through a foreclosure, she went to live with Jarvis in off-campus housing in Baton Rouge while he attended college.

Still, he never lost sight of graduating from college as his top priority. All his life, his parents had emphasized education over athletic prowess, and his success on the college gridiron, even with serious back injuries, didn't change that priority even though he was starting to get glimmers of hope that a pro career with the NFL might lie ahead. "I started off pretty fast my first year, made a lot of plays, got a lot of honors, and that's when I started thinking about it, but it wasn't the most important thing. The most important thing in my head was getting a degree. That's what my mom always preached to us. All of us kids went to college and graduated. When I used to come home, we never talked about football. That wasn't a topic at our table. The topic was, 'How are you doing in school? Are you getting good grades?' "

College continued to be a struggle for him—construction engineering isn't a subject you can get the Cliff notes for, Jarvis points out—but sheer persistence saw him through. He still remembers the elation he felt at his graduation ceremony—and the tears he shed.

Being drafted his first season of pro ball in the fourth round to the Patriots was another wonderful moment. "I was watching the draft on TV when the coach called," he said. He stayed with the Patriots for the next seven years.

"I was so surprised, because I had always thought I would probably go one or two years in the NFL, being what they call a 'tweener': not too big, not too small… in between. But now, nine years later, I'm still playing. And to go to three Super Bowls with the Patriots…It's like being on cloud nine. When you're winning, everybody's happy."

Of course, in his last Super Bowl with the Patriots, they did not win. And Jarvis admits to still being a little bit bewildered by the split-second reversal. "Everything had been like clockwork. The entire season was clockwork and we were beating everybody and everything was perfect. You wake up in the morning and the sun was always shining, put your shoes on right foot first, left foot second, that's the way it was when we got to the stadium."

But things changed in the final two minutes of the game. Looking back more than three years later, though, Jarvis said that "I would say it made me stronger. We all go through adversity all the time, everybody goes through adversity in life. That loss was something that we had to overcome. We had to learn that you can't win them all, you're not always going to get what you want in life. You can work hard, work your butt off, but that doesn't guarantee a win. Some things are predestined."

Today, Jarvis is happily married, a father of three, and a member of the Houston Texans. He is also working harder than ever to spread his message of using adversity for what it can teach us and is looking for new ways to help his community. He started the Jarvis Green Foundation, a non-profit committed to providing support to single working mothers in disadvantaged, low-income areas—other women very much like the amazing mother who taught him the values he carries with him still today.

Proving himself able time and again to counter physical, spiritual and emotional setbacks with perseverance and a belief in the power of good decision-making, Jarvis Green has the true spirit of an Insightful Player™ team member.

INSTANT REPLAY OF JARVIS'S *GUIDING PRINCIPLES*

1. A good education with a priority on graduating from college is the single most important determinant to success of any kind.

2. Everyone, no matter how easy or difficult their life is, faces decisions. Making the right decisions can mean the difference between reaching your goals and falling short.

3. Tell the truth. When you make a mistake, own up to it.

4. Be a team player. Distinguish yourself not with self-promotion but with your loyalty and support of others.

5. Learn to trust other people and be someone others can trust. Hold yourself and others accountable for actions.

6. Treat parents, coaches, teachers and other adults with unflagging respect.

7. Learn to find the message in moments of adversity. Figure out what you can learn from a problematic situation.

8. There are times when losing is not a sign you haven't worked hard enough. Sometimes you lose the game no matter how hard you play.

9. Be a positive role model committed to changing the world for the better.

CHAPTER 13

LEGENDARY PATRIOTS QUARTERBACK

STEVE GROGAN

Set the Gridiron on Fire With Robust Determination and Awe-Inspiring Stamina

New England Patriots Hall of Famer **Steve Grogan** recognizes that it's been a while since he played professional football. When he goes into schools now as part of the DARE program that encourages young people to make wise choices, they often don't know exactly who he is. "So I just tell them I used to be Tom Brady, a long time ago," he laughed. "Then they get it."

If he's not a household name among the middle school set, he certainly is among their parents and grandparents. Steve played 16 seasons with the New England Patriots. The 12 rushing touchdowns he completed during his second season, in 1976, still stands as the most rushing touchdowns in one season by any quarterback. That same year, he led the Patriots to an 11-3 record, winning them their first playoff berth in 13 years. Under his leadership, the team also reached the playoffs five times. Moreover, he said he'd go back in a heartbeat—despite the lasting effects of a physically punishing job. "I've got some aches and pains, but I knew that was going to happen," he said. "I took those risks and I can't complain about it. I'd go back tomorrow if they called me and said they had an opening. It was a lot of fun."

Being a role model has always been important to him. "I'm just a regular person who was in the public spotlight and therefore tried to conduct his life in a good way and set a good example for kids and adults alike," he said. But with the perspective of age, he's also aware of where he fell short. "I have a temper that has gotten me in trouble a few times on and off the field, but I think I've learned to control that to the best of my ability." And the same trait that can be seen as a fault off the field can be an asset to an athlete, he pointed out. "Part of that temper was what made me so competitive and made me successful on the football field. Still, it was something I really had to adjust to and deal with while I was growing up."

At this point, he sees the matter of temper a little differently. "I don't get nearly as upset about things as I used to. I think that comes with age. You get some perspective on what really counts and is important, and what doesn't really count and is *not* that important."

Steve grew up in Ottawa, Kansas, with his parents and one younger brother. His father owned and operated a service station and employed Steve as cleaning help. Meanwhile, father and son together became fixtures on the local sports scene. "My father coached me in a lot of the youth sports that I played," he recalled. By high school, Steve would not only be a rising football star but also led his team to state championships in basketball and track. Meanwhile, the enjoyment his father derived from youth coaching inspired the elder Grogan to start a second career as a teacher, which lasted the next 30 years.

"My parents were both influential in my upbringing," he said. "They had a lot to do with the way I conducted myself and what I held to be important. They were very involved in community and church activities. They set a great example for my brother and me as far as how we should conduct ourselves."

Remembering the fine example set by his own parents helps Steve to articulate the importance of recognizing right and wrong when he speaks now to student groups. "In today's anti-drug programs, they teach the kids to say no. 'Just say no' sounds easy, but it's not. I explain to them how, when I played football, there were a lot of defensive guys over on the other side that were out to get me and to hurt me. Fortunately I had an offensive line that was protecting me, but sometimes the offensive line would break down and I would run for my life to get away from danger.

"And I try to tell them that they have the same type of support system. The offensive line is their parents, their teachers, the police, the business people in their community, all of whom are there to help protect them, but they're going to get into situations where that offensive line is not going to be around. It's a lot easier to run from a dangerous situation than it is to stay and just say no, over and over and over, because eventually people will wear you down and get you to say yes. So, I advise them that if they find themselves in an awkward situation that they're not comfortable with, to get the heck out of there."

Despite the success he eventually had in the NFL, winning was never a given—he has known since childhood that victory is something that must be earned. "On my birth certificate, it says I have a club foot. When I was born, my foot was kind of curled up and withered. My parents refused to accept this as a disability. They spent hours and hours stretching and moving my foot until it finally got back to normal. It never bothered me after that."

Even if Steve can't remember the physical therapy of his infancy, he thinks the spirit behind it imbued him with a sense of tenacity. "It seemed like throughout my career, from high school through college and then professionally, there was always a sense that someone better than me could be playing my position. I just kept working hard and doing the best I could and outlasted all of them."

It wasn't easy, though—physically or psychologically. "It is always tough when you are asked to sit down. I went through it the first time in my career back around 1982 when the Patriots drafted Matt Cavanaugh in the second round and decided he was the better player and should be in the starting position. I did what I had to do to help the team until my turn came again, which it did. Then they drafted Tony Eason, and within a year they had him starting in front of me. I always did what was best for the team. I kept my mouth shut and tried to help Tony, and my turn came again, fortunately."

In part, Steve is simply describing the realities of football, where everything from strategy to injuries can cause today's starter to be tomorrow's second-string, but beyond that, it's the representation of how he was taught by his parents and childhood coaches, he said. "That's the way I was brought up. You're part of the team, you do what they ask you to do when they ask you to do it, and you stay ready to take over when the time comes."

Recognizing he wasn't always the best was an important element of personal growth for him. "On the Patriots, we had a lot of great leaders. I wasn't the only one," he said. "One thing I realized is that humility is the number one asset for someone in a job like mine. It's hard when someone tells you you're not good enough anymore and then sits you on the bench. You don't know whether your career is over with or how long it's going to be before you get to play again. You're waiting for the chance to do something you love to do." But over the years, he developed plenty of coping strategies, he said. "I just found that rather than moan and groan and complain about things, it was a much better approach to just go out every day and practice and have fun. Whatever the coach asks you to do, do it to the best of your ability. Then, no matter what happens, you've got nothing to be ashamed of. Sometimes it will work out, sometimes it won't. But if you start complaining and feeling sorry for yourself, then more often than not, you're not going to get another chance."

Reaching the pros was not only a matter of talent, Steve believed; it was a matter of mentorship. "Like most kids who play sports growing up, I had a dream that I wanted to play professionally at some point. A lot of times, what makes the difference is somebody taking an interest in you, giving you a little extra time, recognizing your talent. I was lucky to have some coaches at the high school level who did that for me. And then my freshman year at Kansas State, I was feeling ready to transfer to a smaller school like the one in my hometown to try to play three sports: football, basketball and baseball. But I had a coach named Jerry Sullivan who spent a lot of time with me after practice, working on my throwing skills until I improved dramatically. If it hadn't have been for him, I wouldn't have stayed at Kansas State when I had a chance to move on."

His decision to stay at Kansas State helped him to be recognized as a potential pro football player, but even getting drafted wasn't the end of his struggle to make it. "When I came to the Patriots, they had three veteran quarterbacks and I was told in camp they were only going to keep two people for the position. So, it didn't look good for me. But I was in the right place at the right time. One guy retired and one guy got hurt, so they had to keep me. I just kept working hard. In the end, I fooled them for 16 years."

Despite the fact that many adults saw his potential early on, the role models throughout Steve's boyhood made sure he understood that getting a good education needed to be his highest priority. "It was always stressed to me that school was important and that sports were not going to last forever. That's why you need an education. I worked hard in school. I was a member of the National Honor Society in high school and graduated with a degree after four years of college. And as much as I loved playing professional football, I knew that I had an education I could fall back on if things didn't work out. I think a lot of the guys at that level nowadays don't take advantage of that opportunity to get an education. Kids need to understand that finishing college puts you a step ahead of a lot of other people."

At the same time, Steve said, balancing a good education with regular participation in team sports may provide the most solid foundation of all. He believes that there are lessons to be learned on the playing fields that are different from those garnered in the classroom. "If you have a strong education plus the discipline, dedication and confidence that you learn by being a part of a team sport, you have an advantage over somebody who has never played competitive sports. You learn special skills by working as part of a team."

For example, he said, "You learn to work with all kinds of different people. On a pro football team, you've got people of different races, different religions, different backgrounds, and you learn to work with all of them. So no matter what situation you find yourself in after your football career has ended, you're well prepared to work with just about anybody. You have to be extremely disciplined to be a part of a football team. You have to take care of your body. You have to study extra hard and manage your time well. When you get benched every once in a while, it can really put a dent in your confidence, but if you learn how to stay confident in your own ability, then you're able to handle a lot of different situations."

For Steve, the life skills he picked up both as a student and as an athlete are still paying off in his current endeavor as the proprietor of **Grogan** Marciano Sporting Goods, a business that he bought seventeen years ago. "I don't have a degree in business, but I had some friends who did know a lot about business, and I was smart enough to draw upon their expertise. I've never had an ego that was so big that I thought that I couldn't learn from other people. That not only helped in football but it's definitely helped in business. I've never been ashamed to ask for advice or help from somebody that I thought had more knowledge or a better talent that could help me.

"Also, through all my years on teams, I knew what it was like to be around a lot of different kinds of personalities. I knew how to deal with people. You don't deal with them all the same way." This awareness is advantageous not only in terms of staying on good terms with customers and employees, he said, but also in making good hiring decisions. "I have developed the ability to recognize talent regardless of whether it is on a football field or in a business setting. These are all elements that have helped us stay successful here in the business for nearly two decades."

Along with striving to make his business ever more successful and enjoying time with his wife, Robbi—the two were college sweethearts in Kansas and have raised three sons—Steve is focusing right now on physical wellness and trying to improve his physical condition. "Iin the spring of 2010 I lost one of my teammates, Mosi Tatupu. Only 54 years old, he died of a heart attack. It was a wake-up call to a lot of us who played with him. We're all getting older, and maybe some of us weren't taking as good care of ourselves as we should have been. I definitely decided to get back in the gym on a regular basis even though sometimes it's painful to do that."

It's all part of his belief that you should never rest on your laurels. With his continuous quest for self-improvement and his faith that there are lessons to be learned from every situation, Steve Grogan exemplifies the qualities of an Insightful Player™ team member.

INSTANT REPLAY OF STEVE'S *GUIDING PRINCIPLES*

1. Recognize your flaws and use them as areas for improvement.

2. Try to develop a sense of perspective as far as what is truly important in life and what is not.

3. Understand that you have your own "offensive line" which may include parents, teachers, coaches, clergy, police, and adult community members, all trying to help you do the right thing as you grow up

4. Sometimes in difficult situations involving peer pressure, the best thing to do is simply run. Rather than struggling time and again to overcome the pressures or temptations posed to you, learn to avoid or escape these situations altogether.

5. Persist at those pursuits that matter most to you. Sometimes success isn't about being the best but rather outlasting the competition.

6. Don't submit to jealousy or over-competitiveness. Keep your focus on your own goals rather than on who is getting there before you; your time will come if you keep working at it.

7. Make your education one of your highest priorities. In the end, it will probably get you farther than any athletic talents will.

8. Develop your team skills: learn to work with others and learn from their differences.

9. Honor your sense of humility. In acknowledging the greatness of others, you open in yourself the potential to stand among them.

10. Take care of yourself physically: make physical fitness and other forms of physical health a priority.

CHAPTER 14

WASHINGTON REDSKINS HALL OF FAMER

KEN HARVEY

An Outstanding Role Model Gains a Boatload of Wisdom from Every Experience, Including Mistakes

Ken Harvey believes in second chances. "Mistakes happen," said the former linebacker for the Phoenix Cardinals and the Washington Redskins and current Washington Redskins Director of Responsibility. "What matters in life is how effectively you rally after making and recognizing a misstep."

Ken's own missteps, from his perspective, date back to his decision to drop out of high school. "It wasn't because I was dumb," he said. "I was fairly smart, but I was a really shy kid and just developed some bad habits. I was trying to manage school and football, but then I would miss a day of school for whatever reason and I'd be too embarrassed to go back. I felt like people would be pointing a finger at me when I came back. So I'd miss another day, and then it just kept adding up. My football coach started saying to me, 'What are you doing? You're wasting your life. You have potential. You could be good. Your parents are on you because of your grades. You're flunking out of classes.'"

But these notions weren't enough to make Ken change his behaviors. His school suggested that he should take vocational classes like woodworking just to get through school. "In my mind, I was thinking 'No, I'm smarter than this,' but everything I did proved the opposite. I was kind of angry about all of it, so I started thinking the best thing to do was to go ahead and drop out because I was going to get straight F's anyway. I figured I'd drop out of school, I could get my mind right, make sure that school was what I really wanted and then make a decision one way or another: either do something where I wouldn't have to have a high school diploma or go back to school."

He did drop out, and then fell into a rut of destructive thought patterns. "If you drop out of school, and if you start listening to all the things around you, which was easy to do at the time, you start thinking 'Okay, maybe I am dumb, maybe I can't make it, maybe I'm nothing.' And you lower your standards and you start getting used to that thought, so everything you do fuels that mindset."

From there his outlook spiraled downward. "Once you start thinking you're not much good for anything, you resign yourself to getting the lowest-paying job, or you go to an interview but you're not fully prepared. Then you wonder why you're not getting a better job or you're not making it. It's because you've set your standards low and everything around you has become that standard. When you drop out of school, there's automatically a stigma. I was a big guy, muscular... so people looked at me like they thought I must be stupid, or a criminal. I was depressed for awhile."

Friends and family members tried to set him straight, but it was a problem he needed to muddle through on his own. Something changed his thinking one day when he picked up a newspaper to see what kind of job he could hope to have without a high school diploma. "All of a sudden I saw that anything I'd want to do would require a diploma. That made me start thinking that maybe I'd better go back to school. I remember meeting a guy who was cleaning floors and he was telling me about what he could have done and what he should have done. I thought to myself, 'Is that how I want my life to be—always telling people what I should have done and how I could have been great?' I knew it was the same thing my parents and my grandparents and even people I hardly knew had been trying to tell me. But finally then, I could say, 'You know what? I can do something. I'm better than dropping out of school. I'm better than all this.' It wasn't that I was being cocky; I just realized I'd let my standards slip too low."

It didn't change all at once after that. "Once you come to the realization you could probably do more, you need to go and set new standards, put in place new habits, which is tough, because now you have to break bad habits and start new habits and identify old faults and all that stuff. So, I started new habits where I had a plan as to how I was going to get into college. I worked out every day and lifted weights and ran. I stopped going to parties .... I started hanging around good people. It wasn't like I'd been hanging around bad people before; I wasn't hanging out with anybody."

It was a lesson in humility, in no small part because upon his return to school, he was in the same class as his younger brother. He sensed that everyone was looking at him, judging him, wondering why he hadn't gotten further in his education. So he looked for divine guidance. "I was on my knees praying. I said, 'God, give me a plan, give me a vision,' and it felt like to me like God was saying, 'You are worth something. You have a destiny, you have a purpose, you are worth something.' That's what I held onto, the sense that I had a purpose and a destiny."

And by seeking out positive role models, Ken found his life starting to change. "All of a sudden, things started happening because I had put myself in a position for good things to happen. I met somebody at the gym who told me about a junior college I could attend in Oakland, California. I flew to Oakland, saved some money, went to school there, and earned a scholarship to the University of California, Berkeley. From there, I ended up playing in the pros. But it all changed because I took a good look at the direction I was headed in and said, 'That's not where I want to be.' So I raised the bar a little bit higher."

It was a philosophy that would serve him well beyond his football career. "Throughout your life, it's important to keep raising the bar or keep adjusting it. I look back now at some of the things I did and wish I could change them, but you are what you are. So you start by looking at that and then you say, 'I'm going to be just a little bit better.' It's just like lifting weights. If I can lift five pounds today and in three months I want to be able to lift ten pounds, the only way to reach that goal is to work out every day and do it the right way."

Looking at the big picture is a practice he's developed through the course of his adulthood. "Life is a journey. You take it one day at a time, but hopefully you learn some lessons along the way, and if you don't deal with those lessons, you're going to run into them over and over and over again. They just come in different forms and different ways and different angles, but you're going to have to deal with them." Believing in this has taught him to view every obstacle or moment of adversity as a potential learning experience. "My biggest fear is to be on my deathbed looking back and saying, '"I never learned that lesson because I didn't deal with it when I was young.' I think it's so important to be able to see growth in your life. I know I can see that in my life. Still, I keep learning lessons and keep growing."

One lesson that has come to him in more recent years is the importance of communication and in reaching out to other people. "You have to be around the right people and you have to have people you can trust, that you can talk to. You want to identify your problems, but you also want to learn how to create new habits, because life is about habits. Habits become a lifestyle, a lifestyle becomes who you are. Once you can identify some of the things that you have to deal with, then you start changing, and creating a new habit."

More recently, he has been trying hard to be more verbally communicative, something his wife has always encouraged. "I used to be really quiet. I didn't want to talk to people. So I started trying to read the newspapers so I had things to talk about. I knew how to talk to the press, I could get by and sound intelligent, but to talk to somebody one-on-one wasn't comfortable for me. When you play pro football, you don't necessarily have to be good at conversation because people just want to talk about football with you. Once I stopped playing football, it was almost like a weight off my shoulders because it was then that I could tell myself that now I didn't have to talk only about football; I could talk about whatever I wanted to."

Ken's diligence in learning to be a better conversationalist paid off; he would eventually go on to work as a motivational speaker before starting his own business development company called Jaka consulting group. "When I went to junior college, the head coach made sure every player took a speech class and so some of that stuff applied. I was trying to read a little bit more so I'd have things to talk about, and recently, it finally occurred to me through prayer and talking to other people that any time someone talks to you, they've spent some time thinking about what they were going to say. And what they say is obviously important to them. So the least I can do is listen to them and give them some time. And so I'm trying to learn now to listen to people as much as I do talk because that's part of a conversation also."

He played 11 seasons with the NFL, but that was only the beginning of a fascinating and varied professional life. Along with being a motivational speaker, he has done video segments for the *Washington Post*, and in 2008 he acquired the landmark title of Washington Redskins Director of Responsibility, a groundbreaking position developed in partnership with DIAGEO, the world's leading premium drinks business. The partnership and proactive corporate social responsibility stance enables Ken to act as a resource and advisor in the development of responsibility initiatives focused on education and advocacy across the Redskins organization and local community.

In September 2008, DIAGEO officials approached Ken in conjunction with the Washington Redskins Foundation to ask if he would take this role with their organization. "It's an outreach program," Ken explains. "We have coaches and players talking about responsible drinking, but the most visible element of their endeavor is a safe rides program that runs during the holiday season and enables adults to get a safe ride home if they've had too much to drink."

Drinking and driving, as Ken sees it, is a bad decision that can often be traced back to pride. "Pride is a big monster in the context of drunk driving because it will always tell you that you're fine and you should go ahead and drive after you've had too many drinks. Meanwhile, your mind is saying, 'It's okay, I can handle it.' It can be like that with football too. You get into a mindset of saying 'I can overcome whatever comes along.' You have to be humble enough to look in the mirror and say 'I know what I need to do. And if I get too drunk, I need to call this number to get a free ride home.' It's a good program."

As a father, Ken thinks a lot about the example he is setting for his children. "If we tell our kids, 'You are something special,' even when they go through bad stuff and the twists and the turns of growing up, hopefully somewhere deep down inside, they're going to hear your voice. It may take years. It may not ever happen. They may not ever go through any difficult times, but hopefully if they do, somewhere deep down inside, they can hear your voice and think, 'I'm better than that.' And that's what I'm hoping to accomplish with my kids."

His creativity has allowed him to write books, while also making the most of his opportunity to help the world through his partnership with DIAGEO. "I always try to stress that I'm not perfect. I make a lot of mistakes. I continue to make mistakes, but by the grace of God, I'm trying to get better every day. We all have issues that we struggle with, but I'm trying always to grow."

His wish to make the world a better place took a dramatic and positive turn when he traveled to Haiti representing DIAGEO to aid in relief efforts after the January 2010 earthquake. "We went out on the streets and saw earthquake survivors just walking around with no place to go. We saw people asking for help and we saw dead bodies. We saw all the rubble and the buildings destroyed, and in my mind I was thinking, even just to get rid of all the debris, it's going to take years. But then you see signs of hope. You see kids laughing. I saw one lady who was clearing out all the debris and stuff right around her just to keep her own little area clean. You see people trying to do their best. What I took from it is that if there is some hope and some vision, if people can see a tomorrow, then all the money that's been raised and all the things that come through will be for the good. If you don't have that sense of hope, then you can fix everything up and make it look pretty, but if your mindset is still the same, it will never change. Hopefully, one day I'll go back to Haiti and see a difference."

Ken is enjoying a life of entrepreneurship and writing. He has published two children's books and recently released his first novel, *Xavier: A Hero No More.* Having gone from being a high school dropout to the NFL and more, Ken is a believer that anything is possible. He believes that his new novel demonstrates some of the struggles players have after leaving the game. He has established his own website, www.transition57.com, as a means for educating players about becoming entrepreneurs after their playing days are over. Ken really has a heart for athletes in transition. He cares about their ability to transition from sports to the marketplace; from inactivity to activity fueled by good health and healthy habits; from a mindset of contentment with life on the field to a sky's the limit attitude off of the field; from irresponsibility to responsibility.

In a way, it all goes back to his decision to go back to high school after dropping out: an attitude of persistence that has stayed with him ever since. "I believe in second chances. I believe in that we can help each other out. I always try to look at the hope and the good inside of people. I think that's it. No matter what, if you look deep enough, there is good in almost everyone."

With his belief in the fundamental goodness of every human soul and his ceaseless quest for self-improvement, Ken Harvey emanates the exemplary values of an Insightful Player™ team member.

INSTANT REPLAY OF KEN'S *GUIDING PRINCIPLES*

1. Maintain high standards for yourself. Low standards become a self-fulfilling prophecy.

2. When you fall into negative ways of thinking, implement new and better habits that will help you make positive changes.

3. Rather than wallowing in regrets or reliving mistakes, use where you are as a starting point and move upward from there.

4. Make it a lifetime goal to keep raising the bar for yourself. Have ever-higher expectations for what you can do.

5. Surround yourself with positive role models and well-meaning people from whom you can learn.

6. Mistakes happen. Growth comes from recognizing when you did something wrong and correcting it.

7. Have goals at all levels of your life.

8. Believe in the inherent worth and goodness of everyone you meet.

9. Be a good listener. Give people your time and attention. Respect what they want to say.

10. Be able to envision a better future and use that as a benchmark to work toward.

CHAPTER 15

THE JACKSONVILLE JAGUARS'

AARON KAMPMAN

#74

Devout Faith, Love of Family and Strength of Character Have Seen Him through the Best of Times and the Very Worst of Times

Aaron Kampman remembers vividly the moment in 2009 when he received shocking and horrible news. He was wrapping up some morning meetings before practice with the Green Bay Packers, for whom he played from 2002 to 2009, when head coach Mike McCarthy said he needed to talk with Aaron privately. Anticipating the worst, Aaron immediately thought of his wife, Linde, and their three young sons.

But the news wasn't about a family member; it was that Aaron's high school coach, Ed Thomas, had just been shot seven times by a former player. Coach Thomas was clinging to life, so Aaron fell to his knees to pray for him. "But that was not the answer that God had for us at that time," Aaron reflected, still heavy-hearted about the tragedy. "And so, he lost his life."

The event was inconceivable to nearly everyone affected by it. As Aaron explained, "Parkersburg, Iowa is a town of 1800 people. Things like this just don't happen there."

What does happen in Parkersburg—or what did over the course of 37 years of coaching—was that Coach Thomas cranked out magnificent football players from a tiny pool of high school students. "Ed Thomas taught all his players the right way to play football—with intensity and passion. The amazing thing is that there are four of us from this tiny town who are in the NFL," Aaron said. "Casey Wiegmann is going into his 16th year with the Kansas City Chiefs, Jared DeVries is going into his 13th year with the Detroit Lions, Brad Meester is going into his 12h year down in Jacksonville, and I'm joining him in Jacksonville after eight years with Green Bay. Talk about beating the odds."

The tragedy of losing his friend and mentor cemented in Aaron's mind the powerful lessons that Coach Thomas had taught him over the years—lessons reinforced by his solid Christian upbringing in a two-parent home. "One of the great lessons that Ed taught was that when adversity strikes, it's not at that moment that you develop the capacity to handle it. Your character is cultivated over time, so that when adversity does strike, you have the ability to handle it with grace, dignity, and perseverance. It doesn't take away the pain but it gives you the ability to manage it. For Ed, those principles were squarely focused in his faith in the Lord Jesus, so that's what he communicated to us as young people. And again, in my own situation, that was communicated first and foremost by my parents, but it was reinforced by my high school coach."

Thomas' sense of character had a ripple effect that would reach more than just his football team. His widow and sons accepted the Arthur Ashe Courage Award, presented at 2010 ESPN's ESPY Award Ceremony. It was an award for their ability to express forgiveness to the family whose son murdered Ed. In the acceptance speech, said Aaron, Ed's eldest son issued a challenge to the country in general and athletes in particular. "He said, 'You've seen the impact that my father, a high school coach of a community that had fewer than 2000 people could have; how much more impact can you athletes sitting here have?' So that shows you the kind of the cloth that I was cut from."

As a student at Aplington-Parkersburg High School, Aaron not only set records in football but distinguished himself in other sports as well. He was first-team Parade All-America selection and USA Today second-team honoree as a senior linebacker and was Named Class 2A Player of the Year. A three-year letterman, he set a school record with 447 career tackles and helped bring his team to three consecutive playoff appearances including a runner-up finish as a junior. He posted a three-year mark of 26-7. Off the football field, Aaron lettered three times in basketball and four times in track, earned all-state honors in basketball as a senior and placed third in state in shotput as a junior and senior. When not competing in athletics, Aaron along with his brother ran a roof shingling business while still in high school.

Growing up as the second of three boys, Aaron believed his childhood was typical. Not until he started college at the University of Iowa did he see how special his circumstances were. "I grew up in a small rural town in Iowa. I could go right out in the back yard and walk past fences and be out in nature. My mom is one of six brothers and sisters and they all live in the area except for one. So every month, the entire family, all the grandkids and aunts and uncles, got together and celebrated birthdays at my grandma and grandpa's house. It was a great way to grow up. But it was also a little bit of a bubble. When I got to college, I first realized the blessing of coming from a two-parent home."

Not only the closeness of his family but also the model his parents put forth regarding community service had a powerful influence on Aaron as he was growing up. "My dad owns a lumberyard. My mom is a registered nurse who works for the county and travels around and takes care of people, particularly elderly people. So from a very young age I saw both of my parents demonstrate an ideal of service and a work ethic that became deeply ingrained in me. Those were powerful ingredients that have really helped shape me into the man that I am today."

"Being the man he is today" means converting a strong commitment to God and family into continuous deeds and actions that reflect his principles. While still in college, he served as president of the local chapter of Athletes in Action and was a regular visitor to the University of Iowa Children's Hospital. During their eight years in Green Bay, Aaron and his wife were deeply entrenched in the Green Bay community. Along with frequent speaking engagements for schools, teams and youth groups there, Aaron volunteered at Paul's Pantry, distributing food to deserving families in Green Bay. He has made several appearances at the Jerry Parins Cruise for Cancer, an annual motorcycle ride benefitting cancer patients and families throughout northeastern Wisconsin. He has also volunteered with the Salvation Army, Brown County Library, March of Dimes and St. Vincent Hospital, filmed a public service announcement for the annual food drive led by U.S. Postal Service and the National Association of Letter Carriers, and played in both the Brett Favre and Donald Driver celebrity softball games. When his hometown of Parkersburg was struck by a massive tornado in 2008 that destroyed the high school, he helped raise funds for the relief effort and delivered the pregame speech to the high school football team prior to the first game following the event.

Aaron's prodigious generosity has not gone unnoticed in the athletic community. In 2003, he was Packers finalist for the Walter Payton Man of the Year Award He was named one of the NFL's "Good Guys" by The Sporting News for his work in the community and received the "Nice Guy Award" at the 2004 Doug Jirschele Sports Award Banquet in Clintonville, Wisconsin.

His Christian faith has also led this two-time Pro Bowl selection into a series of missions overseas. He and his wife traveled to Mannheim, a military community in southwestern

Germany, with the Christian organization Unlimited Potential Incorporated to share their faith with U.S. troops stationed there. In 2007, the couple took a two-week tour of India as guests of Gospel for Asia, a Christian ministry whose missionaries work throughout the most remote regions of southern Asia. Two years later, their destination was Kenya, where they visited Christian humanitarian missions in rural communities. That trip, sponsored by World Vision, also included a visit to a large slum in Nairobi to assist Vapor Sports Ministries, whose mission is to provide humanitarian and Christ-centered assistance for impoverished communities around the world. These travels have alerted him to the pitfalls of what he calls "our sleepwalking society."

To be an effective Christian, Aaron said, you have to "line up with God's word and understand what our mission and calling really is in this life. The foundation of it still comes from God's word, reading the Bible, understanding that I'm called to be an ambassador of Christ and I need to do that in all these particular areas. Those are my marching orders. None of us can do everything, but each of us can do something. In order to attack hopelessness, you have to get your hands dirty. You have to find someone that doesn't have hope and try to help instill that in them, and in the process you'll be giving more than you could ever imagine, and getting even more back."

Even as he devotes his time and energy to aiding the impoverished, Aaron never overlooks the importance of his local fan base. After signing with the Jaguars, he paid for a large ad in Green Bay area newspapers to thank residents for their support. "It was a good way to bring some closure to my long relationship with a great organization, a great state, and great fans," he said of this generous gesture. He also serves as a tireless role model to his team members and other football players. He used the misfortune of an injury at the end of the 2009 season to demonstrate the difference a good attitude can make.

But in June of 2009, Aaron's faith was tested in a way he never could have imagined when he received word that his high school coach had been shot. It was a devastating and unfathomable event, Aaron says now—but one that underscored the many lessons about character that the late coach had taught him throughout his high school years. "Character is built over time, and often during the quiet times. Then it is tested when adversity strikes," Aaron said. "We build our character in these times of peace. For me, that happens to be when I'm reading the Bible and spending time in prayer, and it is reflected in how I love my wife and how I treat my kids and all of these very critical and important things in life that really are the foundation of our identities."

A strong character built on faith in God can stand up to catastrophe, he said. "When something like this happens, if your character has been built over time, you're acting on the wisdom that you're reading in scripture and you're getting stronger in spirit through prayer and how you're viewing life. When adversity then strikes, you have an opportunity to reveal that to others around you." The act of seeking out times for quiet reflection is crucial, he said. "We need time to reflect. We're such a fast-paced society with so much to do. With three little boys, it's hard for me to find the time too. But I try to discipline myself, even if it's fifteen minutes on the way to the stadium. No radio, no cell phone, just time to reflect, time to pray and think and to realize that my strength is not my own. I use the time to ask for strength, to ask for wisdom. And these are ways I think character is built and the soul is strengthened."

But he understands that by some measures, the peace and means for so much quiet reflection is a luxury not everyone has; his charitable outreach efforts have given him plenty of exposure to a grittier side of life. "What I'm saying isn't going to sound real easy to someone who is in the third grade and has a single mom who abuses him and he can't get out of the house without being offered drugs. How do I translate my faith into a context that makes sense to a third grader or a junior high kid dealing with tough circumstances?"

We survive as a people by forging relationships both with God and with other people, Aaron said. He refers to it as "both vertical and horizontal. Our foremost responsibility is trying to get that vertical relationship—the one with our Creator—right. And then after that, the natural outgrowth of a sound spiritual, or vertical, relationship is that it pours into a horizontal relationship, meaning relationships with others. We are created for community and that's why we love to be with people. We're built for relationships."

Observing the actions and hearing the words of the late Coach Thomas' family in the years since his death has cemented Aaron's belief in the strength to be derived from faith and community. "Joy, I believe, is something that is deep seated in your heart and gives you the eternal perspective that no matter what happens in this life, it's okay. It's an ability to see beyond the present circumstances. I've seen how this joy, this sense of peace, has been such a powerful ally for the Thomas family." In fact, Thomas' wife and sons have founded the Ed Thomas Family Foundation in partnership with the National Christian Foundation to benefit those causes that Coach Thomas' family believes will extend his influence and honor his priorities of faith, family, character and integrity. Aaron serves as a board member for the Foundation.

"Whatever is in our heart comes out in our actions," said Aaron, who recently completed a graduate studies certificate program through the Dallas Theological Seminary. "There is a Bible passage that says 'out of the overflow of our heart, the mouth speaks.' We all wear masks, each and every one of us, but when push comes to shove, who we really are in the difficult times, reveals what's inside." The particulars of professional football accelerate this process. "If you're about yourself, if you're about money, if you're about fame and power for yourself, then you will be revealed for that. But if you have values of teamwork and if you're others centered, that will show up. So again, our outward actions are responses to what is in our heart. Whenever we look up in the sky and we see all the stars and we see all this creation, we know that we're not here by ourselves. How did all this get here? Why are we here? I think it's an embracing of the understanding that there is a Creator and He does want to have a relationship with us."

His Christian faith and insistence on living out his ideals, as well as his unflagging charitable outreach and respect for his fans and fellow humankind, makes Aaron Kampman an Insightful Player™ team member worth emulating.

INSTANT REPLAY OF AARON'S *GUIDING PRINCIPLES*

1. Never lose sight of your faith in God. Your relationship with Christ should be the compass that guides you through life.

2. Take time to seek out silence and stillness. These moments are what help you to build inner character strength and foster your spiritual growth.

3. Embody your principles in how you treat others: your family members, your community, your team members, and the less fortunate to whom you minister.

4. Be an integral part of your community. Reach out to others, and stand in for anyone who needs a role model or a source of emotional support.

5. Recognize the opportunities you have been given, whether they are great or small.

6. Leverage your advantages—physical strength, spiritual awareness, the love of family and friends, or whatever you have been given—while finding ways to overcome your weaknesses.

7. In times of greatest crisis, remember you are not alone.

8. Understand the difference between happiness and joy: happiness is the pleasure that come from positive circumstances, but joy is rooted in the knowledge that God is in control, even in the face of adversity.

9. Follow the spiritual imperative to forgive those who have wronged you or others.

10. Let your deeds and actions ceaselessly reflect your most dearly held principles.

CHAPTER 16

THE ATLANTA FALCONS'

REGGIE KELLY

Modern-Day Prophet Calls Forth
the Best in Others and Himself

Reggie Kelly embraces every setback with boundless determination, grace and grit. He bows his head in humility and accelerates his service to others. Reggie's infectious spirit gives off a refreshing warmth, like a roaring fire on a cold winter's day. He is a man of God who calls forth the best in everyone he meets. Reggie's teammates and the media respectfully call him the Reverend, or just Rev.

Reggie grew up in small-town Aberdeen, Mississippi, population 6,000. He was raised by two loving yet strict Christian parents who made him toe the line. When he gave his life to Christ as a very young boy in grade school, he was concerned what other kids would think about him. Reggie said, "I decided to put Christ on the back burner, all for the sake of popularity. By the time I got to high school I did whatever I could to fit in and this included partying and drinking. I did this to fit in because I wanted to be the 'big dog.' I actually believed I was really cool."

He knew exactly whom to hang out with and exactly what to do in order to fit in, and it worked. "By the time I was a senior in high school, I had it down to a science. I was everything in high school. I was voted most likely to succeed, the class favorite, the most athletic—I won all the awards." Reggie didn't realize then that he wasn't being true to who he really was. This created an emptiness inside. He wasn't ready to face this emptiness, so instead he partied even harder.

When he got to college at Mississippi State, he felt like a fish out of water because nobody knew him. He decided on the first day of school that he was going to get back on top fast. Because he lived away from his parents, his partying habits magnified and before long he was once again known as the "big dog." Reggie said, "Even though everything was going the way I wanted it to go, I was empty inside."

He couldn't figure it out and it made him feel restless.

By the time Reggie was a sophomore, the emptiness in his heart became too much to bear and he started to sink. Up until this point, his life was like a roller coaster of emotional highs and lows. The lows became so low he couldn't party them away any longer. He was exhausted from trying to please everyone and trying to prove how cool he was. He didn't understand why he was feeling so empty so he decided to give Jesus a try.

Reggie said, "I already gave my life over to Him and accepted Him as my personal savior when I was eight years old. I was living contrary to how I was supposed to live. I was trying so hard to be what I thought everybody thought I should be. I was a pretender instead of a contender, I guess you could say."

At first he took recommitting his life to Jesus lightly and thought, "I'll try Jesus for a couple of days and if it doesn't work, I'll try something else."

Reggie remembers the day he began to talk to Jesus. "I was sitting in my college dorm room; my roommate wasn't there. I was alone with the Lord. It was a great time, a time I will never forget. As soon as I spoke to Him, He answered me with words that to this day still sends chills down my spine. His message said, 'You can have all the fortune, you can have all the fame; you can be the most popular kid in the world if you so desire. But if you don't have me in your heart, then there is always going to be an emptiness. There is always going to be a void in your heart.' At that precise moment it hit me like a ton of bricks." This was a defining moment in Reggie's life, and it changed his whole outlook. He finally took Jesus off the back burner and put Him at the center of his life. "And I've been on fire ever since," he said.

When he rededicated his life to Jesus, it changed him spiritually, mentally and physically. It enhanced his ability to succeed in everything he got involved with. He had a burning desire to be his very best in every area of his life. He said, "I do everything for the Lord and because of that I have success in everything I am involved in. For example, I stopped playing football so the crowd would cheer for me. I began to play football to please the Lord and this enhanced my ability and my skills soared."

His grades went up and he made the South Eastern Conference honor roll for three straight years. His playing improved so much, the Atlanta Falcons drafted him in the second round.

"In my rookie year in Atlanta, the great fullback Bob Christian took me under his wing. He was a man of God, a real hard worker and was well respected by everyone. He decided that he was going to teach me how to be a pro. He also was going to teach me how to be a man of God and apply it to football. He told me 'You play fast; you play with some power and you play with some aggressiveness. You play the very best you can because you represent God. You play with fire.' He also taught me how to be a professional, how to address the media and how to dress. He really helped make my NFL experience a great one, especially my rookie year. He was a wonderful mentor and friend. We went to church together, we hung out together and he taught me so much. Bob Christian left a lasting impression on me. He knew that life and football were bigger than him. He knew God had given him a platform to be a role model for others. In addition to having a passion for affecting people around the world he was also dedicated to having a positive impact on his teammates.

"Bob's example lit a fire in me and helped me realize that God placed me on earth to encourage everyone to be the best they can be. This includes my family, friends, teammates, adult fans and kids. Knowing that God has placed this desire in my heart, it gives me the fortitude to always set an example and be a leader. The essence of who I am is that I am a man of God. My leadership is displayed by genuine respect and interest in others, my discipline, my willingness to make sacrifices including giving things up for myself when I don't want to. I am very committed to my spiritual, personal and professional growth. This really helps me out when I have setbacks. I always look for opportunities that God is sending me *because* of the setback rather than *in spite* of the setback.

A good example came when Reggie was injured in training camp during the 2009 season. In previous seasons, he had suffered only one other injury and missed just four games. He was sure he'd bounce back this time, too, and was "heartbroken" when he learned he had ruptured his Achilles tendon and would be out for the entire season. Instead of wallowing in self-pity, he decided to figure out a way he could still help the team and decided to concentrate his efforts on helping out the younger players.

Deciding that "this injury is bigger than Reggie Kelly," he vowed to become a role model for how to handle adversity. He wanted to set an example so his teammates and family could see how he handled the bad times as well as the good.

"I believe in my heart that my family and teammates need me as much as I need them. Being injured gave me more quality time to spend with them. It also gave me more time to contribute to the community. I have always been passionate about being a leader and really being there for the younger guys. While I'm injured, I can do a whole lot more of that. I get so excited when I see some of the guys I have mentored mentoring other new players. I believe this can spread like wildfire and keep going on for many generations to come. There are a lot of wonderful men in the NFL and I believe we can all take it up a notch by helping each other more. I want to leave the NFL better than it was when I found it."

Reggie believes that God gave him the NFL platform to have a positive impact on kids. He reaches out to kids and adults too, every chance he gets. He helps them realize that they can achieve anything their hearts desire regardless of their situation. He said, "Life isn't always fair, but whatever hand you get, whatever hand you're dealt, just play it. If you are dealt a bad hand, you can still win. It just depends on how you strategize. Work hard and put your trust in God." Reggie experienced firsthand how God put him in the best position to succeed.

Reggie loves to encourage kids to grow and become productive. He shows kids how to approach all setbacks knowing that great things will come to them if they are willing to learn and grow each time. He teaches them the importance of building inner strength and explains the countless benefits of being resilient.

Reggie treats kids with enormous respect. He lets them know that we need them to be as productive as they can be because it won't be long before they are leading our country and the world. Reggie's genuine passion is contagious and he infects kids with a burning desire to become the best young men or young ladies they can be.

And Reggie has a message for adults: "We have to encourage the grown-ups to reach out to kids. It's hard for kids to reach out to the grown-ups. We all need to create a warm and safe environment for the kids to feel at home, to feel like they can talk to us. Teenagers are not going to initiate conversations with adults. We need some passionate grown-ups who are willing to go out and reach the kids around the world. How can we do that? I'm not quite sure. But I know that there are all kinds of opportunities to do so.

"One thing that I also would like to stress is the importance of being unique. You don't have to be like the next person. Just because this is the way the in-crowd does it, you can go against the grain and still be a success. You can be different, you can be unique; this is what this world needs.

"A lot of time when you follow the in-crowd it's going to lead to some form of destruction. It worked that way for me. I was trying to be like everybody else because being accepted meant everything to me… it ran my life and it was exhausting! I finally figured it out that I didn't have to be like everybody else, that I've got my own style. If you have your own flavor and you maximize your own uniqueness, MAN! There are all kinds of possibilities out there for you. I think that's the way that God wants it. He made each of us different. He gave all of us different gifts and different talents. You are here to maximize your talents and create a life that dreams are made of.

"I am inspired to help kids avoid a lot of stuff that I've gone through. The Bible says that to whom much is given, much is required. So, I know that God has given me a great platform being in the NFL. He put me here so that I can have a great influence on kids."

Reggie is committed to a life of learning and growing. He is the first to admit that he has a lot of room for growth. Out because of his injury in the 2009 season, he worked on becoming more patient. Sometimes he found it hard to be on the sidelines rather than on the field because of his injury. He became antsy and wanted to be out on the field. He reminded himself to calm down, relax and let the healing process take its time; let the rehab process get him in the right position to perform for the upcoming year. He knew that in due time this would pass and God would bring new opportunities his way.

Reggie is most grateful for his family. He is married to his high school sweetheart, Sheila. They have two children, a boy named Kavan and a girl named Kyla. He is also grateful for his fabulous parents and wonderful big brother Floyd. Recently he co-authored with Barton Green a book called _Prepared: Body—Mind—Spirit: Using the Gridiron's Boundaries To Reach Your Limitless Potential,_ in which he explores the timeless lessons that shape the three ever-developing parts of mankind: the body, mind and spirit.

Reggie is an Insightful Player ™ team member who is spiritually rich and inspires the same in others. He casts a warm and lasting glow inside the hearts of everyone he meets. He is the exact kind of role model our world yearns for. We could all learn a lot from Reggie.

INSTANT REPLAY OF REGGIE'S *GUIDING PRINCIPLES*

1. Look for opportunities with every setback rather than in spite of them.

2. Let go of trying to impress others.

3. Be unique by honoring your greatest talents and gifts.

4. Be a leader by always setting an example.

5. Believe you can achieve your biggest dreams regardless of your situation.

6. Treat everyone with respect, always.

7. Turn your life over to God.

8. Commit to learning as a lifelong process.

9. Offer your support and share lessons learned with others.

CHAPTER 17

THE NEW ENGLAND PATRIOTS'

DEVIN MCCOURTY

Leveraged "Speed Bumps" to Pave the Way to Tremendous Success and Enduring Inspiration

Being a member of the New England Patriots—a first-round 2010 draft pick, no less—may well be the realization of a lifelong dream for **Devin McCourty**, but being part of a team is nothing new for the young New York native. The cornerback was born to one: the lifelong team comprising himself and his twin brother Jason, who plays the same position for the Tennessee Titans.

And it was that sense of being half of a whole that made what happened his freshman year in college so difficult. After a stellar career playing opposite each other at St. Joseph Regional High School in Montvale, New Jersey, the two went off to Rutgers University together, but while his brother started playing right away, Devin was red-shirted, meaning he practiced with the team but with the expectation that he wouldn't see any game time until sophomore year. "The coaches at Rutgers felt that I needed to develop more," he said.

"I think it would have been easier to take if I didn't have a twin brother. For our whole life, everyone saw us as the same, and then we got to college and faced someone who was saying, 'He [Jason] can play, but you're not ready yet.' It was the first time that we were treated differently. Everyone had always seen us as the same and this was our realization that in the real world, we were different."

Seeing the team leave campus for weekend games was particularly difficult for Devin that year, so he often went home to spend weekends with his mother. A supportive roommate—a football teammate from high school—who also happened to be red-shirted helped him get through that year as well. "Since that time, I've talked to different guys who couldn't play for whatever reason— being red-shirted or being injured—and they talk about how easy it is to start feeling disconnected. You go to college to play football, so then when you can't play, you start to feel aimless."

Devin refused to let that sense of aimlessness get the best of him, however. Instead, he worked harder than ever to ensure that he would have a spot on the football team his sophomore year. "The whole freshman year experience made me realize what it would take to really get to where I wanted to be. So I worked out and lifted weights and did everything I could do, because I said to myself, 'There is *no way* that I'm not going to play next year.' I had played football since my freshman year in high school; this was the first time I'd been in a situation in sports where it felt like, maybe I'm not that good. It really takes your confidence away at first. But I chose a path to just work and keep believing in myself."

That attitude paid off not only when he started playing regularly for Rutgers his sophomore year but on into his present-day life as a pro, Devin believes. "It made me the type of athlete I am as far as not being high maintenance. I've seen some athletes where the coach will tell them to do something, but they're so used to doing everything their way, that they won't believe it will work and they won't do it. Whereas my early college experience was that I had to do everything that the coaches said just to try to get on the field. And now, other players sometimes say to me about a particular instruction, 'You don't have to do that, you're the first rounder here. They're not going to cut you!' But it's so ingrained in me to try to do everything the right way and to do it the way the coach is asking for it to be done. I think that attitude will stay with me no matter what kind of success I reach."

Up until their freshman year in college, the twins had done everything together, Devin said. The two of them were raised by a single mother who was widowed when the boys were just three. Their brother Larry, older by 17 years, acted as both brother and father figure to them, although he was often absent during their teen years because he was on active military duty as a tanker in the Gulf War.

Their mother made it clear that spirituality was a high priority. "We went to church on Sundays when we were kids. It was within walking distance. That was one of the strongest forms of mentoring I had. In a community church, everyone knows your situation, so when you to different people in the church, they can give you all kinds of guidance and encouragement. Later, when we were playing a lot of football, we had Sunday morning games and couldn't always get to church, but we still were always aware of our spiritual background."

At Rutgers, a college chaplain named John Maurer helped Devin to continue his spiritual development; the chaplain led Bible studies on issues particularly relevant to college-aged men. Today, Devin continues to try to grow spiritually with ongoing Bible studies on his own.

Devin refers to the obstacles he has overcome throughout his life as "speed bumps." One such speed bump was being red-shirted at Rutgers, but the very first one was losing his father at such a young age. "At first, since I was only three years old, I didn't really understand it. As I was growing up, I kind of just went about life as if I didn't have a father and the only time I really noticed was on Father's Day and times like that. It wasn't really until college that I started to realize what I had lost. Playing in my first college football games, and then graduating…at those times it started to hit me, like, 'Wow, I wish my father was here so he could see this.' That speed bump motivated me because I always felt like he was looking down on me. He left the world early, but Jason and I are what he left on this earth and I always felt we represented his presence here, and that made me want to try to do good."

Paradoxically, his mother's on-the-job injury was one factor that had a positive influence on Devin's athletic career. "She got hurt on her job when I was five. She had to fight to get disability and go through that whole process, but in the end it gave us an advantage growing up because it meant she was home a lot. That meant me and Jason couldn't wander too far away from staying on the right path because she was always on us. She was always able to go to sports practices and games and parent-teacher conferences. And she meant everything to us."

Devin's mother inspired the growing boy with her astonishing sense of determination. "As far as me being where I'm at right now, I really, truly don't think it would be possible if it wasn't for all the things she sacrificed," he said. "My older brother was born when my mother was nineteen. She was in college and she had to drop out to get a job so she could raise him. She wouldn't buy herself things as far as going out shopping and getting clothes. Probably the biggest sacrifice was to send us to a private high school. In all actuality, it was really too expensive, but she made it work. She just took out loans and did whatever she had to do."

Devin said his mother took pains to make sure her investment was sound, however. "She challenged us to make sure we did the right things in high school so she wasn't wasting her money. She put everything she had, all her savings, out there and put it on us to do well in high school and get a scholarship to college and make something of ourselves."

Only later did he fully understand how much his mother was willing to sacrifice for the success of her children. "After we graduated, she ended up having to file for bankruptcy just for paying for our high school and all the loans she took out after I graduated college. She always used to tell me and Jason how important it was to have good credit and pay your bills on time, but she was willing to sacrifice all of that for us. She gave everything she had just so we could have a better future than she'd had."

From his mother he learned not only self-sacrifice but self-reliance. "Once my older brother left for the Army, it was really just my mom. She had to do double duty with Jason and me because there was no one else around. Now, she tells me that back then, she looked at it like she had no choice. She didn't have anyone there to help her, so she couldn't turn and say, 'What should I do now?' She didn't even think about it, just did what she had to do."

As much as his mother was the guiding influence of his childhood in terms of what she did and the example she set, he and his brothers never forgot their father's presence, either. "I always thought of playing sports as a gift from my father. When we were two years old, he would have us walking around with a basketball in our hands. So I always felt like my love for sports was kind of connected to him. His birthday is in September, right around the time we usually play our first game of the season. Jason and I both always feel like in some ways we are playing in his memory."

When Devin had to sit out his freshman year at Rutgers, his mother offered encouraging insights that he remembers still to this day. "She said you have to realize that everything you want to do doesn't happen the way you want it to happen. But there are reasons. Just keep going. My mom always used to tell me that if you're talented and you work hard, someone will notice it someday."

And his mother proved herself to be right when both twins ended up on professional teams: first Jason on the Titans and then Devin on the Patriots. When Devin got the news that he had been drafted, he and his mother both cried. "It was her fault; she started crying first," Devin said. But even the triumph of being a first-round draft pick for the Patriots didn't mean the end of self-doubts, Devin discovered recently. In Patriots strength and conditioning coach Mike Woicik, he has found inspiration when the going gets tough. "After we played the Jets and didn't do too well recently, Mike told me about pole-vaulters. He said when they go to pole vault they have to be totally on point, because if they're hesitant at all, they can be too short or be too long and instead of hitting the net, they'll hit the concrete. It's just like playing cornerback, Mike told me: You can't go out there to play and be hesitant. You have to go out and attack it."

Mike Woicik also gave Devin a quote he treasures. "Every day, a lion and a gazelle wake up. The lion will starve to death if he doesn't catch the gazelle. The gazelle will perish if he can't run away from the lion. No matter who you are, every day you have to get up running because either way is survival."

And even though his career is prospering right now, Devin looks ahead. "In the past, when I talked about playing professional sports, someone would always say to me, 'Well, what's Plan B? What are you going to do if you don't make it as an athlete?'" Now, Devin passes along that same advice to young people who talk to him about their own dreams. "I tell them, don't let people tell you that you can't make it. It's true that you need a backup plan. But at the same time, don't ever let your backup plan be more important than your original plan."

He can still bring to mind the image of his mother watching game after game throughout his teen years, and he still believes that made all the difference. "To make it professionally, you need someone there saying, 'I'll come to your game to watch you play just to show my support for you.' I was lucky enough that my mom got hurt on her job and was able to be there for almost every game I played in four years."

But even as a cornerback for the Patriots, he knows he has more goals yet to reach. "It's important never to forget that whatever you accomplish, there is always something else. Don't relax whenever you get somewhere no matter how hard you thought that goal would be to reach. Don't let that be good enough. Keep pushing yourself. And wherever you are, never forget to try to inspire other people to reach their own goals."

With his persistent refusal to let adversity defeat him coupled with his determination to learn all he can from life experiences and those around him, Devin McCourty walks the walk and talks the talk of a remarkable Insightful Player™ team member.

INSTANT REPLAY OF DEVIN'S *GUIDING PRINCIPLES*

1. Take inspiration from the stories of others. Believe that if they can overcome their obstacles, you can overcome yours.

2. Never stop striving to learn and to grow spiritually. Read a lot and think a lot.

3. Find mentors wherever you can: at church, among your coaches, within your family.

4. Recognize the good that results when you make sacrifices.

5. Appreciate and acknowledge the ways other people are sacrificing for you.

6. Be a fighter, remembering that every day of existence is in some way a fight for survival. Do all you can to stay on top.

7. Rather than submitting to defeat, overcome it.

8. Follow a spiritual path.

9. Don't let comparisons to others distract you from recognizing your own accomplishments. Whether you are a first-round or a sixth-round draft pick, you still get to play for the pros.

CHAPTER 18

THE TENNESSEE TITANS'

JASON MCCOURTY

An Exceptional Role Model Who Pushes Himself to the Limit In Honor of His Parents

Some of the circumstances of **Jason McCourty**'s childhood might seem like disadvantages. His father died when he was just three years old. His mother faced a tall task, raising Jason and his twin brother Devin on her own. And yet Jason said from his young perspective, everything was ideal for their little family. "My father passed away when my brother [Devin] and I were three. We never really got a chance to get to know him. Any memories we have are kind of distant because at that age you tend not to remember a lot of things that are going on around you. So, growing up there was just me, Dev, my brother Larry [17 years older], and my mom. I didn't ever look at it as a disadvantage because my mom didn't make it seem that way. She was tough, and that made it less like we needed a father figure because if disciplinary action needed to be taken, my mom was there to do it. She had no problem with it. She never second-guessed herself or anything like that."

The twins inherited their father's love of team sports, but their mother made it clear that participating in sports necessitated maintaining good grades. "From Day One, we wanted to play sports, and from Day One she required us to keep an A or B average. Those were her values, and they were very important to me growing up. Just watching the way she coped with adversity helped me to develop strong values as I grew."

The adversity his mother faced included not only widowhood at an early age but also a car accident when the boys were young which left her disabled due to serious knee injuries. "It must have been hard for her," Jason reflected. "At the time of the accident, she had been working for twenty years. You get used to working everyday and surviving, and then it's tough when something like that happens."

But the result of his mother's injuries was that she was more present in her young sons' lives than many of their peers' parents were, and so they studied harder, felt safer, and could participate in more extracurricular activities. "Other kids would come home from school and go straight outside and go run around before their parents got home from work. We didn't have that opportunity, because as soon as we got home, she was there telling us to get to our homework, but at the same time, she was always there to take us to any type of sporting event we wanted to do. So in that respect, it was kind of good just to have her home."

His mother's oversight turned him into a strong student with a value on studying that carried him successfully through his years at St. Joseph's Regional High School in Montvale, New Jersey, and then Rutgers College. "I was always pretty good at sports but also able to do well in school, and I think it was just because my mom forced me to work hard at it."

Much as he loved sports and was a naturally gifted athlete, developing a commitment to regular practice took almost as much pushing from his mother as did his academic habits. "I started Pop Warner football when I was ten," he recounted. "The first year was great. The second year, we had practices starting August 1st from 6 to 8 p.m. every single night, and by the end of August I was tired of going every day. I'd be outside playing and when my mom told me it was time to get ready for practice, I just wouldn't want to go. In fact I wanted to quit. But my mom said no way: I'd already signed up for it and started the season, and as far as she was concerned that meant I'd made a commitment. She let me know that when you commit to something, you see it through."

Even though he was only eleven, Jason understood that the issue was about commitment and not about football; his mother didn't mind if in the future he gave up the sport. "She said I had to finish out the year, and if I wanted to quit, I would have to wait until the following year and make the decision not to play before it started."

The lesson was crystal-clear, Jason said. "That taught me plainly that quitting wasn't the right thing to do. And by the time I got to college, I saw that when you're not willing to make the best of an opportunity, there's always someone right by your side who is going to take that opportunity away from you."

He was glad he saw the season through—that year and later when he looked back on the experience. "It made me realize that my mom was right; she knew that I didn't want to quit. It just happens, you know, when you're a kid and you're doing one thing—which in my case was running around with my friends having a good time—it's hard to give that up and do something else, like go to football practice every day. But she knew in the long run, I'd be happier if I stayed on the team, and she was right. I had fun and I had a lot of friends on the team. So, once I stuck it out, I never second guessed it. It taught me that quitting in the beginning isn't always the best thing. Stick it out and you'll see that that hard work you're putting in at that time will start to pay off."

Both twins went to Rutgers University and joined the football team; while Devin was red-shirted their freshman year, Jason played, but it wasn't a spectacular season for him, he said. Not being a great success right away pushed him to try harder. "After my freshman year, I worked extremely hard to get stronger, bigger and faster. A lot of times it happens to guys that if they are not successful at something right away, they don't know how to work through it. I think that was where I was able to make up ground and catch up with the other guys I was competing with. Even though my college career didn't start that well, I didn't give up. I put in that extra effort and continue to work hard to do well."

Once he hit his stride as a college player, it was only natural for Jason to start to look to a career in the NFL, but he said he felt unusual in this regard. Professional dreams were not always taken seriously in the community in which he was raised. "My brother and I didn't grow up around a lot of people saying they want to become a professional athlete, or a lawyer, or a doctor, or anything. When you say you want to play pro football, a lot of people look at you and try to tell you that the odds are that you can't do it, or that maybe you should plan to do something more generic. But my belief is that it's important to understand that if this is something you really want to do, and you're willing to focus and really work for it, you can accomplish it." Still, these were thoughts he often kept to himself. "I knew I was in college to get an education. I'm not a guy who is flashy or likes to boast about things. For me, it was more fun *not* to talk about my dreams of playing pro ball and just show more with my actions. So, my strategy was to work hard in football, try to get better, and not talk about going to the NFL."

Both of his parents, each in their own way, played a part in inspiring his dreams, Jason said. "Growing up, a big part of my drive and motivation to do something with my life was to be able to provide for my mom one day. I guess when you see a parent do as much for you as my mom did for us, when you go to school with a variety of kids who talk about what their situation is like with their family, even things you see on TV… well, the older you get, the more you realize the kind of impact that a parent has on your life. By the time I got to high school, I knew that whatever I did in the future, I always wanted to be able to provide for my mom."

Not only does he credit her with his happy upbringing and strong moral compass; he continues to rely on her advice to this day. "We talk just about every day. Whenever I'm going through a problem or issue, no matter what it is, I feel like I can call her and talk to her. She's older than me, she's wiser than me, and there are a lot of things in life that either she's gone through or she's seen someone go through. Just my ability to have that relationship with her, where I feel like I can talk to her about anything, helps me to make better decisions. I can bounce ideas off her, knowing she's not going to tell me exactly what to do; she's just going to provide some input. Without my mom, there's no way I'd have made it as far as I have."

At the same time, the distant memory of a loving father nudged him toward his aspirations as well. "Before I go out on the field before each game, I look up in the sky, kind of having a conversation with my dad and thanking him for everything that he did for me and Dev. Just because of him, I have the opportunity to be where I am today. I ask him to just continue to watch over me. That's something that I do before every game. Once I forgot and I felt like I had a bad game, so that's my pre-game ritual."

If his relationship to both parents was paramount to his personal victories on and off the field, his bond with his twin brother was just as influential. "Growing up, Dev and I had one another to lean on. That was huge for both of us. And it is even now, because we've gone through a lot of the same things: we both played college football, we're both now in the NFL [Devin was a 2010 first-round draft pick for the New England Patriots]. If I'm going through an issue—for example, right now I'm injured—he's a person that I can talk to knowing we're not affiliated through either of our teams, but this is still somebody who understands the situation and also is looking out for my well-being. I can talk to him and he understands everything I'm saying."

After graduating from Rutgers in 2009, Jason was drafted by the Tennessee Titans as a sixth-round draft pick. That hardly made him feel like his ticket to success was written, he said. "The scariest stretch I've gone through was my first year in the NFL, that first camp. I was drafted in the sixth round, and a lot of people back home were congratulating me, saying 'Wow, man, you got drafted! You made it!'" But that wasn't how it felt to Jason. "When you're drafted that late in the draft, the likelihood of making the team is slim. The longest stretch for me was going through camp because I had heard so many stories of guys who make it through the draft but because of various factors like money and numbers end up not making the team."

With a mix of superstition and pragmatism, Jason took one obvious step in acknowledging his sense of precariousness: he avoided getting an apartment in Tennessee. "During training camp, I stayed at a hotel, because I didn't want to get an apartment until I knew for sure I was on the team. There was so much uncertainty. You have a good day and you're feeling good, then you have a bad day and you're a little worried. I remember that last day of cuts, I saw the roster go from 75 players to 53 players. To see so many guys get cut and still be standing and then know I'd made the team was an awesome feeling. But at the same time, throughout the process you start to build bonds and relationships with a lot of guys. Seeing so many of them have their dreams cut short was kind of disappointing."

Having embarked upon the pro football career he dreamed of ever since childhood, Jason knows how fortunate he is. He spends a lot of time thinking about what principles carried him to success, and he encourages others who look to him for inspiration to understand how vital his core values remain.

"When you make it to the NFL, on that journey you meet a lot of people. The more people that you can have a positive impact on, the more support you're going to have. My mom always tells me you never want to burn bridges. If you can be respectful toward people, it leads them to say, 'Wow, he's a nice guy. I hope he makes it.' And it's a good feeling to have a lot of people who are pushing for you and want you to succeed.

"When I talk to young people about reaching their dreams, I tell them this: 'Whatever your dream is, make sure that everything you're doing is contributing to your opportunity to make it.' A lot of people look at my brother and me and say, 'Wow, you're so successful, you're a superstar!' I say to that, 'We're just regular people who have gone through some of the same struggles that you've gone through. And we've overcome some of the same obstacles. So you can, too.'"

A fundamental belief in the importance of adhering to his core principles and values has defined the winning spirit of Jason McCourty, a superb Insightful Player™ team member.

INSTANT REPLAY OF JASON'S *GUIDING PRINCIPLES*

1. Keep your focus on realizing your dreams, and avoid detractors who try to tell you what is and is not possible for you.

2. Working hard and succeeding academically should be a top priority no matter what your goals are for the future.

3. Recognize the sacrifices your parents or caretakers have made for your success.

4. Once you make a commitment, follow through on it. Don't quit once you've agreed to do something.

5. If you're not willing to work hard enough to succeed at a goal, you'll lose the opportunity to someone who is.

6. Treat everyone with courtesy and respect. If you don't get along with them, minimize your interactions, but don't give them any reason to think less of you.

7. Resist the temptation to "rest on your laurels." Enjoy the successes you meet, but remember that they are stepping stones to the next stage of accomplishment. Even after being drafted by the NFL, you still have to make the final cut to play on the team!

8. Recognize—and bear gratitude for—those blessings that come from a higher power and not from anything you've done yourself.

9. Focus more on the process than the results of what you do. Rather than thinking constantly about someday playing for the NFL, be the best player you can at whatever level you are competing.

CHAPTER 19

DENVER BRONCOS LEGEND

KARL MECKLENBURG

All-Pro Author and Speaker Inspires Long-Term Positive Change in Individuals and Teams

When **Karl Mecklenburg** was a boy on the junior varsity squad, a tough football coach sentenced him to a week of grueling workout drills.

It was a punishing practice in more ways than one.

The coach was angry because Karl had to miss a rescheduled game to go hunting with his father. So, the coach insisted the teenager run up dozens of long, steep hills five days in a row. The coach figured the boy would surely quit the team. Instead, it hardened young Karl's resolve. "I'm going to be a great player," Karl told himself. "If I can do this, I can do anything."

And he did. Karl would play in six Pro Bowls and three Super Bowls. He was such a versatile linebacker he played all seven defensive front positions. He amassed 79.5 sacks, the second highest total in Broncos history.

But to succeed, on the gridiron and off, he ran an obstacle course dotted with professional and personal challenges. And his start as a pro player was hardly auspicious. Back in 1983, when the Denver Broncos drafted Karl, it was in the 12th round with the 310th pick overall.

As a young athlete, Karl was, by his own description, stiff, small and slow. He wasn't naturally gifted. He had to work at the game. He left one college when the scholarship he thought was coming never did, and then toughed it out as a walk-on at another school. Ineligible to play, Karl had to sit out for a year. To hang out with the team, he swept the weight and locker rooms.

If it seemed like a ref had thrown him a penalty flag, Karl simply shook it off. He didn't let the housekeeping chores bother him.

"It was worth it to me, because I had this passion that I wanted to be the best player that ever played the game of football, and that was something that I made my decisions around day to day," said Karl. "I worked super hard at it, and I also worked hard at school."

Even after he was injured, and forced to rehab in the women's training room (a punishment he believes was designed to rattle him and get him to relinquish a hard-won college scholarship), he pushed on, driven to make a comeback.

Talent, he concluded, was just a tiny piece of the path to success, especially since Karl knew talented players who never made it.

"I think God has given each and every one of us more talent than we can use in a lifetime," said Karl. "And along with that, He's given us free will. What that means is that it is up to us to go out and find out where our talents and abilities lie and then work hard to develop those talents and abilities. It doesn't happen by accident."

For Karl, a good and successful life required a smart game plan. The ingredients? Hard work, the courage to try new ventures and the persistence to pick yourself up and try again if you fail.

Family support was also key. Loving parents stood by young Karl, even as he pursued a sometimes brutal sport. Unlike today's so-called "helicopter parents," Karl's mother and father didn't try to rescue him when the sport, and life, administered some hard hits. The JV player who ran those punishing hills learned resilience.

Supportive parents stood by young Karl as he worked to correct a noticeable lisp. Over and over, he repeated the phrase: Sister Sally sells seashells down by the seashore.

He battled dyslexia, too. It's a learning disability that haunts him still. "I have to watch my pen form letters or the 'p,' 'd,' 'q,' and 'b' will be mixed up," said Karl.

The challenges made him a cheerleader for a can-do attitude. And at least for Karl, there were some advantages to being dyslexic. For starters, he is ambidextrous. "I think a little differently, and that's a great advantage when you are out in the world … As a football player, I played all seven defensive front positions, and they moved me around, left side, right side. It didn't matter. I am just as strong with my left side as my right side."

Karl insisted the big potential he found in himself, despite his handicap, exists in us all. "The path you take and the success that you ultimately achieve is up to you," said Karl. "Don't let anyone else tell you you can't, because you can. It's up to you, and you have to make the right decisions and work hard and then you have a chance. And even if you make wrong decisions, because everyone does, you keep going in the direction that you want to go. Find that passion and chase it."

Karl positively ran after his passion, and he snared his dream early. Even as a young boy, he had already figured out how he would spend a huge chunk of the next couple of decades.

He recalled his dad, a physician, asking the 10-year-old what he thought of football. "And my response was, 'Dad, I really love to smash guys.' You know, 10 years old, and I'm already a linebacker."

Along the way, the lessons Karl learned could serve as a playbook for other youth. He learned teamwork, the key to any successful organizational endeavor, whether it's football, soccer or social work. In football, teamwork is nearly as critical as the helmets. If the offensive line doesn't protect the quarterback, ruinous sacks may follow. But if the star wide receiver picks up the blocks he needs from skilled teammates, a sprint into the end zone may follow. Teamwork is a concept Karl now stresses in speeches to corporations and groups, and for the football great, leadership is the highest expression of teamwork.

He also reminds kids to wisely select their teammates off the field. "Your team of friends is the only team that you get to pick," he said. "Choose a team of friends that have dreams and aspirations, who value friendship and respect you. My friends have always added so much value to my life."

For Karl, family is his most precious team. "I am a devout Christian, and I take my love for my family very seriously," he said. "I want everything I say and do to reflect God's love."

In the community, Karl puts his words into action. This father of three works with his wife, Kathi, on behalf of kids and families in several charitable groups. Through his REACH Foundation (Rewarding Experiences for All Children), the Mecklenburgs encourage youngsters to read.

He recalled that the 2009 winner of his REACH for a Book program had been transformed from a disinterested student and poor reader to an enthusiastic bookworm reading above grade level.

Through the group Aspen Youth Experience, the Mecklenburgs help introduce urban kids to nature. And in Colorado Youth Outdoors, he works with others to pair kids and their families with the kind of traditional outdoor sports he shared with his own father, grandfathers and uncles—hunting, fishing and camping.

As a resident of Littleton, Colorado, Karl sat by the bedsides and rehab tables of kids injured by the shootings at Columbine High School in 1999. He spent months visiting the recuperating teens weekly, awed by their grit and optimism. "Those kids inspired me with their toughness and positive outlook as they struggled through the long months of rehab," said Karl.

In addition to his motivational speaking, Karl is the author of two books, *Meck for the Defense* and the newly released *Heart of a Student Athlete, All-Pro Advice for Competitors and Their Families*.

Karl's passion to help others lead a successful life is a commitment he has made. He is an extraordinary Insightful Player™ team member who has his feet planted firmly on the ground with his head way up in the clouds.

INSTANT REPLAY OF KARL'S *GUIDING PRINCIPLES*

1. Act in the best interests of the team. Think "we," not "me." Leadership is critical to business and all relationships. Leadership is the highest expression of teamwork.

2. Have the courage to try new things; you will gain confidence and develop new skills that will carry over into every area of your life.

3. Have the courage to be decisive. Trust your intuition and take action. Being decisive will expand your perspective and give you easier access to your wisdom.

4. Own up to mistakes and then forgive yourself. Learn to be 100% accountable to yourself without self judgment.

5. Work hard, continue your education and refuse to quit.

6. Nurture a big dream, a passion. Think big picture and long term. Your passion will make it easier to overcome obstacles.

7. Use your desires to help you create and follow through on specific short-term and achievable goals. Make sure they move you forward to fulfill your dreams.

CHAPTER 20

NFL FREE AGENT

BILLY MILLER

#83

Avoided Major Fall, Letting God Wow Him On and Off the Field

By his own admission, **Billy Miller** was on his way to joining an elite but unfortunate group. "After their playing days are over, many NFL players' lives fall apart: 80% go bankrupt, 50% get divorced, many experience both. For guys who, at one point, were on top of the world, it's a staggering statistic."

By the third year of his football career, Billy was heading down that road, "living recklessly," in his words; partying and spending; trying to keep up with the older guys. How he caught himself before a major fall and transformed his life to one of focus and purpose is an inspiring story.

Billy Miller was born in Los Angeles and spent the majority of his childhood in South Central L.A. "I didn't grow up with a lot of money; didn't have a whole lot of role models," he said. "My parents worked hard to try to keep a roof over our heads. It was me, my mom, my dad, and eventually we had my brother, and then my sister.

"I saw my first shooting around five; I probably saw my first dead body at eight. We had an alley behind our house and there was a lot of drug activity going on, and sometimes those deals went bad. When you grow up in a neighborhood like that, you're never able to really be yourself, because you're always concerned about what could happen next. You're always on guard."

From the time Billy was very young, his father planted the seeds for ideas and dreams that would set him on his path in life. "When my dad was frustrated because of a situation we were in, he would always tell me that I would be better than this. He was really fond of football and always told me, from a very young age, 'You're going to play in the NFL one day.' And, he said it so often, I believed that was what I was going to do. It kept me focused. I didn't look at it as pressure. It gave me something to try to change in my life; a goal to set for myself: to not be satisfied with my environment, to not settle, to not go down the wrong path and do things that would keep me away from that goal.

"Now, did I believe that I was actually going to the NFL? Absolutely not. But it was just a dream and a goal that kept me on the straight and narrow. My dad definitely started that dream in me."

One of Billy's strongest characteristics, then and now, is his desire to please his family. "I was driven by the fact that I wanted to make them proud, that I wanted them to see that I was going to be an example of positive change, of growing up a certain way but then having an opportunity to become something different.

"I think that the reason that I made it, and some of my other friends who are by far better athletes than I am, didn't, is choices—choices that I made and things that I did to stay on the straight and narrow. That's the reason that I'm able to have a career in NFL. Some of my friends did not make good choices, which led them to jail, or not doing as good in school as they needed to, or other things that might have held them back. Sometimes it comes down to those simple choices that make the difference in the direction that your life takes." Billy is grateful for his Dad's constant reminders that his life will be better. This gave Billy confidence and helped him develop the inner strength and insight to make the right choices.

Billy remembers a nomadic existence in those early years. "We lived right in the middle of South Central Los Angeles, for the most part. We went from apartment complex to apartment complex, to living with my grandmother at South Central to living with my other grandmother in Carson to having our own place here and there. We just bounced around a lot until, in my freshman year of high school, we moved out to a city called West Lake Village, California. My mom got a really good job up there."

That move took Billy from one extreme to another. "Being half white and half black, I grew up in South Central Los Angeles and was considered the only white guy in town. Then, in high school in West Lake Village, I was considered one of a very few black guys. It was kind of a funny change of events."

Billy's new environment was life-changing. "By that time, my parents had gotten separated, which was tough for me. To have the opportunity to move to West Lake and see families still together, to see how very successful these parents were, it just seemed like it automatically built confidence that there was no such thing as failure. Their parents were successful in whatever job that they did—not that they all were making a tremendous amount of money, but they just seemed to get up every morning and go to work, have a sense of stability and it kind of breathed that confidence into my friends.

"Before I got to high school, I played football, a little bit of basketball and baseball, and I did some other sports. But I never at any point thought that I was good enough to play with the guys that you see on TV. When we moved to West Lake Village, I had an opportunity to get around a lot of positive people who were all doing positive things. I got around a bunch of really good coaches at a young age that mentored me and helped me along in the process.

"My freshman year of high school, I played fullback. After that season, I said to myself, 'You know what? Maybe I'm not too bad at this football thing. I might have an opportunity at least to play college ball,' never thinking that the NFL was attainable, but maybe I could get a scholarship. And my sophomore year, I got moved up to varsity and had the same experience. I played okay and started to get noticed a little bit by colleges.

"And then, in my junior year, my parents both decided they were moving back to L.A. My dad was moving back to Carson with *his* mom, and my mom was moving back to South Central Los Angeles with *her* mom. I was overwhelmed and shocked. I'm in an area where I feel really good about myself; I can finally relax and I can be myself, and now I have to go back to Los Angeles? That really hurt me.

"I called my football coach, Jim Benkert, and said, 'Hey Coach, I'm leaving. I have to go back to Los Angeles.' I explained the situation and he said, 'Let me talk to your parents and let's try to figure something out.' My best friend at the time was a guy named Steve Aylsworth, and I told him the story. His parents asked my parents if I could stay with them and continue going to high school in West Lake. That all happened within a week. And so, my junior and senior year I stayed with the Aylsworths, and they were like second parents to me.

"They definitely saved my career. It was a point that probably formed the outcome of the rest of my life. Maybe I couldn't have resisted some bad decisions if I'd had to move back to Los Angeles. Being able to stay at that school in West Lake, I was able to play football, and do it in a very comfortable area and get a scholarship to go to college. It was huge."

Steve Aylesworth is still Billy's best friend. "I had five really, really close friends when I was in high school and I still consider all five of those guys my best friends to this day."

Billy's NFL career has had many twists and turns. "I was at the University of Southern California, where I led in catches for my junior and senior year. Most of the time, an accomplishment like that when you go to a major university means that you're going to get drafted really high and make a ton of money. But, I didn't. I was selected by the Denver Broncos in the seventh round and spent half of my first season on the practice squad.

"When I was going into the second year of my NFL career, my father passed away, which took a toll on me. It was the first time that anyone had passed away in my life, let alone someone close like my father." The loss of his dad was difficult for Billy to handle. "Instead of saying, 'Life is short, enjoy it and take care of yourself,' I looked at it as, 'Well, life is short, so I might as well do all of the silly and crazy stuff that I can possibly do.' I lived recklessly. I was drinking to dull the ache of missing my dad. I was going out and partying every night and used spending money as a bandage; I was hanging out with the older guys and doing what they were doing.

"While I was with the Broncos, I fell into a rut of not truly paying full attention to my job. It's not just the time that you go to practice, you have to take this home, you have to study, to understand your opponent. When you're in a football season, there's never a time when your mind is not somewhere on football. And when you're home with your kids and your family, you can enjoy that time with them, but whether you notice it or not, there's still this video being played in the back of your head. Have you prepared enough? Are you ready? I never really studied my playbook and never really took the job seriously. I just said, 'I am here now and I'll be here forever,' which is a sad mistake. I got cut in my third year.

"It was a huge learning experience. I had a year off and then I went to Houston. I led the Houston Texans in catches that first year. I scored the first touchdown and led the team in catches as this unknown, nobody tight end. It was a phenomenal thing in my career.

"I was there for three years, and then I got released. During that period of time, I had several stress fractures in my ankle but was stubborn enough to say, 'Hey I just want to go play football', so I went to Cleveland. I tried to hide the fact that I was hurt, and lasted there for about eight weeks until the pain got too bad. I got released and spent the rest of that season out of the NFL, and really was going to retire.

"Then I got a call from my agent and he said that the New Orleans Saints wanted me to come and try out. I told them no the first two times, and finally said, 'Okay, well, let me see if I still love this game.'

"I came out and fell in love with football again with the New Orleans Saints. At the end of pre-season, they cut me. So, I was really done with football, but Coach Peyton said, 'Hey, if something ever happens, we'll bring you back.' So, I stayed in shape and six weeks later, he brought me back. I finished out that season and the next season, and then in the 2008 season, ironically, things are going well, and they released me for one game. And I finished out that season and led all the tight ends in catches the whole time I've been here as a Saint ."

His team won Super Bowl XLIV in the 2009 season, though an injury prevented him from playing in it.

Billy grew up in the NFL, and, as he matured, his outlook on life changed dramatically. He is eager to tell the story of what gave him that different perspective.

"I definitely did not get here by myself. God has put people in my life that have helped me stay on course. For example, before I got picked up by the Houston Texans, my financial advisor, Craig Jones, gave me a personal loan to sustain myself until that season started. He pretty much said, 'I have faith that you will make this team.' And that's just one of those people in my life who have been a positive influence.

"Going into my third year in the NFL, I met this lovely young lady named Rachael. Very shortly after we began dating, I decided that this woman is going to be my wife. So, I moved her up to Denver with me. I was actually playing for the Broncos at that time. Well, that third year, I got released. We went back home and stayed with the Aylsworths, and Rachael got pregnant with my son, Jaden.

"I had a lot of depression and confusion; I had a lot of worries. I now had this girlfriend who was pregnant. The one thing that I loved at the time more than anything in my life—football—had been taken away from me. And, I'm about to start a family and I have no source of income. All that together was pretty scary for me.

"In that year off before I went to Houston, I was part of that group of the 80% of NFL players that go broke. I did not work at all. Part of that was stubbornness, part of that was being depressed and not really wanting to face the fact that I was no longer an NFL player. To me, especially living in my hometown where I was this football star who made it, it would have been embarrassing to have to go back and ask someone for a job. I did not want to accept that the game was over. I dwindled down to my last dollar.

"My depression came from my view that I thought other people had of me—that they wouldn't see me the same way if I wasn't playing football anymore. In my life, depression has always been kind of an outside pressure. Maybe I've let someone down, or maybe I feel they will look at me differently. Since becoming a Christian, that's changed for me because I have God who tells me who I am to him whenever I read my Bible. I learned that external pressure is something that you have to get rid of; you have to know who you are, and, no matter what your circumstances, it can always get better.

"During that period, two teams called and said they'd like to try me out. I decided to go and play for the Houston Texans. They were a brand new organization who didn't really have any players; and I thought, what a better opportunity to just start over fresh. And so, we packed up our stuff, what little we had left and drove to Houston, and I began that process of practicing with the team.

"There was a gentleman named Tony Boselli who had gone to USC as well. He was a two or three time All-American, and at the time had been to several pro bowls; in that era of football, he was probably the best left tackle playing. Every day, Tony would say,

'Hey Billy, we're having Bible study, I think you should come.' And I'd be like, 'Nah, I'm okay.'

"At that time, my wife Rachael was atheist. And so, I thought, 'Okay, I'm going to fix this once and for all because I don't want to go to this Bible study. I'm going to ask my wife in front of Tony.' So he says, 'You know, hey guys, I'd love for you to come to this Bible study.' And my wife says, 'Okay.' That puts me in a weird position because I definitely don't want to go to Bible study. Now, because I'm trying to pull a fast one on Tony Boselli, my wife says yes.

"We were arguing every day. I probably drank more than I should have. If there wasn't some drastic change, if we kept going down this path, it could lead to disaster. And I knew it, but I couldn't stop these patterns that I had started. We both decided, 'OK, our life isn't heading in the right direction, so let's just go and see what happens.'

"We went to the Bible study and Tony starts to speak and it's unbelievable. And he's doing a phenomenal job and at the end he says, 'Is there anybody in the room who would like to accept Christ into their life?' So now, I'm ready to go. Okay, we did the Bible study and it was really touching. It was unbelievable, but really now, it's time to go home. And we bow our heads to start praying—and my atheist wife raises her hand.

"I open my eyes and she's crying. She raised her hand and she went over to Tony's wife, Angi, and they began to talk. Now Tony Boselli is about 6' 8" and about 340 lbs. So, I see this big old man starting to walk over to me and I know what's coming. He's going to ask me, 'Hey, where you at?' So we go out in the hallway and we just begin to talk as friends and I start to lay down my life's pattern, where I'm going and where I've been.

"I felt my spirit crying out for help. I said, 'You know what, Tony, I do need to change my life and I need something different.' And that day, my wife and I both got saved. And, from that day forward—and I'm not saying this because I'm some overly religious person—my life has changed completely and 100% for the better.

"Now, Tony said, 'If you're really going to have faith, I think you should actually test God.' I'm thinking, 'Test God, that seems kind of ironic.' Tony says, 'Just ask him for something and I want you to have faith that it's going to come true.'

"So, me being the selfish guy that I still was, I don't ask for me and my wife's relationship to get better or to have a healthy baby. I just asked to make the team, because to me that was the most important thing at the time. The next thing you know, I make the first round of cuts. And Tony says, 'Hey man, just keep praying.' And I said, 'Hey man, I made the team so far, this prayer thing is great.' Tony says, 'Ask Him for something bigger.'

"So, I say this prayer that I want to do something so special that I'll be remembered and they'll have no choice but to keep me around. Now, that seems like a pretty big prayer to hope for. What happened? The very first pre-season game, the very first game that the Houston Texans ever played, the very first time that they're ever on television, I scored the very first touchdown. They kept that ball and put it in the Hall of Fame. So, that happens and I'm thinking, 'You know what, this prayer thing is fantastic.'

"I make the team and then, there's the opening game—Houston, Texas, first year against the Dallas Cowboys. I've got this prayer for the last two weeks, 'You know God, that was really special, but it was pre-season, so God, what I really want is to see something really special during the season, because pre season doesn't really count.' And about a minute into the game, I score the first touchdown in Texas history in the regular season. And from that point on, you can just say, Billy Miller loves Jesus and my wife and I have never wavered from that.

"Rachael and I went two years without having any alcohol; we didn't drink at all, just to break the cycle. And we started making little changes within our relationship and in our lives. Through all these trials and tribulations, my perspective has changed so much and for that I will always be grateful."

Thanks to the lessons learned from his many challenging experiences, Billy knew that he needed to think about life after football, and how he'd support himself and his family. He was determined not to rejoin that unfortunate elite group—the 80% of NFL players who go broke when their careers are over. The idea for his business, Elite Performance Factory, started during his brief stay with the Cleveland Browns. He was dealing with stress fractures and it was looking like the end of his career.

"I said to myself, 'OK, what am I going to do after football?' Every year that I'm in this game is a tremendous blessing, and I don't want to depend on that. I wanted something that I could put my attention to once I was done playing. What was it that I wanted to do? So I put my passions together—sports and kids. I have three of my own, but, besides that, I love to be able to give anything that I can back to children.

"I believe that I was not put here to keep this to myself. I've had a very interesting upbringing. A lot of kids on both sides—black and white—relate to me because of my bi-racial background. And I thought that I could bring something into the community where I went to high school.

"At Elite Performance Factory, we teach kids the value of sports in the way of integrity, trust and respect. We also try to make them better athletes so that they can play as long as they possibly can in the sports that they love. We go from the professional athlete, whether it's NFL, NBA or major league baseball, to guys in college who are getting ready to go to the pros, all the way to about the eighth grade.

"The thing that's great about the facility is that, at any given time, you can have a bunch of high school seniors in there working out right along with guys like Reggie Bush or Marcus Colson or Drew Brees. The younger athletes in my facility are able to see how these pros work, and how much it takes to actually get to the next level. It can be used as a tremendous learning tool."

Billy has made the journey from adolescent party boy to mature adult. He's got a clear purpose and deep desire to give back to the community that he loves.

"Having played for over eleven years, I've been extremely blessed in being able to play much longer than I should have. I'm able to build a facility in West Lake and give back to kids and do so much more than I ever thought was imaginable."

Billy gives his mother a lot of credit for shaping his approach to life. "My sensitivity, the person that I am today, that comes from my mom, and the way she loves and she cares. My attitude and personality definitely come from her!

"Every day is a growth opportunity for me to become a better father and husband. If you were to ask me why I was placed on this earth, I would say, 'It's to raise my children—Caine, Jaden and Celeste—and to be a good example.' If I can't raise my own children correctly and show them love and respect, then how can I go out and try to speak to other kids about doing things right? So, that is first and foremost in my life."

Billy knows that, at some point, his football journey will be over. When that time comes, he plans to devote himself full-time to being a husband and father and running his business. "I'm taking the same drive and focus and compassion and resilience I have here in the NFL, and pouring that into Elite Performance Factory—to not only make great athletes, but to make great people."

Billy's down to earth perspective, his kindness, his passion for kids and sports, his steadfast faith and willingness to grow make him the perfect addition to the Insightful Player™ roster!

INSTANT REPLAY OF BILLY'S *GUIDING PRINCIPLES*

1. Set goals that are so compelling that they catapult you out of bed each day.

2. Push yourself every day to be your very best, and never let up. Take your work seriously. Prepare yourself to succeed. Don't settle for a poor environment or difficult circumstances. Strive to be an example of positive change and growth.

3. Choose your friends wisely. Surround yourself with people who want to make something of their lives, and who will challenge you to make something of *your* life

4. Find role models and mentors who will help you succeed. No one ever makes it on his or her own. And while you're at it, mentor someone else to succeed.

5. Pay close attention to the choices you make. What looks like a simple choice can determine the direction of your entire life.

6. Don't just rest on your current successes. Consider your next move. How will you continue to contribute and be productive?

7. Take actions that make you and the people you love feel proud.

8. Create a relationship with God. Put this at the center of your life and expect to be blessed with grace.

CHAPTER 21

NEW ENGLAND PATRIOTS HALL OF FAMER

STEVE NELSON

PHOTO COURTESY *of the New England Patriots*

A Passionate Leader Who Is an Ultimate Teammate As a Player, Coach and Person

You can't reach every single one of your goals, said former New England Patriots Hall of Famer and former college coach **Steve Nelson.** And he's learned not only to be philosophical but to recognize how much there is to be learned from that lesson. For example, he played in three Pro Bowls, but said that, "I would trade that experience a hundred times to play for one team that won the Super Bowl."

When he did finally make it to the Super Bowl in 1986, his team lost. Naturally, that was disappointing, Steve said, but only served to underscore his belief that "as you dream and you set goals, you also come to realize that you don't make all your goals, and that's okay."

The linebacker who missed only three games during his 14-season career with the Patriots explains his longevity as a function of his passion for football—and its underlying structure. "You really have to love and enjoy the sport, enjoy your teammates, and be able to have a great experience playing, no matter what sport you play," he said. "It doesn't matter whether your sport is football or another team sport or even an individual sport; there are still the same fundamentals required to reach your goal."

The fact that he believes so strongly in being part of a team may partially explain his commitment to football. "The first thing you have to recognize about playing on a team is that the team comes first. Once you understand and accept that, you really start enjoying what team sports are all about."

In some ways, the Minnesota native has made a career for himself out of recognizing the value of the team over the individual. Following his 14 seasons playing for the Patriots, he worked as an assistant coach for that team and later became head football coach at Curry College. "When you're part of an effectively functioning team, you appreciate everyone else more. You understand people more. You get to know them better when you're all doing something for a common cause. You develop greater relationships with your teammates." And yet that doesn't mean giving up your sense of worth as an individual, he emphasizes. "When you understand everyone else's job, that understanding paves the way to individual success. You get a chance to appreciate what each of your teammates has to do and the difficulties their positions pose. And as you become a better teammate, that translates into you becoming a better person."

After all, Steve pointed out, as part of a team, you can be playing at the top of your game and still end up losing because of other players. When that happens, "You understand that things don't always go the way you planned and you have to make adjustments. Sometimes no matter how much you adjust, you're still going to be beaten. These are all the little life lessons that football teaches you about not giving up. And about the fact that working hard really does count toward your success."

This is why he believes that identifying wins and losses is a meaningful distinction that should not be minimized in the interest of building children's self-esteem. "I think we've become so politically correct in this country. Everyone has to get a trophy and everyone has to get an A. That defeats the whole purpose of working hard. If you give your best effort, you have nothing to be ashamed of. If you lose by five touchdowns, but you tried your best and you just weren't good enough, that's nothing to be ashamed of."

Recognizing the value of teamwork was woven into the fabric of his childhood, Steve said. His father was a high school coach, and Steve grew up with an understanding of a coach's role in his players' lives. "My father had great teams and great players, and I saw firsthand the impact he had on high school kids. I understood how hard he worked, and his teams were successful for many years because everybody bought into what my dad was selling. He taught his players that it's important to work out in the off season. It's important to be a good student. It's important to be a good person. All of these things add up to being a good teammate, and if you have a bunch of good teammates, you're going to have a good team."

Steve's father, now in his nineties, remains one of his most powerful role models. "He's 90 years old and he's still my hero. In World War II, he was part of the fighting on Omaha Beach. He took care of my mother after she developed Alzheimer's for as long as he could, and when she finally had to go to a rest home, he visited her every day. He still lives in his own house, cuts wood, mows his lawn and plays golf. And this is someone who really grew up with nothing. He was one of four kids, they had no father in the house, and my grandmother earned a dollar a day. Her message to them was, 'We're not poor. You're going to have to work for success, but that's the way it should be. Don't ever accept a dime from anybody.' That's what he did and that's what he taught his kids to do. Until ten years ago, I almost never used a credit card. I bought everything with cash. If I didn't have enough cash, I wouldn't buy it. Because that's what my father taught me. I had great examples of parents and I had incredible friends and it was just a great way to grow up."

He recognizes that many kids are not as blessed as he was with a father who taught valuable life lessons. But what matters, Steve believes, is that kids find someone else. "I think there has to be some type of adult in their life that kind of fills the void of what they're missing. Somehow, the community has got to rally around the young people and provide leadership and good role models. Being a good role model is not somebody taking them to the ice cream store every Saturday; it's someone who sits down and tells them to knock it off, or don't do that, or that's not the right choice. When you're growing up, you need someone there to correct you, which is what my dad did for me."

But even as he admires strong parenting and has always prioritized setting a good example for his five daughters, as a coach, he has also had to deal with his share of over-parenting. Mothers and fathers whose pursuit of what they believe their children were entitled to—such as more field time—often made it difficult for him to do his job.

"When I started coaching college, I couldn't believe that parents of 18 and 19 year olds were asking me to do things for their kids," he said. "Parents would call to ask why I wasn't playing their kids more. One father said that he couldn't understand why his son didn't get more playing time, especially since his son could jump from the floor to the top of the kitchen counter. I never did understand what that had to do with being a quarterback. But I would always respond by telling them that these kids were not children, they were young men. I'd say, "You have to let him fall down and get himself up. That's not my responsibility. My responsibility is to make sure he understands the rules that our team has and that he abides by them and he gives me his best effort.'"

As a coach, Steve practiced tough love with his players: they had to demonstrate their commitment and passion for the game if they wanted to play. "As far as I'm concerned, the two most important things are to show up on time and have a good attitude. It's not asking too much. But if kids were late and didn't demonstrate a good attitude, I took that to mean they didn't want to be a part of the team. So right from the start of the season, I would say, 'Well, you're late, well you're going to stay afterward. Everyone else is going to go in and you're going to run because you missed part of practice. Next time you're late, you're not going to play in the game. Next time after that, you're not going to be part of the team, unless you've got a late class or you have a legitimate excuse. If you have no excuse, you accept the consequences.'"

And despite his aversion to the kind of overbearing behavior he sometimes saw among parents at the college level, he acknowledges that parental interest is paramount to children's success. Parents whose kids play team sports should find a way to be part of the team, he said. "I would really encourage moms and dads [of younger children] to get involved directly in coaching. If you don't feel comfortable as the head coach, be an assistant coach. If you don't want to do that or if you don't have the time, be involved in the banquet. Just be involved. At the very least, attend the games. No matter how the team is doing, make sure your kid sees you up in the stands being proud of them."

And then engage your child in discussion about the game afterwards, he urges. "Don't tell them how they played. Ask them, 'How do you think you did,' or say 'Tell me about this play.'" It's not just about sports, Steve said; this kind of dialogue paves the way for open communication in all areas of a child's life. "When they see that you care and that they're important to you, it becomes natural for them to open up when they have issues and problems."

Part of what makes Steve such an effective coach is that he truly believes in a holistic approach to learning, something he demonstrated by switching traditional roles with his daughters when he asked them to teach him to ski. At the time, they ranged in age from about 8 to 14 and were all good skiers; he was 36 and had finished his football career. "We'd get on the chairlift and they'd tell me to be careful. And I would get off the chairlift and fall down or my pole would get stuck in the chair lift and go around the whole cycle again. They would get frustrated with me. They had to wait for me. But then when we stopped for lunch, all they wanted to talk about was how I was improving. They were able to see me saying, 'I tried it this one time, it didn't work, and I want to try it again. What do you think?' It was a reverse mentorship. I think it was really good for all of us. You learn a lot about kids when they start teaching you stuff: not just about their knowledge level, but how they hold their frustrations in, how they re-create learning experiences, how they think on a different level."

As a pro, Steve said, one of the most important lessons he learned was dealing with injuries and recognizing when it's time to take a back seat to another player. "Early on in the pros, I learned to distinguish between being hurt and being injured. You can play when you're hurt but you can't play when you're injured. You have to be a good teammate and understand that the guy who is your substitute will play better than you will if you're injured and he's not. And you have to sacrifice your own personal goals by letting the sub take your place so your team has a better chance of winning. That's why I have such great respect for Steve Grogan: he was a starting quarterback and then he was a backup. When he was a backup, he never felt sorry for himself. He always tried to prepare the starter as best he could from his own experience. He was a great example to all of us."

An unshakeable sense of Christian faith has always guided him as well. "I believe that there is something much bigger than me," he said. "People are special and I believe that we didn't happen by two meteors running into each other. If you go to Alaska and look at the mountains, you realize how insignificant you are in the whole grand scheme of things. If you believe there is something bigger than you, then you believe that all these mistakes you made and all the sins you commit will be forgiven. You're human and you're going to make a lot of mistakes. You're going to wish you could take things back that you said. You wish you could take things back that you did. But you can't, so apologize and forget about it."

Along with his four adult daughters, Steve and his wife Angela have a much younger child named Gracie. After ending his coaching career, he went into business: first as a restaurateur and later in the high-tech field. His number, 57, has been retired by the Patriots, and the 14-season linebacker now has what he believes to be the means for happiness. "I think fundamentally, the key to being happy is to be appreciative," he said. "If you don't appreciate anything, you're not going to be happy. You're always going to be searching for something. If you appreciate your health and you appreciate all the good things that life has given you, you're going to be happy."

This sense of profound gratitude, along with his sense of commitment to and respect for other people and his abiding faith, make Steve Nelson the embodiment of an Insightful Player™ team member.

INSTANT REPLAY OF STEVE'S *GUIDING PRINCIPLES*

1. Recognize that in football, and often in life, you win or lose as a team. How you are playing individually at any given time matters less than how your team is doing.

2. Children thrive when they have strong role models who are not afraid to guide and direct them.

3. Playing to the best of your abilities always matters more than getting a win; and losing is nothing to be ashamed of if you've put in your best effort.

4. Respect the abilities and expertise of other people, who may have important skills that you do not possess.

5. Help other people—whether they are your teammates, the players you coach, or your own children—to realize their goals.

6. Dream big, but also know how to set small, attainable goals for yourself as steppingstones to a bigger goal.

7. When you have wronged someone, possess the capacity to apologize sincerely and move on from it.

8. Put forth your best attitude in whatever you choose to do.

9. Develop a sense of faith, wonder and gratitude.

CHAPTER 22

JACKSONVILLE JAGUARS PRO BOWLER

MONTELL OWENS

PHOTO COURTESY *of SS Wedding Photography*

Hard-Driving Hunger to Be His Best Puts Him on the High Road On and Off the Field

Montell Owens' path to the NFL wasn't easy. He got there through sheer determination and hard work. There were many times when it looked like things weren't going his way, but instead of letting his frustration stop him, he took the time to refocus on the priorities that he learned from his parents: faith and family.

Montell grew up in a middle-class family in Wilmington, Delaware. His father had a good job in the construction industry. When he was working, times were good, but sometimes the economy or bad weather would lead to stretches of unemployment.

His parents, being smart and savvy people, used those occasions to teach him some valuable lessons—like the time his mother brought home Brussels sprouts for dinner.

He questioned why she had bought them and his mother explained they were on sale. At dinner, he ate everything on his plate, but left the Brussels sprouts. His mother was firm. "Look, son, you're going to eat these Brussels sprouts. You're not going to come in here and waste this food that we worked so hard for. You want to be a good football player, a good baseball player, then you have to eat."

His dad tried to calm his mother down. "I'll tell you what, honey, if he's hungry enough, he'll eat them."

There was something about his father's words that made Montell really listen and think. "Maybe it was God speaking to me that night," he remembered, "teaching me a lesson. I guess I realized that I *was* hungry—and this was not just about food—I was hungry to be a better person."

He ate the Brussels sprouts.

Later in life, when he didn't want to do things that seemed hard or uncomfortable, he realized he had two choices. He could make excuses, complain and avoid doing them. Or, if he was hungry enough, he could do what he knew was right, do what would make him a stronger athlete, a stronger person.

At Concord High School in Wilmington, Montell excelled in schoolwork, music and sports. He was a member of the National Honor Society, a lead trumpet player in the jazz band, and a letterman in football, baseball, and track. As graduation approached in 2002, he began to get offers from schools. The best offer—a full football scholarship to a Division 1AA school—came from a surprising place: The University of Maine. Montell didn't know much about Maine—just that it was cold and nine hours away from his hometown. Still, his parents could not afford to pay for college, and Maine was the opportunity he had been waiting for.

The first two years of school were lonely and hard. He was far away from his friends and family, and the person he spent the most time with—his football coach—never seemed to give him a break.

Jeff Cole was Montell's running back coach. Every day, month after month, no matter how hard Montell worked, it seemed that Coach Cole was not satisfied. He always wanted more out of Montell. He wanted him to work harder, to get better, and he wouldn't let up. Although Montell fell back on his work ethic and did what he had to do, his heart wasn't in it. He began to see Coach Cole as a mean old guy who just pointed out all his mistakes and didn't appreciate him.

But after about two years, Montell and his teammates began to notice a change in Coach Cole. He didn't have as much energy as he used to; he started to lose a lot of weight. He would wave off questions, saying he was just trying to stay fit. But then it seemed like Coach Cole was always coming down with yet another cold. About halfway through Montell's third year at Maine, Coach Cole started to lose his hair and the players realized that something serious was going on.

One day at a team meeting, the team found out that Coach Cole was going overseas somewhere, for how long they didn't know. The players thought maybe he was taking a vacation, and didn't think much about it. But three weeks later, after practice, they saw Coach Cole walking toward them. He looked like he had lost almost 70 pounds. He was skin and bones and his hair was gone. That's when the team found out that his trip overseas was a last-ditch effort to try a treatment, unavailable in the U.S., for the brain cancer he had been quietly battling for the past three years. Within two weeks, Coach Cole was dead.

After that, Montell's whole mindset about his experience in Maine began to change. Instead of feeling victimized and unappreciated, he began to think about the lessons Coach Cole had tried to instill in him, not just with his coaching, but in how he lived his life. For three years, Coach Cole had awakened each morning knowing he was dying. But he lived each day with drive and determination. He chose not to use his cancer as an excuse, but saw each day as an opportunity to battle back, to give his best. Montell realized that his coach had wanted him to know that it wasn't about getting it right the third or fourth time. It was about getting it right, right now. There was no time to wait.

Looking back at his first two years at Maine, Montell wondered if Coach Cole had ridden him so hard because he saw more potential in him. He wondered if God was also sending him a message through the coach. During the cold and lonely time at the beginning of school, he had let his frustration affect his attitude. But now he realized that, like Coach Cole, he could change his attitude and use it to push through any adversity that came his way. This change would be the ticket that helped him get through the many barriers that stood between him and the NFL.

So for the rest of his time at school, Montell dug in and gave Maine his best. But although he was a good player and a hard worker, he didn't have the kind of playing opportunities that would have showcased his talents to NFL scouts. During his senior year he had only about 750 yards rushing, not enough to display his talent. Maybe that was why his coaches did not encourage him to get his hopes up for life in the big leagues and tried to talk him into a career in medicine.

But Montell was not ready to give up on the NFL. In his mind, he had a shot, however small, and he intended to go for it. What did he have to lose? He went to a training camp with fellow students to prepare for the NFL tryouts. Just by showing up at the training sessions and doing his best, he started being noticed by NFL trainers.

When the training and tryouts were over, there was nothing Montell could do except wait. Weeks went by; no phone calls. Montell went back to the Maine coaches and asked them to help him put together a highlight tape, to make a few calls on his behalf. The coaches helped him out, but he knew they thought he was wasting his time.

Finally, it was draft day. Montell was at a friend's house, a wide receiver named Kevin McMann. Kevin had had a great year, and Montell knew his chances were good. When Kevin got the call—the last pick of the draft—Montell jumped and shouted. Later, while picking up the popcorn and pizza boxes after the celebration, it hit Montell that when Kevin was selected with this last pick of the draft, there went his chances for playing in the NFL.

Then his phone rang.

"This is Coach Pola here with the Jaguars. Montell, do you want to play some football?"

Montell could not believe it! "Yeah!" he answered, "I'm in!"

When Montell got to Jacksonville, he realized he had his work cut out for him. In some ways, it was like being a freshman in Maine all over again. There were already seven other running backs—six veterans and a second-round draft choice—to compete with. Montell knew he was last in line, and he would need to work hard to make the final cut.

He focused on his predicament. Even if this was his only time in the NFL, here at this training camp, he thought, he was determined to enjoy it. And he gave it his best.

But it wasn't easy. Many of the offensive plays were new to him, and he wondered if he was in over his head. It seemed like he kept making mistakes; he just wasn't playing well.

One night, sitting alone in his hotel room, he felt his frustration overwhelm him. He knew the cuts were coming up soon, and he didn't think he was going to make the team. Tears started to well up in his eyes and he felt like giving up. But then he began to pray. "Where are you, Lord?" he asked in despair. He prayed for comfort, and he prayed for help. He found himself almost trying to bargain with God, promising he would be a better Christian, a better person, if he could just make the team.

But as he listened to himself pleading with God, he was hit by a sudden realization. He had been so consumed by football, with making the team, he had lost sight of his real priorities. He had lost sight of his faith.

He realized that it didn't really matter if he made the team. He wasn't playing for the coach, or for the guy next to him. He was playing to give his best to God. And before long, he found that this change in perspective, this change in priorities, started to impact his playing in a positive way. Instead of getting frustrated, and having his frustration lead to more mistakes, he was able to bounce back more quickly, to let things go and stay in the present.

Montell made the first cuts; he made the second cuts. And then he got a chance to play in a preseason game in Miami. He had to wait until the fourth quarter and then he heard "Montell, you're in on kick-off." Montell said a quick prayer: "I'm enjoying myself, I'm having fun, thank you Lord Jesus, I'm going to give you my best on this one play." Then he was in there, making play after play after play. The next thing he knew he had made it and was placed on special teams. And he knew that his success had stemmed from the night in his room, when he had almost given up hope and turned to God for comfort and help.

A few years ago, Montell was visiting a friend in Jackson, Mississippi, during the off-season. He was a little bored, and was just wandering around, looking for something to do. He came across a little art museum. There was a picture hanging there that caught his eye. It was a simple one: just some trees and a dirt road that split in two directions. Just a picture of a fork in the road. He bought it and took it home.

The picture reminds Montell of that night in the hotel room, that night of despair. He could have taken a different road. He could have told himself it was just too hard.

Today, Montell's success with the Jacksonville Jaguars has made him a rising star in the NFL. He made the Pro Bowl in the 2010 season. But he knows that the road ahead will continue to include obstacles and forks and will require him to remember those lessons that helped him get where he is today.

As an NFL player, Montell knows there are millions of kids who look up to him and other players for inspiration. In Jacksonville, Montell has connected with local high school kids through music via his support of a new jazz band, the St. John's River City High School All-Stars.

Montell has a dream of starting a TV show that highlights the positive efforts that many players in the NFL have made in their local communities. He knows other players who work in soup kitchens, who volunteer at their church, whose lives are shining examples of dedication to faith and family and community.

He aspires to be able to push kids in the right direction, without pushing them away by being too rigid and harsh. He knows that many of them are standing at a fork in their own road, trying to make the hard decision about which way to go. What he wants them to know is this: follow the road that will lead to your dreams, but don't travel alone. Bring along your faith, your family, your friends and your passion, and you will go far.

Montell Owens is an admirable Insightful Player™ team member who is dedicated to being his best. He hopes to share the lessons he has learned with kids: that focusing on priorities like faith and family and personal passions like music and sports can bring real satisfaction, real joy.

INSTANT REPLAY OF MONTELL'S *GUIDING PRINCIPLES*

1. Develop a relationship with Christ.

2. Take full responsibility for your life and give your best every day.

3. Be willing to try new things.

4. Trust and act on your yearnings for success.

5. Push through obstacles to gain inner strength.

6. Tap into your passion to move forward.

7. Believe in yourself, especially when others don't.

8. Maintain a positive attitude regardless of your situation.

9. Rearrange your priorities so that the important things in life come first.

CHAPTER 23

NFL FORMER PLAYER

KEVIN REILLY

Transformed Tragedy Into an Inspiring, Purpose-Driven Life

I f Academy Awards were given to remarkable people who transformed a personal tragedy into an awe-inspiring life, Insightful Player™ team member **Kevin Reilly** would surely win one. He started out living the kind of life dreams are made of. Growing up as one of six children with two loving parents, he was an exceptionally talented high school football and basketball captain and won a football scholarship to Villanova University, where he was voted MVP.

One of Kevin's most memorable moments was when he was recruited to play professional football. He was drafted by the Miami Dolphins, traded to the Philadelphia Eagles, and ended up finishing his career with the New England Patriots. Not only was being drafted in the NFL a dream come true, but so was being traded to the Eagles, as this was the team he had fallen in love with as a young boy.

Unfortunately, Kevin's football career came to a screeching halt when he was diagnosed with cancer. He went from living a dream to enduring a nightmare. Although his life was saved, radical surgery took his left arm, five ribs, and a large portion of his left shoulder.

Just before he was rolled into the operating room, a priest gave Kevin communion and the sacrament of the sick. Growing up Catholic, he knew the sacrament of the sick was a prayer for people on their deathbed. This was shocking since he hadn't been told his life was in jeopardy. At that moment, everything changed. The NFL no longer mattered to him. All he could think of were his wife and three young children. Frightened and overcome with a penetrating sorrow because he didn't get a chance to say goodbye to his family, he felt horrible that he hadn't spent more time with the people close to him and wished he'd extended himself more to others.

Kevin did survive the surgery, but the doctors were not certain they had removed all of the cancer. This began his journey down the long road to recovery.

When it came time to take the bandages off, the nurses wanted Kevin to have someone with him. He chose his friend John Bunting, an Eagles linebacker, to be there. John had just come back from a horrendous knee injury the year before. Kevin was stunned to see how much of the left side of his body was missing. John was equally stunned. Trying to make light of the situation, John said, "At least you have two good knees." Kevin still laughs when he recounts the story.

Kevin remembered, "Immediately following the surgery, everyone treated me differently. I was getting pampered in a lot of ways, and well meaning people were feeling sorry for me. That wasn't my M.O. I didn't want people feeling sorry for me. It just made me feel sorry for myself. I began to spiral down into a sea of negativity."

He started to worry about what he could still do and desperately questioned everything. What if he couldn't button shirts, tie his ties, or even drive a car? What kind of husband and father could he be? With these questions, he faced great fear and self-doubt.

One day when Kevin was feeling particularly sorry for himself, he got a surprise telephone call from Rocky Bleier, former Steelers superstar. After Rocky's 1968 rookie season, he was drafted into the Army and sent to Vietnam, where he was severely injured. The doctors told him he would never play football again. Rocky defied all odds and went on to play for the Steelers and winning four Super Bowls.

Kevin said, "Rocky asked me if anyone had been in to talk with me about my limitations. I told him they talked to me about a multitude of limitations and how they painted a picture for me that was very bleak. I also told Rocky I needed to accept what they said because they were experts and I was an amateur.

"He pointed out to me that the Titanic was built by experts, too, and the Ark was built by amateurs. Rocky's words created a real turning point for me. I finally had the courage to read all the unopened cards and letters I had received from family, friends, and fans I had never met. They all had the same message: They were praying for me and knew I would come back. I felt I owed it to my family, my supporters, and the general public to make a comeback. It solidified that I was going to be the best one-armed person going forward."

After that, Kevin took on his rehabilitation with all his might and pushed himself further and harder than anyone thought possible. He proved "the experts" wrong about the limitations they set in front of him.

They claimed he wouldn't be back to work for a very long period of time. Kevin was back to work in two months. Not only that, but he built a successful career as a senior executive at Xerox while simultaneously becoming a radio announcer for the Philadelphia Eagles on stations WYSP and WDEL.

They told him he would never be able to tie his own tie and would have to settle for a clip-on. In fact, one of these experts had tried for 25 years to tie his own tie after losing an arm and told Kevin it couldn't be done. In two months, Kevin was tying his own tie, again proving them wrong.

They told Kevin his athletic abilities and physical capacity were severely diminished and recommended he dramatically lower the bar for his fitness goals. As soon as Kevin went back to work, he joined the company racquetball team and immediately figured out how to compete without a handicap. He was a great competitor and played on the team for five years. This gave Kevin the confidence to try other sports. He said, "If I can play racquetball, I can play golf. I broke 90 twice and I never did that when I had two arms. I can putt as well as the best of them."

Kevin thought if he took up running, he would be able to keep extra weight off. The experts insisted running wasn't even a remote possibility for him. Yet again he proved them wrong and completed six half-marathons and one full marathon. He has even run in races with all three of his children. In the fall of 2009, he ran a 5K race with his 10-year-old grandson, Jake. Kevin is committed to his physical fitness, and in addition to all the sports he plays, he works out three to four days a week.

Even though Kevin was successfully slaying one dragon after another, he had that gnawing fear in the back of his mind that the cancer might come back. He would wake up in the middle of the night fighting off gut-wrenching fear. He often questioned whether the surgeons got the entire tumor; whether his family would make it without him; what he needed to do to take away their fear; and what he had to do to prove to his bosses at Xerox he could do the job with one arm. It took Kevin 12 years to finally gain some peace, and that was only after the doctors gave him a clean bill of health.

Once cancer-free, he started appreciating everything he had to be grateful for. His drive to be the best one-armed man he could be grew stronger every day.

Throughout the years following his surgery, Kevin experienced additional tragedies. His 20-year marriage dissolved when his kids were in college. He said, "I never saw it coming. That was a much bigger crisis for me than losing my arm. I felt humility, and rejection. It took me a year to come out of it. I had to put my fractured family back together. I said to God, 'You took my arm, now you take my marriage?' This was much harder for me to accept, because family is my most important value." The combination of his Catholic faith, his strong will, and support from loved ones pulled Kevin through this, but not without other struggles.

Early on in his career at Xerox, Kevin developed a habit of drinking a couple of glasses of wine to wind down. Shortly after the marriage broke up, the number of glasses he drank escalated. Kevin stated, "After a while, my friends told me I was out of control. I didn't see it, because I never missed a day of work nor a workout. I finally had to admit to myself that I did have a problem, and I joined AA. I am happy to report that I haven't had a drink in several years."

Kevin looks at his tough times with tremendous respect and humility. He said he clung close to being "consistently persistent" and made that his declaration every single day as he put one foot in front of the other, one day at a time. He said, "If I took away some of those bad times, maybe I wouldn't have the experience to be where I am right now. Each crisis has made me stronger. It is important to prepare for downs and lows. We need to find that middle ground."

Today, Kevin thrives on giving to others and has realized that the more he does for others, the better he feels about himself. He joyfully volunteers his time to work with amputee soldiers at the Walter Reed Army Medical Center in Washington, DC. He said, "I get so much out of this. The soldiers are very proud of their service to their country. One thing I have never heard any of them say is, 'Why did this happen to me?' They have so much courage and are determined to live the best life possible in spite of their injuries. They inspire me so much and I can feed off of their positive attitude for days, and sometimes even weeks."

Several years ago, Kevin retired from a 30-year career at Xerox to pursue a career as a motivational speaker and trainer. He inspires his audiences to become relentless in finding the very best in themselves regardless of their circumstances. Howie Long, Fox NFL Football Analyst and NFL Hall of Famer, said, "Kevin literally brings audiences to their feet with his inspiring story. They should create a special Hall of Fame for people like him." Kevin may be the only person in the entire world who receives a standing ovation *every time* he speaks.

Kevin still hosts the Eagles pre- and post-game radio shows. In fact, he was even selected by the Eagles to be the play-by-play commentator for their 2009 exhibition pre-season games. He always wanted to become a television sports commentator, but never thought it possible with only one arm. Artie Kemnar, Fox Senior Producer, told Kevin he literally broke the handicap barrier for an NFL telecast because he was the first handicap person to host an NFL telecast. For this accomplishment, Kevin feels very proud.

Even though he has been through some extremely difficult circumstances in life, he is now a realistic optimist. His sights are set very high, and he recognizes the importance in building resilience because bumps in the road are inevitable. According to Kevin, "We need to make sure we really enjoy the good times and hunker down during the tough times. We will be stronger for it. Sometimes the bad things that happen to us can result in unforeseen future opportunities that transform our lives."

"We all need to be on the lookout for people, and in particular kids, who are going through rough times. Many people are great at hiding their suffering from others and could really benefit from a loving gesture. Next time you find yourself judging someone, go into your heart and reach out to them, or reach out to someone else who could use a lift. Better yet, set out to give every person you meet something to smile about. You'll be better for it, and your kindness could be the very thing that sets them on their own 'best track.'"

Kevin feels this is a message for kids too. He wants to encourage them to reach out to other kids who are alone in the cafeteria or on the playground; make friends with them not just for the moment but for good. This simple act of kindness could have a positive and lasting impact on the rest of their life. When asked what one quality he thinks is most important for people to cultivate, he said, "Empathy. If we all exercise empathy, we'll see more kindness in the world."

Kevin has three happily married children, Brett, Erin and Brie, and has been blessed with eight delightful grandchildren. As Kevin said, "This extended family is my pride, joy, and love of my life!"

Kevin Reilly is a tremendous role model. His ability to get back up, no matter how low he has fallen, is exceptional. The tragedies he has faced in his life have opened his heart, strengthened his character, and given him an amazing ability to love more deeply while judging others much less. He has recognized that adversity has given him an insatiable appetite for helping others. He believes everyone deserves a second chance and recognizes if he wasn't given one he wouldn't be here today. These are the qualities that have earned him a spot on the Insightful Player™ team roster.

INSTANT REPLAY OF KEVIN'S *GUIDING PRINCIPLES*

1. Always be grateful and content with what you have. The more grateful you are, the more you will have to be grateful for.

2. Let other people support you; don't be a "Lone Ranger."

3. Face your fears but don't let them consume you.

4. Find a compelling reason to have a great life, regardless of your circumstances, and make it happen.

5. Follow your heart and don't let anyone tell you what you can't do.

6. Build resilience: When you fall down, get back up. You'll be better for it.

7. Show empathy to people going through tough times and always be on the lookout for kids that could use your support.

8. Reach out. For kids especially, when you see another kid sitting alone, show kindness and befriend that kid. Acts of kindness such as these change lives.

9. Give other people something to smile about every day, especially those days when you can't find anything to smile about yourself.

CHAPTER 24

THE NEW YORK JETS'

TONY RICHARDSON

PHOTO COURTESY *of Laurel Austin*

God-Driven Life Makes Him a Champion
On and Off the Field

hile other boys were passing the pigskin in the backyard with their dads, Insightful Player™ **Tony Richardson** was growing up in a country where football was really soccer. His father, a sergeant major in the United States Army, was stationed in Frankfurt, Germany, when Tony was born.

The only American football he saw was Monday Night Football on television until his family moved back to the U.S. when he was in seventh grade.

Tony did not even start playing football until high school. On his first day, he secretly studied the other players gearing up, to see how to put on his pads. He was too embarrassed to ask for help. Despite proving himself a talented running back, he knew that no one in his small Alabama town had ever received a Division One scholarship, and his odds were slim of being the first.

Tony was not deterred from the quest to get a college scholarship, and he succeeded in being accepted by Auburn University. Once there, his sense of resolve again saw him through, and he gathered his strength to become the second running back ever to start as a freshman. (Bo Jackson was the first.)

The great success he enjoyed as a college football player seemed to assure that he would be drafted by the NFL, but when it came time for the draft pick, he was passed over. "God," he prayed, feeling devastated, "if this is what you call me to do, you've got to make a way because what I have been doing hasn't worked."

As a free agent, Tony could be approached by any team. After he turned everything over to God, he got a call from the Dallas Cowboys, and was invited to their training camp. He did not make the team, but was put on the practice squad instead. It was a very humbling experience. Even after completing his seventeenth season, Tony continues to be inspired by what happened to him. "Every day, you have to prove yourself," he said. Tony tells his current Jets teammates that "this still makes me hungry now."

God is still a very strong presence in Tony's life. He continues to work hard, but when he faces storms in his life, he puts God in the center as his best resource. "I get up each day with a smile on my face because it isn't about me, it is about Him," Tony said. "I cast everything over to God."

His deep-rooted faith and trust in God has brought tremendous joy to Tony's life. He is amazed by how his faith gives him the ability to live with a sense of freedom because he recognizes that much of what happens in life is out of his control. He also feels less attached to material things. "All the stuff can be gone tomorrow. My faith, and God's presence, is the only constant I have."

Tony went on to have a successful career, playing for the Kansas City Chiefs and the Minnesota Vikings before landing with the New York Jets. He has been recognized for his talent and received numerous awards. He was selected by NFL Commissioner Roger Goodell to the six member Player's Advisory Committee in Spring 2007. And, in 2008, he was named Walter Payton Man of the Year for the Jets. He currently serves on the NFLPA Executive Committee.

In 2003, he was named Pro Football's Weekly's "Arthur S. Arkush Humanitarian of the Year" and was voted an "NFL Good Guy" in 2002, 2003, and 2004 by The Sporting News based on civic responsibility and character. He was also chosen by teammates as the Chiefs' NFL Man of the Year nominee and the NLFPA's Byron "Whizzer" White Award nominee. In 2005, Tony received the Distinguished Citizen Award from the National Conference for

Community and Justice, an organization dedicated to fighting bias, bigotry and racism. In 2010, Tony was named the Jets Man of the Year and won the NFLPA's Byron "Whizzer" White award.

Interestingly, out of 300 players in his "class," Tony is the only one who is still playing in the NFL. And, he was a free agent! He believes that his career has survived this long "because God knew what I would do with the platform (of football) which is to help people."

Tony went from being a champion on the field to being one off the field, dedicating his free time to helping others. Through his Rich in Spirit Foundation, Tony sponsors The Dictionary Project, which provides new dictionaries to schoolchildren, while promoting literacy and education. The program has donated more than 45,000 dictionaries to elementary school students in the Kansas City area alone. It is also active in Minneapolis and New York. Tony wants to see the project grow. "It would be grand if the Rich in Spirit dictionary project could put a dictionary in the hands of every child across the nation. The impact that it would have would be amazing."

In his own childhood, Tony remembers sitting in the back of the classroom, sliding down into his chair when the teacher asked, "Who can use this word in a sentence? Who can spell this word?" Tony is very passionate when he talks about the Dictionary Project, "A dictionary can give you power and helps kids build confidence."

He knew his project was working when the father of one of the students who received a dictionary approached him at the grocery store. He told Tony that his daughter took his suggestion about taking the dictionary with her everywhere so seriously that she even slept with the book. The father was grateful for the positive impact Tony had on his daughter. Tony continues to meet kids who tell him how much the dictionaries have helped them in their lives. "With education, anything is possible," Tony said enthusiastically. "Education prepares you for life."

The Rich in Spirit Foundation has also done a lot of work for the Special Olympics and Athletes in Action. Tony hosted the Special Olympics Punt, Pass and Kick competition in Kansas City annually, from 1999 to 2005. The foundation was created "to extend a helping hand and uplift the lives and spirits of individuals who society has turned their back on."

"It is great to be an inspiring football player, to be a Hall of Fame Pro Bowler or to win a Super Bowl, but it is most important to invest in yourself, invest in your future with education," said Tony, who received a bachelor's degree in education from Auburn in 2000 and a masters degree in business from Webster University in 2004. "Education prepares you for life and gives you a greater opportunity to get a lot more out of life. It is important to continue to learn."

Through the NFL Entrepreneurship program, Tony has taken classes at the Wharton School of Business and Northwestern's Kellogg School. He has also studied at Stanford and Harvard.

Insatiable in his thirst for knowledge, Tony makes it a point of knowing what is going on in the world. To keep current, he watches documentaries, and reads newspapers and magazines. He especially loves reading about people overcoming challenges and obstacles in their search for success. It is important to learn from your mistakes, said Tony. "Failures were the very thing that made them become the best person and business person they are. That's knowledge, that's power."

A good habit to get into is to learn from mistakes and failure by asking your self, 'how can I turn this into something positive?' Over time, it will become easier to put into practice. Faith is the main component for Tony. "Never allow anyone to tell you that you can't do anything," Tony advised. "Often, the people who tell you that you can't do something are the same people who can't visualize themselves doing something great, or they may not be willing to make the sacrifice."

An early role model, Tony's father, Sergeant Major Ben Richardson, is the person he admires the most. "He got up every day at three or four a.m. to polish his boots and never complained. I wanted to get up with him." Tony was impressed that his father, a Vietnam veteran, received such reverence and respect when they were out in public or on the army base. "This made me think," said Tony. "Why should I be a knucklehead and give my dad a problem?"

Growing up in Germany, Tony was exposed to many cultures, which made him more tolerant of people, regardless of race, economic status, intelligence, gender or religion. His parents taught him discipline and encouraged him to do everything to the best of his ability. He remembers when his father asked him to wash the car. He scrubbed the side closest to the house, hoping he could fool his father into thinking the entire car was clean. His father went looking for him and made him clean the rest of the car. This taught him to give one hundred percent to anything he does and it set the stage for his future accomplishments. "Dad always said, 'if it is worth doing, it's worth doing right.' This is what I tell young people."

He looks forward to having his own children someday and teaching them about character the way his father taught him. "I would like to be that person for my kids that my father is for me. Hopefully, I can be half the person he is."

Another valued mentor for Tony was his high school coach, who took over the team during Tony's junior year. "He built a strong foundation for the football program," Tony remembers. "He took it seriously and a lot of kids quit. I really appreciate him for giving me the framework for working twice as hard as I originally thought I was capable of."

Today, Tony tells kids to look at athletes as role models, but to also have role models closer to home, such as parents, teachers, coaches, aunts, uncles, and even older kids. "If you don't have anyone in your life, go to the Boys and Girls Clubs," Tony advised.

He meets kids who are in rough situations, many live in poverty. "I always tell them to not get caught up in where they live or where you go to school," Tony said. "An education will get you out of that."

Tony has a dream that the kids he has helped will go back to their old neighborhoods and help out. They will be able to relate better to the kids because they have been in the same situation, and they will be a tremendous source of inspiration because they made something of their lives.

In his own life, Tony is inspired by the words of Charles Swindoll, a pastor in Texas who is known for saying: "Life is 10 percent of what happens to you and 90 percent of how you respond." In life, there are successes and failures, good days and bad days, Tony said, but what counts is how you respond to them. "Every day I have an opportunity to do something and put my best foot forward. If something doesn't work in my favor, can I become a better person from it? Can I learn from it? Can I walk around with a smile?"

He sees his own future as being a positive influence for other players in the NFL, helping them to make good decisions and maximize their playing time.

Tony faced a lot of negativity from people who said he could not make it to the NFL, but he never gave up and eventually reached his goal. He was supported by a strong, loving family who taught him to work to the best of his ability. He found strength through his faith in God, and he found inspiration in the lives of successful people who overcame challenges in their lives. Giving back to the community is important to Tony so he reaches out to young people through the Dictionary Project and other programs sponsored by his Rich in Spirit Foundation. Tony is a truly remarkable role model who lives his life with integrity. He is indeed a valuable member of the Insightful Player™ team.

INSTANT REPLAY OF TONY'S *GUIDING PRINCIPLES*

1. As long as you work hard and do the right thing, good things will happen for you.

2. Set a goal and go for it! Find something you are passionate about no matter what it is and become great at it. Opportunities will show up once you are committed to your goal.

3. Surround yourself with positive people. Don't let negative people tell you that you cannot do something.

4. Use athletes as role models, but also find mentors closer to home, including parents, teachers, coaches, relatives, and religious leaders.

5. Find inspiration from the lives of successful people who have faced and overcome challenges.

6. Advance through education. Read books, go to school, and keep a dictionary with you at all times so you can learn new words.

7. Trust in God. Have faith that God will take care of you in good and bad times. This will free you up to feel the joy of life. Don't be attached to material things. They don't last.

8. Get rid of the distractions in your life that tempt you away from being great.

CHAPTER 25

NFL FREE AGENT

GEROME SAPP

Enduring Resilience and an Open-Minded Approach Are the Keys to His Success

Growing up in inner-city Houston, there were times when **Gerome Sapp** and his siblings had to cope without water or electricity. Not all the time, but occasionally for a day or two at a stretch. Other children in those circumstances might grow up with an embittered view, but for Gerome, it was formative to his remarkably positive outlook. He used the experience to learned two important lessons modeled by his mother, Angelia. "First of all, she would tell us that tomorrow would probably be better," Gerome recalled. "And second, that it would be a good idea to do our homework early instead of putting it off."

This reflected Angelia's approach to life, which was always to balance the ideal with the realistic. Ideally, she would be able to pay the electric bill or water bill within another day or two and all would be well: realistically, it would make sense to finish homework during daylight hours in case the lights still weren't on later. And today, her son embodies the resilience and spiritual strength for which Angelia set an example in those difficult days.

"We didn't always have what we wanted, but we always had what we needed," Gerome said. "My mother loved each of us unconditionally. Love and religion were the basis for everything that happened in our lives. We were Southern Baptists and went to church most Sundays, but more importantly, my mom stressed having your own relationship with God and knowing that you can depend on Him no matter what is going on in your life. That really inspired me and stuck with me. No matter what is going on in my personal life, I know that there is a greater power protecting me and guiding me."

This core of resilience has carried Gerome through every stage of his life thus far—from his hardscrabble childhood and an absent father to his ascension as the number one ranked high school football player in the entire state of Texas; the years as an undergraduate at Notre Dame, during which he demonstrated both athletic and academic success; and five strong years in the NFL. And Gerome's quests are not yet over: he and some former teammates have launched a company called Morph &Thro, LLC.

"I knew my father but I had no relationship with him. He was always in and out of jail, on drugs… he missed probably 90% of our life," Gerome said. In the absence of a father's leadership, his mother signed up her two sons—Gerome and his brother Charles, just one year older—in the Big Brother program. Both boys were matched with young men to whom they stay in touch to this day. To seven-year-old Gerome, Big Brother Todd Freeman was a godsend. "He was 23, fresh out of college. We would go out and play catch and talk about sports." As the years went by, the two talked about far more, and Todd eventually opened Gerome's eyes to a wider world. "He told me that to play in the pros, you should go to college first. Before that, I thought Notre Dame was a football team. I didn't know it was an actual university. I went to my first hockey game with him. He kind of opened me up to a whole other side of life that I hadn't seen." The two stayed close; Todd attended Gerome's college football games and his first pro game, and Gerome was in Todd's wedding party. "He was the first consistent male figure in my life," Gerome commented.

In high school, Gerome connected with the second major father figure of his youth: his football coach, Lee Malowitz. The players generally considered Coach Malowitz to be tough and not always kind, but Gerome and his brother saw behind the façade. Malowitz lived near them and frequently gave them rides to and from school, and during those rides, Gerome said, "we basically broke each other down. He realized that me and my brother weren't just the average teenage black males. And we realized that even though a lot of people thought Coach

Malowitz hated them, he was hard on us because he didn't want to see us mess up."

The boys learned also that Malowitz had lost his wife to cancer just a few years earlier. Like Angelia, he was a single parent trying to do his best at raising children. "He was a fiery person, but at the end of it, I understood him," Gerome said. "If he cussed me out, I understood why he cussed me out. Our relationship is still strong."

The insights into their coach's personal problems reinforced a lesson Gerome had already begun learning on the urban streets of Houston: don't judge people. His mother had encouraged a nonjudgmental attitude which has always helped him to treat people fairly and kindly, but back then his open-mindedness made it all the more difficult when the young man felt himself being judged. He still recalls a moment of childhood mockery that bruised him deeply. "My family received food stamps, and one day my mom sent my brother and me to the store. I put the food stamps in my shoe. On the way, my brother and I got into a game of pick-up football with some of my friends. During the game, my shoe came off and the food stamps flew everywhere and everybody was laughing about the food stamps. I guess looking back on it, that situation was extremely impactful to me in terms of how I wanted to shape my future. But still, part of me was wondering why these kids would laugh at something like that." Rather than being traumatized by the mockery, Gerome countered with his innate sense of resilience, knowing it was the other children who were being ignorant and that his family did not merit blame for their circumstances.

The tight bond between Gerome and Charles grew ever stronger as the boys became high school football stars. "My brother and I were always very athletic," he said. "We weren't always the best, but we knew we had potential. I come from good genes, and that's obviously advantageous for athletes. From my freshman year to my sophomore year, I gained about thirty pounds of muscle. So I had the opportunity to start as a sophomore on varsity. My brother was the strong safety and I was the free safety. It was cool having two siblings starting on varsity, like the culmination of our hard work, all those push-ups and sit-ups when we were young. By my junior year I was *Parade* and *USA Today* First Team All-American. In my senior year, I was the number one player in Texas, and number five or six in the country."

College recruiters were watching, and Coach Malowitz knew it. He took responsibility for helping to shape Gerome's college outlook. "Basically, his lesson to me was 'Keep doing what you're doing and don't mess up. There's a lot of good things that can come to you from how you play on the football field, but you also have to make sure that you always handle the academic part of it too.' Well, academics have always been important to me. That's something else I learned from my mom. I always do my work."

Along with athletic prowess and academic diligence, another factor fueled Gerome's potential: his commitment to clean living. It was a set of beliefs shared by his best friend, Robert. The two had been pals and teammates since middle school and would eventually be drafted the same year by the NFL. "We had other friends drinking and smoking weed and stuff like that," Gerome said. "That wasn't important to us. We knew people were doing it but we had the attitude of, 'That's not my thing. Right now, my thing is making sure that I'm where I need to be physically and mentally to take this next step, because I know this next step is coming.'" Instead, the two friends would egg each other on in the weight room and on the track, pushing each other to even greater physical challenges. "It's good to have a friend with similar interests," Gerome said. "You have to find somebody who is positive."

At Malowitz's urging, Gerome kept his grades up—earning a solid B average, as he recalls—and listened to the college coaches who wanted to sign him. At first smaller schools visited, assuming that he didn't have the grades for a more impressive institution; but once they saw his transcript they backed off. Gerome eventually chose Notre Dame, in part because he valued the opportunities it would give him to experience something different.

"My mom didn't tell me where to go. Her only wish for me in choosing which college to play for was that I do it for the right reasons and make it a chance to expand my horizons. I'd never been to Indiana. I'd never lived in the snow. Notre Dame is a hard school. That was my first big adult decision in my life, choosing to go to Notre Dame. I did it because I knew it would be a challenge to me."

Even though he knew he was answering his mother's wish that he experience something new, he still recalls how hard it was for her to watch him leave. "I remember my mom walking me to the gate. She was waving goodbye and I had tears in my eyes because I knew from that point on, it was my transition from being a teenage boy to becoming a man. It hit me at that point that this is where my mom has to say goodbye to her baby boy."

The four years at Notre Dame were fundamental to shaping not only Gerome's football career but his adult personality as well. "A lot of guys I knew who went off to college couldn't handle the mental burden, because the first time you're away from home, school is hard, football is hard. You're no longer the big shot anymore. So you have to learn how to play a role of a lesser athlete, not what you were in high school. I was able to handle that though."

And his peers at Notre Dame were in for a surprise. Though his upbringing was not as privileged as most of theirs, he had brains and intellectual ambitions. "There are a lot of smart people at Notre Dame but I hung in there with all of them academically. That was a time when I kind of had to come into my own and further expand my horizons, especially being a black male from the South, coming to South Bend, Indiana. The most challenging part was not really me having to adjust to a different culture, it was that other culture having to adjust to me." For example, Gerome said, when students were assigned to work together in groups, others would often assume he didn't know as much as they did. He would calmly wait them out, learning to exercise patience as he listened to their misinformation. "Then I'd just be like, "'Whatever, man. I'm right, you're wrong, let's move on. Now we have an A on the project instead of a C.'"

His classmates' incorrect assumptions about him extended beyond the classroom. Many of the other students at Notre Dame had attended private Catholic high schools and had little experience with any minorities at all—not just African-Americans. The first time he played R&B music in his dorm room—the music he had grown up with in Houston—his roommate was appalled. "He was like, 'What are you doing? Why are you playing this music?' He was half joking, but that was his way of telling me to cut the music off. Guys would ask me if I knew how to barbecue because I was from the South. I'd say, 'Not really, you throw some meat on the grill, right?' Little things like that were amusing. There were only two black guys in my whole dorm and they were both football players."

But even though he can laugh at the memories of his classmates learning to adjust to him rather than vice versa, Gerome values the lessons that his social interactions at Notre Dame taught him. Like with the food stamps when he was a child, he used their perceptions to improve his own understanding of the world. "Looking back on it, the most important thing I learned at Notre Dame was how to get along with people in different social environments. Notre Dame is very international. I learned to talk to people from China and ask, 'Why is or isn't this acceptable in your culture? How would this be looked upon?'"

Even his two American roommates had cultural differences with one another: one was a deeply religious young man from Washington state who looked down on anyone who didn't attend chapel services and the other was a non-religious hockey player from a suburb of Detroit. Gerome played the middleman, telling the more pious student that he needed to develop tolerance and understanding rather than try to impose guilt upon someone who did not share his religious beliefs. Gerome credits his exposure to a range of values during college with his ability to be resilient in social settings as an adult. "If you throw me in a jungle, I can interact. If you throw me in a ballroom, I can interact. It doesn't really matter to me where I am, people are going to be people no matter what."

Entering the NFL was another culture shock. "When you make that kind of money and have that kind of free time, you can get into a lot of different kinds of trouble. But it was a good time for me, because I had my head on my shoulders, so I never was in danger of going off the deep end the way some guys did. It was the first time they had the financial freedom to do what they wanted to do. If you give guys without a lot of financial education a bunch of money and they don't know what to do with it, it can cause a lot of trouble. The reality is, only 5% of the guys in the NFL make the kind of money where you never have to worry about working again. If you're in the other 95%, you have to save your money and know what you're going to do when your football career is over."

As for Gerome, after five years as a safety in the NFL—first for the Baltimore Ravens, then the Indianapolis Colts, then back to the Ravens—he became a free agent. Though he doesn't rule out a return to pro football, his priorities lie elsewhere right now—with his wife, Tracy, and son Aiden, and with the business that he co-founded with two Notre Dame teammates. "We realized that the way apparel is manufactured can have damaging ecological effects on our environment. So we researched sustainability and sustainable fabrics and fibers. We realized that we could create athletic apparel and fitness apparel out of plastic recycled bottles. We teamed up with companies that provide recycled yarns and now we are able to manufacture a full line of fitness apparel out of recycled bottles, which is converted into polyester."

It's an idea that Gerome speaks about with just as much passion as his earlier football career. "The cool thing about it is, there are so many environmental benefits in terms of the water consumption you save, the emissions that you save, even the energy savings. We save one half gallon of gasoline with a pound of yarn we use. Multiply that across our entire product line. That's a lot of pounds of yarn and a lot of gallons of gasoline saved. Everybody has a carbon footprint, but if we can limit our carbon footprint on the environment as much as possible, I think we've done our job. Not only are we making highly technical and durable performance and fitness clothing, but I think we're making a statement saying that the environment is important to us too and our society is important to us."

The company has a charitable arm as well, an initiative called Go the Greener Mile through which proceeds from apparel sales will be used to assist charities and urban groups involved in athletic endeavors.

It is important to Gerome that young followers understand how many different facets make up one man's personality. "I always tell kids not to just look at me as an NFL guy," he said. "To understand who I am, you have to see everything leading up to this point and everything I've gone through. That's the most important thing, to have a perspective when you're looking at something."

And his own perspective right now is one of patience. Things move quickly in the world of professional sports, Gerome said, but as a father, he is learning to take his time with his young son, and as a company president and CEO, he is discovering that launching a company can take time as well. "A play in the NFL that lasts 10 seconds is a long play. The off season goes by fast. You live fast. In professional sports, slowing down is a detriment, because when you slow down, somebody else around you is speeding up to take your job. But right now, things have slowed down a lot for me. I'm just trying now to take things slower, enjoy all that God has given me, and think about how blessed I am."

Demonstrating self-reliance, ethics, faith and loyalty from childhood right to his present-day role as a father, husband and company president, Gerome Sapp is someone who lives by his principles and in doing so fits the definition of an Insightful Player™ team member.

INSTANT REPLAY OF GEROME'S *GUIDING PRINCIPLES*

1. Nourish family relationships with love, care and loyalty.

2. Develop a relationship with God based on the understanding that God is always there to sustain you.

3. Use other people's differences as a learning opportunity. Find out why they see things the way they do.

4. Don't take ignorant comments or reactions to heart. Be able to let judgments slide off of you.

5. Don't judge others, and don't judge yourself too harshly either.

6. Find friends who are good role models and who exhibit values you want to emulate.

7. Stay on the straight-and-narrow, avoiding drugs, alcohol and misbehavior.

8. Study hard and persist academically so that you have the greatest range of options in life.

9. When times are tough, remember that "this too shall pass" and easier days likely lie ahead.

10. Know your own beliefs and values. Don't just accept what you are told or taught; think critically about why you believe what you do.

11. Appreciate the many gifts you have been given.

CHAPTER 26

NEW ENGLAND PATRIOTS HALL OF FAMER

ANDRE TIPPETT

#56

A Giant of a Man In Football, Karate, and Everyday Integrity

As a New England Patriots Hall of Famer, **Andre Tippett** has worked with some of the best coaches and players in the NFL. So you might guess that football and the professionals associated with it are what formed his work ethic and life view. But according to Andre, other people and even another sport were just as formative. For his work ethic, he credits his grandmother. For his commitment to doing what's right, his mother. And for his belief in the interconnectedness of physical ability and mental balance, he credits the martial arts he has studied since he was 11 years old.

"In the martial arts, you take a holistic approach," Andre said. "Karate instructors always talk about mind, body and spirit, and how you can't have one without the other."

Martial arts also taught him to never sit on his laurels. And as an AFC Linebacker of the Year, player in five Pro Bowls and franchise record-holder for sacks, he has many he could sit on if he chose to do so. But that's not his philosophy. Practicing martial arts, "you just continue to push yourself. You don't concern yourself with thoughts like 'When am I going to get my next promotion' or 'I hope I win my next karate tournament.' It's about getting on the floor, putting in the actual time and training; the blood and guts and the sweat and the tears, and doing it one more time."

Just as with the martial arts, he learned never to stop striving on the football field, even throughout the eleven seasons he played for the New England Patriots. "When I got to the pros I always took the attitude that every year we drafted a new linebacker, that kid was coming in to take my job, so I needed to work hard. I never let myself get caught up in a mindset of 'I'm too good to do that' or I' don't have to do these drills 'or 'I don't have to work that hard in training camp.'"

Born in Alabama, Andre spent his earliest years with his grandmother, who imparted a lifelong message about the importance of hard work. "My grandmother, my mother's mother, was a very strong woman who had an unbelievable work ethic. She worked all of her life, even past the time when she was supposed to be retired. She was the matriarch of our family and even after I got to college, she would still call me to advise me and talk to me about things. She was a very good example."

Nonetheless, when Andre was seven, his mother opted to leave the south, believing a better racial climate existed elsewhere. They ended up in Newark, New Jersey, where life was "difficult and different" for Andre. "My mom was trying to work and trying to provide for her two children without having a whole lot. This was during the mid to late sixties, the time of the racial riots. A lot of things were going on." With no father in the picture, Andre's family struggled with a combination of poverty and a tough environment in which children had to watch their backs. But it made the young Andre stronger. "The three of us had to stick together. We had each other and we dealt with things. I was poor but I really didn't know what poor was. I just knew that when I wanted something, my mom said, 'No, you can't have that.' So, I learned to deal with that. It was just plain and simple that early on we didn't have a lot of food in the house. We barely had the ability to have breakfast and dinner. But my mother would always figure out a way to put some food on the table."

It wasn't only the poverty. Although neighbors kept an eye on each other, it wasn't exactly the proverbial village, Andre said; street life could be hard on a child. "I was the oldest in the family and big for my age. When I had trouble with other kids, I didn't have a big brother or anybody to go to and say, 'Look, I need help. These kids are giving me a hard time.' I had to figure out what to do on my own. You can't keep running; at some point you're going to have to learn how to step up and defend yourself."

The necessity of self-defense skills led him to the martial arts—but what he learned in the karate Dojo turned out to be more far-reaching than just how to avert a street fight. "With karate, I found myself in an arena with guys who were trying to share their knowledge and discipline and training with me, a young person who showed some potential to be a good karate student. Just as important was the fact that I was a part of something; I was in a structured environment away from other temptations."

Even as a child, he understood the value of hard work and self-discipline. "My sister and I had our chores that we had to do. I would get sent to the corner laundromat to do the laundry when I was just nine or ten years old. You learn to grow up fast in that environment. I've always been mature for my age, even as a youngster. My mom was a disciplinarian, she was a caretaker, she was the person that we feared the most from a disappointment standpoint, and so we tried not to do anything to disappoint our mother and do the right thing."

And as he grew, Andre came to believe that his mother's words held the key to distinguishing right from wrong—a belief that compels him now to urge young people time and time again to listen to their parents and other elders. "I'd say at least half of the time, when young people who get in trouble, it's because of the environment that they're brought up in, specifically whether there is accountability and love. If the love is there, if there are constant conversations about what the expectations are for a child, then when your buddies tell you, 'Hey, let's go do something that we shouldn't be doing,' there's always that voice on your other shoulder saying, 'What would your mother say? Do you understand the price you'll have to pay if you get in trouble?' And for me, even in high school as I became a young man, there was always that question: What would my mom say?"

Even as his values were taking shape through the influence of his Sensei (karate teacher), his mother, and life experience, challenges cropped up. As a freshman in high school, he submitted to his friends' urging to try out for football with them. Knowing little about the game, he didn't make the cut—but his friends did. Rather than turn him off to the sport, the brush with rejection strengthened his resolve to improve at it. "I watched every JV and varsity game and I started working hard to make sure I'd be on the team the next year," he said. Andre joined the wrestling team to build his strength and practiced football skills on his own. "After a while, I found myself thinking, 'You know, this is a pretty good feeling. I can see myself making my way here.' "

He learned something else from the experience. The same friends who made the cut when he *didn't* make it had quit the team within weeks, lacking the commitment to see it through. "These guys who were probably better athletes than I was at the time—stronger, faster—had the opportunity, and then they quit. They threw the opportunity away. I kept thinking, That could have been me on the team. I was determined that I was going to make that team the next year." As a sophomore, Andre made the JV squad and was then sent up to the varsity team before the season ended. His team won the state championship.

Along with developing the football skills that would lead him to a career in the NFL, Andre met one of the great influences of his life at this time: his high school coach, Frank Verducci. "Coach Verducci became an inspiration and a disciplinarian for me, a father figure in my life who was constantly on all of us to lead by example and do the right thing. To this day, whenever I need to talk to somebody, I can call him and tell him just about anything."

Through Coach Verducci's example, Andre became aware of what it meant to be a role model. He knew about his own role models—not only his mother and grandmother but his karate teacher and championship athletes like former Chicago Bears tight end Greg Latta, who grew up in the same area and had overcome similar challenges. At the All-State Championship banquet celebrating his high school team's triumph sophomore year, Andre heard Latta speak about his career. "The way he talked about his mom and dad showed so much respect. The fact that he was playing in the NFL and he had come from where I'd come from gave me the idea that I could do the same things; someday have the opportunity to stand up and thank my mom for the fact that I'm now playing in the NFL." And Andre still thinks about his responsibility as a role model when he speaks to audiences now. "I always assume that if there are 100 people in the room, if I can reach one person, then I've done my job. So, whenever I share my experiences, that's the outcome that I always wish for."

But as his own prestige as a football player grew, he was ever mindful of the watchful eyes of younger family members—by this time, his mother had remarried and he had stepbrothers—as well as kids in the community. "Being the oldest in the family, I wanted to make sure that the younger kids would never have an excuse to say, 'Well, Andre didn't do this, so I don't have to do this.' I wanted them to say 'You know, Andre went to college and got his degree so now I have to go to college and I have to follow my big brother.' So, I basically tried to lead by example."

He grew up to marry the love of his life, Rhonda, and the couple had four children. Spiritual faith has always played a significant role in his attitude toward family. Though his religious affiliation has changed over the years—he was raised Methodist, then converted to Judaism as he and his wife made plans to marry—his belief in a higher power has not. "It goes back to my grandmother. When I was in high school and college, whenever I went to go visit my grandmother down south, the last thing that she would say as we talked about travel plans was 'Make sure you bring a suit with you because you're going to church with me on Sunday.' It wasn't *maybe* you should bring a suit. My grandmother was a very religious woman. She spent a lot of time in church during the week, on the weekends, volunteering. So I guess the faith has always been there for me, always there in the back of my mind."

Ultimately, there is perhaps no tenet that Andre holds higher than the necessity of seeking out role models and advisors—and then adhering to their advice. "As a kid, I could have taken the right turn versus the left turn just as easy as the next kid. But because of the people that were constantly giving me good advice, I made the right decisions."

He knows that it's a two-way street; the same people who counsel him seek his advice. "I've been with my Sensei (karate instructor) Steve Banchick, since 1982. He's been like a brother to me and he and I constantly talk and confide, sharing advice and leadership. He listens to me and I listen to him. The roles are constantly intertwined."

For a child raised in poverty who becomes a high-earning professional athlete, questions always loom about how to provide generously for his own family—he has three daughters and a son—while ensuring that the lessons of his hardscrabble childhood are not lost. "I joke with my kids that I didn't have a winter coat. I didn't have snow boots. If I walked home, my feet were soaking wet. But it didn't deter me or weaken me......it made me stronger. My kids have more things than I ever dreamed of when I was a kid growing up. Sometimes when they ask for things I say no, sometimes I say yes, sometimes I surprise them and I go get something they've asked for."

Those who know him comment on his amazing ability to be present and to embody values and integrity in the way he lives his life every day. People who come into contact with him are struck by how carefully he listens and how easily he earns their trust. His sincerity is striking. A giant of a man physically, he also awes people with the magnitude of his kindness and sincerity, and with his enormous devotion to family and faith.

As he turns 50, he continues his work in the NFL as Executive Director of Community Affairs for the New England Patriots. Andre recognizes the many forces that have contributed to his success, and he's a strong proponent of staying humble, even at the superstar level he has attained. "It's important for all of us not to take ourselves too seriously. Humility makes you step back and not mind saying 'Hey, I was wrong, you were right.' I still get bashful when people recognize me and they come up and they say all these nice things. I understand that there are people out there that have been affected by some of the things that I have done as an athlete, but I also understand that I'm just an athlete. There are people out there who are saving lives, curing cancer, so many things out there that are much bigger than who I am, who most celebrities and professional athletes are. So, I have to have the humility to understand that I didn't get here alone. I had people who were watching my back and helping me along the way."

And his work as a role model has not ended. Along with being an important part of the Insightful Player™ campaign, he is featured in the Good Men Project, an endeavor that recruits male role models to tell their stories in an effort to build and sustain national discussion about being a good father, son, husband, partner and worker in America today. For this project, Andre wrote an essay focusing on how martial arts have influenced him as an athlete and as a man.

The project is produced by the Good Men Foundation, a nonprofit dedicated to helping organizations that provide educational, social, financial or legal support to men and boys at risk.

Tom Matlack, co-founder of the Good Men Project, explained the importance of Andre's participation in the endeavor, by saying, "I have enormous respect for Andre. He is a consummate good man. He is a great husband, father, son, worker and friend. He starts each day fresh, with a beginner's mindset. This approach gives him an amazing ability to push harder, reach further and give more each day. He's tenacious, gentle, humble and incredible. I am fascinated with how he used the martial arts to help him overcome challenges in his youth. His commitment to the martial arts goes hand and hand with his inspiring path of greatness."

INSTANT REPLAY OF ANDRE'S *GUIDING PRINCIPLES*

1. Children raised with discipline, love and expectations from their parents will develop a strong ethical compass and always have principles to follow.

2. The mind, body and spirit must be developed in harmony with each other for a well-balanced perspective.

3. Never rest on your laurels. No matter what level of success you have attained, you are obligated to keep working and keep striving.

4. Recognize your responsibility as a role model. Whether there are younger siblings, community members or fans watching you, be aware of how your choices and behavior affect their decisions as well as your own.

5. Don't quit or squander opportunities. If you encounter rejection or failure, double your resolve to make the cut next time around.

6. Seek out mentors, ask their advice and follow it. Surround yourself with people who have your best interests at heart and listen to what they tell you.

7. Believe in God and acknowledge the positive influences of a higher power.

8. Retain a sense of humility. Remember that there are always people doing more important or worthy things than what you are doing.

9. Allow yourself to have dreams and to do all you can to follow them.

CHAPTER 27

NFL FREE AGENT

BEN UTECHT

Grit and Grace Create Harmony
On and Off the Field

Graced with what outwardly might seem to be conflicting gifts—movie star looks, NFL-caliber athletic talent, rock-solid faith, a soaring tenor and a tender heart—**Ben Utecht** has managed to create harmony among his many facets. His journey in becoming a renaissance man has been a lesson in self-discovery and acceptance.

Ben grew up in Hastings, Minnesota, in a loving family, surrounded by music. His dad, a Methodist minister, had been a vocal music major, and his mother was also a singer. Ben always valued the deep love his parents shared and knew that was exactly what he wanted for himself. "I grew up in a wonderful family," Ben said. "I saw success in marriage and in relationships, a strong work ethic and loving people. That's why I was drawn to my belief system, because I really saw it lived out correctly. I looked at it and said,' Now that's something that I would really like to have.'"

Ben readily admits that he was far from perfect. One of the things he got caught up in, along with so many kids, was the popularity game. For a while, he bought into the idea that he was better than others because of superficial things. "When I think back to high school, I remember things that kind of make my stomach ache a little bit," he sheepishly admitted. "There are definitely some mistakes from that time that I wish I could change. I remember many times feeling conflicted about things that I would say or do because it really wasn't me, but I was doing them purely because of the influence of the people that I was around, wanting to look a certain way. I remember things I said about people, or how I treated people that were not a part of the 'in crowd.' There were times when I put myself on a higher pedestal than other people. That created a selfishness and pride in my heart that began to change how I viewed myself."

Ben has an interesting perspective on those early years. He's glad he had some character problems at that time in his life. It was because of those that he was confronted and realized that there were things he needed to change about himself.

"I was fortunate to have people in my life that told me the truth. I had a couple of accountability friends—they were able to confront me on things about myself when they saw that my behavior was not consistent with who I was and what I believed in."

Ben specifically remembers a high school friend telling him that he had some issues with pride, and that he needed to get a grip on that because 'arrogance is not a quality that represents what you stand for.' "She really had a point," he mused. "It wasn't easy to hear. I remember getting very upset about it, but it's one of those things where, once it's settled, it was a revelation. I know my true friends are the ones who tell me when there are things I need to work on. It's great to be around those kinds of people."

These early experiences taught Ben a priceless life lesson. Change, especially within the heart, doesn't often occur overnight. For him, it was a process of having to be confronted a number of times. And, there were definitely moments when he became angry, argumentative and very defensive.

"I remember calling my dad one time and he said, 'Ben, have you ever asked yourself why you get so defensive?' And I said, 'No.' And he said, 'Well, you would think that if pride really wasn't an issue, then your response would be one of peace, but obviously there's something within you that is trying to defend.'"

Ben learned that the fact he was so defensive showed that he actually did have some problems with this issue. Striving towards humbleness and humility, he believes, comes with a number of different breakdowns that have to happen to us.

Towards the end of his high school career, Ben started to mature. He remembers going to a couple of church retreats that really brought him to a new understanding. That's when the message of faith and love started to penetrate. He started to change. "My attitude when I left high school was that I wanted to be someone that stood against the flow. I wanted to be somebody that didn't have to do things to please a crowd. The only thing that I was going to strive to do was to love people and to love God. And that in itself just changed my perspective about popularity and all those things that we deal with at that time."

Ben's faith would be put to the test when his plans for playing football in college and going on to a pro career did not work out. He went from being a potential first- or second-round draft pick as one of the top tight ends in the country to not even being drafted at all. He spent half of his college career with two different injuries that ended up taking him completely out of the NFL draft.

It's not often that players going undrafted have a successful career. What happened for Ben is what he calls "one of my miracle stories."

"I went to the University of Minnesota, which is where Tony Dungy, coach of the Indianapolis Colts, went to school as well. Two months prior to the draft, we both attended the same conference and, when I got up in front of everyone to speak, I razzed him a little bit being an alumni. I told him, 'Coach, alumni have to stick together, so please feel free to draft me.' When it was his turn to speak, he kind of did the same thing, but he made a promise that if for some reason I slipped through the cracks, that he would be the first person to call.

"I didn't get drafted because of my injury. I went through a tremendous trial at that point in my life, a gamut of emotions, tremendous fire, not knowing at all what's going to happen with me, being fearful, being very afraid, very embarrassed about not being drafted."

When Ben wound up a free agent, the first person to call, as promised, was Tony Dungy. "He said, 'We know the talent that you have. We're going to get you surgery. We're going to give you a year to heal, and we're going to pay you for it and we're going to give you a chance to play.' Three years later, I'm one of the starting tight ends on the Super Bowl championship team, led by one of the most respected coaches in the league."

Without those injuries, without going through those trials, Ben would never have been on the Indianapolis Colts and never would have won a Super Bowl. If anything gave him hope in those times, it was that experience.

Ben's faith, strong character, and balanced view of life are helping him navigate this most challenging time in his professional football career. He was recently released from the Bengals due to injury and is now a free agent.

Ben's approach to life is to grow in a multi-dimensional way—personally, professionally, spiritually, musically—while staying true to his values. He certainly has not put his eggs in one basket! Thankfully, he had the wisdom to listen very well when his college coaches told him that the average career of an NFL player was only 2 ½ years, and that it wasn't something on which he could base his entire life. He has been preparing himself for life after football, whenever that day comes.

Ben put that wisdom into practice when he began recording his debut inspirational music CD. It was released in April 2009. "It was a lot of fun to do. I've been group singing, and, as I've said, my family is musical—I grew up surrounded by music. It's always been something that I've wanted to do, like being a professional athlete, but the thought of actually singing professionally and pursuing more of the entertainment side of things was always a little out there for me." Being a part of the NFL has opened some new doors and allowed Ben to meet the right people. Ben's music reflects his personal mission of "striving to bring the attitude of love to the world."

"One of my favorite songs on my album is called 'Generation.' The song says that we need to be a generation that is going to bring the message of love and a new light into the world. I know that it's something that's been said before, but I just think that if our focus was on love, and how we can better serve people, it would change so much of how we approach everything—from politics to religion. It's something that gets swept under the carpet, and I think that we need to try and revisit it."

What does an attitude of love look like to Ben Utecht? "There's is a well known and used passage shared at many weddings," he said. "I can't quote it perfectly, but it talks about a definition of love: it's not boastful; it's not proud. It rejoices in the truth. It has no stereotypes. I think it's a passage that everybody agrees with. It really paints a great picture—no matter what your faith or your background—of what kind of an attitude we should be having in regards to love."

Once of Ben's most striking characteristics is quite the opposite of the stereotypical macho football player. When he gives speeches or performs, he always tells people that one of his main goals is to be vulnerable—in his music and in his words. "I'm not going to hide my mistakes," he said firmly. "If anything, I want people to hear them. I want people to know my weaknesses, so that maybe those who have dealt with the same things that I have can learn something."

Ben has an inspiring attitude about his missteps and challenges. He likens them to a trial by fire. "What's one of the greatest qualities of fire? The thing that comes to mind for me is refinement. Some of our most precious metals are forged in the greatest heat. When you can grasp and believe in that, it gives you a lot of peace whenever you're going through the flames. You know that out of it you're going to become a more refined and strong individual. That's how I tend to approach these things—that great growth can come from the greatest adversity."

Ben has experienced this so often in his life that, whenever he's faced with tough times, he doesn't retreat anymore. In fact, he almost looks forward to seeing what's ahead because he knows that there are going to be some great changes and growth as a result.

When asked what advice he has for kids, Ben grew thoughtful. He reflected on his upbringing with gratitude, and acknowledged that he was pretty lucky. "I can't really put myself in the shoes of someone who grew up in difficult environment. I do know that so much of a person changing begins with their heart. You have to have a change within the heart in order to truly become something different."

Ben believes that people really do understand right versus wrong and good versus evil; that, no matter where someone grows up, they understand that stealing or getting involved in similar activities is breaking the law and not something that we should do.

"I would say, go to the root of it. Find out what you believe, what is right and wrong. Trust in your instincts in your heart. I think, more often than not, people will make the right choice. I'd encourage them to see that it's like a snowball effect. When you continue to make good choices and good decisions, and start seeing the positive effect it has on your life and the people around you, then it becomes easier to keep on doing that."

Ben is facing his future with confidence. "When the foundation is strong, then all of the buildings that are built on that foundation don't crumble. That's been an important factor in all of this. I've got such a strong support system—my family, my wife, other interests outside of football—that life doesn't seem so scary and uncertain. I've been able to step back and say, 'I know things are going to be okay', and that's been a huge help during this process."

Ben looks at football as a job. He believes we've all been given talents in different areas, and that his abilities are in athletics and music. Therefore, he wants to take those talents and do the best he can to refine and accomplish his best with them. At the same time, he's also very clear about the fact that there are a lot more important things in his life, such as family, that make him who he is.

From the outside, it looks as if Ben Utecht has everything, and could easily rest on his laurels. He grew up in a strong and loving family. He's married to the love of his life, Karyn, who happens to be a former Miss Minnesota. They have three daughters: Elleora Grace, and identical twins Katriel and Amy. He's handsome, kindhearted, charismatic, multi talented and a strong leader. He's achieved success and national recognition in one field and is poised to conquer another.

Ben takes none of this for granted. He believes that his work has just begun. "Because of my foundation and platform, I realize that I'm called to do great things. My focus will be to build up and serve others and to achieve my goals, so that I will leave this earth fulfilled, feeling as though I accomplished my purpose."

"The ultimate fulfillment for me, first and foremost, is that I'll never be afraid to stand up for what I believe in. Also, to strive to be the best husband and father that I can possibly be; and lastly, that I will be able to have a positive impact by spreading the message of love to the world through my platforms of athletics and music.

"I understand that God has given me talents and abilities to do something with them. I believe my job as an athlete and, hopefully, my job in the future as a musician, is so much more than just giving a performance. It's a platform to create change that affects everybody positively. So my promise is that, no matter if it's football, no matter if it's music, I'm going to do whatever I can to help bring a new message, to bring a new light to inspire a new generation to change the world in a positive way."

With his many gifts, his grit and grace in the midst of the fire, his passion for gaining wisdom no matter what life brings him, his solid faith and the balance he strives to achieve in all of his endeavors, Ben Utecht indeed deserves the title of an Insightful Player™ team member.

INSTANT REPLAY OF BEN'S *GUIDING PRINCIPLES*

1. Surround yourself with people who care about your well-being and your character, and who will be honest with you. Even if you don't like it what they have to say, pay attention anyway. You will grow into a better person.

2. Be willing to accept that having a change of heart is a process. It doesn't happen overnight. If you truly want to grow and be a better person, be prepared to be confronted on the same issues a number of times. Notice when you're stubborn or defensive—that's where you need to do the work.

3. Develop faith in God. Faith is the key to getting through tough times. It carries you through and gives you hope that things will always work out for the best.

4. Trust your instincts and your heart, and stick to what you believe in.

5. Know what you stand for, and act on it. When you continue making good choices and good decisions, and start seeing the positive effect it has on your life and the people around you, it becomes easier to keep on doing that.

6. Adjust your attitude about tough times—they teach us important lessons. Look beyond them. Some of our most precious metals are forged by the greatest heat. Great growth can come from the greatest adversity.

7. Ask yourself how you can fulfill others' lives as well as your own.

CHAPTER 28

NFL FORMER PLAYER

DAMIAN VAUGHN

Catapults Growth of Young, Collegiate and Pro Athletes by Revolutionizing the Role of Parents and Coaches

Being a professional football player is a powerful role, said former NFL tight end **Damian Vaughn.** But he also emphasizes that it's just that—a role. It's what you do, not who you are, not the sum of your spirit or even your personality. In order for professional athletes to reach their ultimate potential, in Damian's view, they need to look beyond their capabilities as professional athletes and tap into a deeper well of potential.

"In their mid-20's or 30's, when an athlete might be peaking in their career, there's a misconception that this is as good as it gets," Damian said. "Athletes come to think that nothing they will ever do in the future will have as much impact as what they are doing by having a pro career." As a result, they avoid thinking about the future—which Damian sees as a significant waste of potential. Too often, he said, athletes retire from pro sports and spiral into a downturn. "So the very people that youth are looking up to are winding up in serious depression, divorce or bankruptcy."

Damian has spent his life thus far contemplating the meaning of success and how it can be used toward a greater purpose. He was conscious of those questions as a child and has made a career out of them as an adult. And one reason he was able to transition so seamlessly from being a pro football player to helping others realize their personal potential was that he sees sports as a metaphor for life and a positive way to unite society. He uses the New Orleans Saints, winners of the 2010 Super Bowl, as an example. "A high school team plays the very same role within their smaller community that an NFL team plays in a city or in a country. Any small farm town high school team has the same potential within their community that the New Orleans Saints has in this entire country. Sports function as the glue in so many towns and cities of every level that it's played at, whether it's high school, college or Olympic or pro."

The key to greater self-actualization, he said, is for athletes to better understand themselves and connect with a higher purpose in their lives. He believes this is a way of thinking that athletes would do well to start developing while still in childhood. But unfortunately, he often sees just the opposite occurring. "It is something of a paradox that as athletes start getting more serious about their athletic careers, they're putting all their eggs in one basket. In one regard, that's great, because obviously the more attention and energy you put into it, the more effective you'll be. But what happens to a young athlete is that they start to overly self-identify with a particular athletic role so that they are actually not able to perform at their best."

In Damian's own case, the drive to be the best player he could be had both a down side and an upside. To his enormous credit, he demonstrated superlative effort and stamina as a young athlete working his way to the top. On the other hand, he believes it was this determined bent toward overachieving that caused him to ignore the physical symptoms that led to what would ultimately be career-ending injuries. Today, one reason he has devoted his post-sports career to helping athletes recognize their potential is with the hope of helping others avoid the pitfalls into which he stumbled.

As Damian sees it, parents and coaches need to understand that it is incumbent upon them to help children strike a balance between working hard to develop athletic abilities while also keeping sight of the other areas of potential in their futures. "Across the board, we all need to become more mindful and more aware. If parents can cultivate more consciousness, then they'll be better mentors or guides for their own children in this path that we hope that the kids will take."

Damian recalled an incident that took place when he stayed with friends in Florida not long ago. While sleeping in the room of his hosts' teenage son, he spotted a poster on the boy's wall that posed the question, "Why do I play football?" Also on the poster was the boy's answer: something along the lines of "So that I can get more girls and be popular and people will respect me." Though Damian admits he felt the same way as a fourteen-year-old high school player, he found it alarming to see the sentiment so baldly expressed.

Damian poses this as a question of intrinsic versus extrinsic motivation. Wanting to impress girls or be popular is an extrinsic motivation—as is having a goal to be an All Conference player, go to the championship game, or be a leader in your position among your peers and your league. By contrast, he said, "when you're intrinsically motivated, your focus becomes much more about presence and awareness, being fully present in everything that you're doing."

The value of developing these intrinsic goals, he said, goes beyond becoming a better player. "What I teach most athletes is that you can cultivate a lifestyle that allows for you to be in a 'higher zone' or zone of greater mental flow more often. Regardless of what you're doing, it's setting the tone for success in every other aspect of your life as well. This very practice allows you to be more tuned in your relationships at home, with your teammates, with colleagues, with people in the media, and so forth." The practice also has benefits as athletes reach the end of their careers. "When the time comes for you to transition into the rest of your life, you're able to approach it with a more creative response and a more intuitive response, rather than one that's more fear-based."

A parent of a young son and daughter himself, Damian believes many parents make the mistake of micromanaging their young athletes' games. "When you see parents getting overly aggressive with their kids' coaches, they're not allowing their kids to really shine and develop for themselves," he said. Moreover, kids sometimes start playing for the wrong reasons: to appease their parents. "It's amazing, but even when I'm talking to pro athletes in their twenties and ask them why they play, they'll say their motivation is to impress the coach or to impress their parents or impress a father who is not there or prove someone else wrong. In doing that, they've placed their own sense of identity in someone else's hands." Again, it's an extrinsic rather than intrinsic motivation.

"The best thing a parent can do is create an environment in which their kids are able to fully express themselves as athletes, but first are able to actually understand why they're playing. As a parent, you might put kids in sports hoping someone else will discipline your child or teach them fundamentals and life skills of how to become successful and how to deal with failure and adversity. That's definitely an advantage of team sports, but I think that too often parents fail to facilitate that growth. More often than not, they impede it."

On the other hand, parents who are able to look for teaching moments in children's sports can do a great deal of good. Resilience is one of the key lessons adults can model to children, Damian said. In one typical scenario, a parent whose child is not getting as much playing time as the child would like has to decide whether the appropriate response is to confront (or criticize) the coach or to help the child accept the reality of not getting to play a lot.

"If the kid is not getting the time that he wants, he sometimes starts an internal conversation: 'My coach doesn't like me' or 'I'm not good enough' or some kind of self-loathing story. As a parent, you can teach your kids to have the resilience to keep giving their full effort and just stay true to their passion regardless of what the results appear to be. It's so critical at every single moment to recognize that you're either contributing to positive growth or moving in the opposite direction, regardless of what level you're playing at. When some kind of adverse situation arises, you have that choice based on your internal dialogue or your internal conversation."

A favorite quote of Damian's comes from Coach Vince Lombardi, who famously said that the Green Bay Packers never lost a football game; "They just ran out of time." "That is such a great thing to remember because we put time constraints on sports events, and we tally up the score, simply because there has to be some ending within a specified amount of time. Coach Lombardi is saying that it's not about winning or losing, it's just that in this particular game, we ran out of time. We didn't have the momentum that we needed and the amount of time that we needed to come out of this with more points than the other team."

This kind of attitude goes farther than a simplistic, "It doesn't matter whether you win or lose" response, Damian said. "It creates a conversation that is more about taking responsibility for what's going on and for your actions as opposed to blaming and pointing fingers."

Looking back at his own childhood and career, Damian said his experiences gave him a solid foundation on which to contemplate parents' and coaches' roles in young athletes' lives. "For so many athletes who make it to the NFL, it's as if genetically, they were born to do it," he reflected. "I was not like that. My talents were in music, writing and composing, but then I just became enamored with the sport of football. I appreciated to the opportunity it provided for immediate feedback. You could go into a practice or a game saying, 'I'm going to give them my all and see if this works or doesn't work.' Within the space of two hours, you can tell what kind of results you're going to get and you can make adjustments right there, right then and there."

He played high school football in his home town of Orrville, Ohio, then went to Miami University in Ohio as a walk-on after turning down smaller schools that offered him football scholarships. "The fact is, I wanted to play Division 1A football because I felt like I could do it. So my dad said, 'I'll pay for this one year, and if you don't get a scholarship then you're on your own.'"

Through ceaseless effort and tenacity, Damian won that sophomore year football scholarship. "Even then it wasn't like I was the most naturally gifted athlete on our team," he said. "I just worked so hard for it. And I succeeded to a point, but my motivations became increasingly more extrinsic in nature. All I wanted to do was prove to myself that

I could play at that level. And so I worked and I worked and I worked and I showed up in such great condition and with such strong energy that I brought to it, that they recognized that right away and gave me a scholarship. But then my motivations became focused on being better than this guy and that guy, and I was always comparing. I got in my own way through my whole college career. It wasn't until my senior year that I kind of remembered what it was like to go step by step, just be present and let go of my goals. And I did that, and became the first person from Miami University to be drafted by the NFL in ten years. So, that story alone was a huge learning experience for me, to just reconfirm what works and what doesn't."

Damian went on to play two seasons as a tight end for the Cincinnati Bengals and one for the Tampa Bay Buccaneers, then spend another two seasons with the Barcelona Dragons in NFL Europe. Although his stats were good with the Dragons, injuries plagued him, cutting his pro years short.

But he has always believed that the most important learning opportunities lie within moments of adversity, and having injuries end his career were the kind of adversity that he looks to for a greater message. "We can all develop an amazingly powerful relationship with adversity," he said. "The fascinating thing is to figure out what lesson it brings us."

In Damian's case, the lessons he learned from both his triumphs and his adversities would serve as a launching point for his subsequent careers: first as an entrepreneur who founded two companies—a countertop manufacturing company and an importer, wholesaler, and distributor of rare and exotic stones—and later as a personal coach for athletes and coaches.

After studying meditation practices with Deepak Chopra and other New Age leaders, Damian founded The Vaughn Center in Phoenix, Arizona, which helps athletes focus on their minds and bodies through meditation, with the goal of helping them find their ultimate athletic and personal potential while also transitioning from athletic careers to new endeavors. It is in that role that he hopes to effect genuine change in the world of sports. "In programs such as this, athletes start to recognize that they can leverage the platform they have through sports for something beyond their own personal gain; that is, the accolades and financial benefit. What you miss when you're not playing anymore is the feeling of being the hero, the feeling of being the warrior that is able to overcome obstacles and then be a leader for that kind of strength and courage. But once they realize they can leverage that same kind of leadership for a higher purpose, their careers after sports can be truly amazing." The reality is that there's no reason why a star should just fizzle away when his sports career is over, Damian said. "Instead, the transition should be a stepping stone to ever greater achievement and impact."

With unremitting focus on how athletes can extend their fame on the field to help make the world a better place, Damian Vaughn embodies the far-reaching goals of the Insightful Player™ campaign.

INSTANT REPLAY OF DAMIAN'S *GUIDING PRINCIPLES*

for Parents and Coaches

1. Educate your kids about the importance of being a role model and reinforce their learning process. Commit to being a shining example in what you do and in how you approach life.

2. Use concrete questions to help kids think introspectively about their greater purpose beyond playing a sport well or winning a game.

3. As a parent or a coach, help your young athlete strive for balance in his or her life.

4. Help young athletes to cultivate their intrinsic motivation—making success its own reward rather than a means to impress others.

5. Demonstrate to young people the importance of being present in what you do by articulating the ways in which you focus on your current goals rather than being too attached to past accomplishments or too concerned about future possibilities.

6. As a parent or coach, use losing as a learning opportunity rather than a reason for blame.

7. Encourage kids to stay true to their passions, regardless of external measures of success.

8. Facilitate discussions with kids about how they can leverage their innate gifts: not just talents in sports or other pursuits but gifts such as leadership and empathy.

CHAPTER 29

THE CLEVELAND BROWNS'

BENJAMIN WATSON

Recovering Perfectionist Embraces Scripture and Receives a Gift of True Grace

ot every man can trace his spiritual awakening back to a moment with a giant teddy bear, but **Benjamin Watson** is unusual that way. He still remembers the moment when he was six years old and experienced firsthand a lesson from the Bible that has provided him with sustenance ever since.

"When I was a little kid, my family had this big teddy bear, about my size. I used to look at the teddy bear eye to eye. Every other night or so, my dad would ask me if I wanted to fight the teddy bear. And I'd say yes, so he'd get behind the teddy bear and make the teddy bear box with me. He'd knock me down; then I'd get up swinging. Even then, I was so competitive and hated to lose. My dad tells me now that if I lost to the teddy bear, I'd go to bed screaming, "Daddy, you bring that teddy bear back out here! I'm not going to sleep until I beat the teddy bear!"

Finally, the six-year-old Benjamin triumphed over the teddy bear. But his father, a pastor as well as a former college football player who considered it his fundamental responsibility as a parent to teach his six children the word of God, used it as a teaching moment, not just horseplay. "After I beat the teddy bear, my dad asked me if I knew what would happen to me if I were to die that night. He wanted me to understand that we all have a soul and we are all going to spend eternity in heaven or hell; this is not the end when we leave this world. When I said I didn't really understand, he explained to me about the verse John 3:16. "For God so loved the world that he gave his only begotten son, that whoever believes in him should not perish, but have everlasting life." That was the moment that I first remember repenting for my sins and believing in what Christ did for me on the cross."

Benjamin now believes that was the beginning of his lifelong commitment to living a Christ-centered life. It was the first step on a journey toward the recognition that, in his words, "it's not about me. So much of the time we focus on ourselves and what makes us happy and what we can do for ourselves. We think about getting as much money as we can, being as successful as we can be, and being upset when somebody doesn't treat us right. With that way of thinking, it's always about us. That may be a natural way to think, but the message I started learning when I was still a child is that it's not about me, it's about what Christ has done for me and how people can see his love through my actions."

Raised in a stable and loving two-parent home, Benjamin saw his father as a giant. Both parents strove unflaggingly to pass messages of faith on to their six children. "I'm so thankful for the fact that my mother and my father were there for us kids," he said. "They taught us how to treat people. They taught us right from wrong. They taught us about the Lord. It's such a blessing."

But despite his many acknowledged blessings, Benjamin said one fatal flaw hung over his youth and persisted into his years as a pro football player: his own perfectionism. Even when he was a boy, his parents were trying to correct their son's sense that he had to do everything perfectly, every time, but it wasn't a lesson easily learned.

And injuries in his career didn't help. Benjamin now sees as a turning point his first season in the pros. Drafted by the New England Patriots as soon as he graduated from the University of Georgia, he initially thought he'd reached his life's goal. "I never felt certain that I was going to make it into the pros. Even at the draft, I wasn't sure I was going to get in until they called my name for the Patriots. Then when they called my name, I thought that was it. I thought I'd made it. I started out with the Patriots so excited to play, and then it was still my rookie year and I tore my ACL. With that particular injury, you're pretty much out for the whole year."

Looking back, Benjamin sees how his sense of letdown went beyond the mere disappointment of missing out on his rookie season, but at the time he lacked that perspective. "I was so disappointed. I felt useless, almost. People put a lot of expectations on you as an athlete and sometimes you definitely feel it. You want to do well for yourself, but also, you know that your family is proud of you and people back in your hometown are excited, and even the Patriots fans and the people who drafted you expect certain things from you, so I really felt like I let people down."

He missed a big year in Patriots history, too. "That was in 2004, and the team won the Super Bowl. I wasn't able to play because of the ACL injury, and I just felt miserable. I had this bad attitude the whole week. I didn't want to enjoy the experience of being at the Super Bowl because I wasn't participating."

In retrospect, Benjamin sees this as an example of a time when he was too inwardly focused to see the real message in what he was doing. "At the time, I had the attitude that it was all about me. I had this injury that kept me off the field, and my family had gone down to Jacksonville for the Super Bowl and I had the perception that I was embarrassing them. I felt like I was a failure because I couldn't play."

Eventually, he would come to see the problem with that kind of thinking: he was over-identifying with his job. "During the 2004 Super Bowl, I was so tied up in the belief that my importance was in football, I couldn't even enjoy my family being around. They were all happy and having fun, but I couldn't enjoy it, and I made it miserable for everybody else just because I had a bad attitude."

Even off the football field, perfectionism proved to be perhaps Benjamin's greatest flaw. As a young teen, he played tuba in the middle school band. "Even there, I was trying so hard not to mess up any notes because I don't want to embarrass anybody. The whole perfectionism is definitely a theme that goes throughout my life. It has always showed up as a kind of an unhealthy anxiety. It's normal when you perform, whether on the football field or with an instrument, to have a certain degree of nervousness and anxiety. But for me, it was more of a fear of failure. And then if I didn't play well, I would hide. Maybe not physically, but emotionally. I'd be short with everybody and not want to engage. Whereas now, if something doesn't go my way, I'm still upset about it but I'm able to say, you know what? That doesn't change my worth as a person because this didn't go well."

He now sees that 2004 season as the identifiable moment when he realized that his presence or absence in the Super Bowl did not define him as a person or even as a football player. It was a revelation that would be further underscored the following season, when he executed not one but two of the most astounding plays that Patriots fans had ever seen, both occurring during the 2005 season playoffs. First, during a game against Jacksonville, he broke three tackles and outran five defenders, taking the ball a total of 63 yards for a touchdown. He then amazed fans even further during the AFC Divisional Playoff game against Denver when he intercepted a pass from the quarterback in Denver's end zone and ran it down the full length of the sideline toward his team's end zone, tackled by the opposing player at the two-yard line.

Benjamin now looks back on that season as the time he finally started internalizing the message about separating his work from his worth. "It's when I began to understand that your value and your worth aren't tied up in what you do," he said. "Your value and your worth are tied up in who you are as a person and who God has made you, and your worth is the fact that Christ died for you."

For the ability to make this transition, Benjamin credits his parents, who he now knows had been trying to communicate this message to him since childhood. "Finally, I started actually listening to what my parents were telling me, things they'd been telling me for years, but in the past I didn't listen because I was too involved in myself. This was the point at which I really heard what they were telling me, heard them say that if I never played ball again, they would still love me as a son, they would still be proud of me, they wouldn't think any less of me because I couldn't play ball anymore."

But it wasn't only his parents he was listening to, Benjamin said; it was also Scripture. "I re-read the Bible and came across that verse in Chronicles, 3:23, that says 'Whatever you do, do it wholeheartedly unto the Lord and not to men.' It's basically saying that whatever we do, whatever our occupation is, we're doing this to the glory of God, and not to get accolades and not to get ourselves a pat on the back. Ultimately, that's what we're doing it for. I had always said I loved that verse and believed in it, but really deep down, I don't think that I was acting like I believed it. But at that time in my life, I was reading the Bible a lot and speaking to the Lord and praying and dealing with the hard times."

For Benjamin, the hard times were generally associated with injuries that affected his ability to play. "There were always times I thought I wasn't going to make the team," he said. "In the off-season, the Patriots brought in some other tight ends. I had a hamstring injury. There was a lot of speculation in the press, and people were asking me if I thought I was going to stay with the Patriots or whether I was preparing my family to move, and I learned to say, 'People can do only what God allows them to do I trust God and I trust whatever He's going to do. These people can't do anything to me that God doesn't allow them to do.'"

The self-acceptance he began to develop after the 2004 Super Bowl would take several more years to become ingrained in his personality and his way of thinking, according to Benjamin. Several years later, he finally found the avenue to talk over his perfectionist instincts with his father in greater depth than the two had ever talked about it before. "I'm still like a kid in the sense that I still look up to my dad and see him in some ways as infallible. And in the 2009 pre-season we had a conversation about me putting him on a pedestal, and he talked to me about how he makes mistakes just like everyone else. That allowed me to better understand grace, the awesome grace that God gave us through salvation."

Benjamin now sees the 2009 pre-season as a transformational point in his life, and not only for the change in his perspective on his father. That was when, for the first time in his career, he faced a huge struggle to hold on to his place with the Patriots. Speculation swirled in the media that he would be cut from the team. But Benjamin surprised many fans by countering not with fear and defensiveness but with pure faith. Rather than fighting tooth and nail to prove himself worthy of the team, as he explains it, he turned it over to God, trusting that God's will would result in the right outcome. As much as he wanted to stay with the team, he says he could hear his soul speaking to him and telling him to allow this divine presence to take control. Coping with that difficult issue made him fully acknowledge the reality that "football is what I do and not who I am," he said. "Up until then, I knew it in my head but not truly in my heart."

In the end, the Patriots kept him on for the 2009 season, and his enlightenment led to what he now sees as the most enjoyable season of his career so far. "We didn't win the Super Bowl. We didn't even *go* to the Super Bowl, but having finally recognized that I needed to stop worrying so much about stats and numbers and pleasing people, I felt so much more free. My wife Kirsten always says to me, 'Benjamin, it's not about you. There's a bigger picture here.' She's been saying that ever since I met her, but this was the year it all started to make sense to me. And I feel like that made me a better husband and, in general, a more enjoyable person to be around."

Today, he still struggles with his perfectionist tendencies, striving ever more to find the balance between staying motivated and becoming obsessed with his own success. "God doesn't require perfection from us. At the end of the day, I see so many guys who are struggling, feeling like life isn't making any sense to them, and they wonder, 'Is there more to life? Is the only reason that we're here to make a lot of money and have a nice house and have nice cars and all that stuff?' No, it's not. It is about recognizing that God created us and God wants to have a relationship with us."

This is something that Benjamin strives to communicate to young people who look up to him as an athlete. "Kids need to understand that it is okay to be different. Too many kids perceive success as getting money and women and cars, and making x amount of dollars. Kids need to know that they must not be scared to say, 'Is this really what it's all about, or should I maybe not be running with this crowd? Do I have to be part of the "in crowd" all the time? Do I have to be like everybody else to be accepted?' Everybody wants to be accepted, but don't be afraid to step out and say, you know, this isn't right. I want to do things the right way, search for truth. Just because you see it on TV, just because you read it in a magazine, just because your best friend is doing it this way or that way, doesn't mean that it's the right thing to do."

Benjamin left the New England Patriots in 2010 to begin a career with the Cleveland Browns. And now he is directing his energies in a new direction as well. He and his wife, Kirsten, recently founded a public charity called One More (www.watsononemore.org), which Benjamin said is "devoted to spreading the love and hope of Christ to One More soul by meeting real needs, promoting education and providing enrichment opportunities through charitable initiative and partnerships. The foundation recently awarded its first college scholarship, named in honor of their daughter Grace.

With his lifelong beliefs in the wisdom of his parents and the grace of God, as well as his commitment to selfless living and demonstrating to followers that faith is far more important than materialism, Benjamin Watson embodies the principles of an Insightful Player™ team member.

INSTANT REPLAY OF BENJAMIN'S *GUIDING PRINCIPLES*

1. Question what you see around you rather than blindly complying with what others do. Be courageous in your quest for knowledge and understanding.

2. Have faith in God, and use that faith not only to make your own choices but to better understand the actions of others. Believe that whatever happens is according to God's will.

3. Respect your parents and learn all you can from them.

4. Remember that the most important thing about you is your soul and spirit, not your job or your accomplishments.

5. Striving to be good at something is admirable, but obsessing over being perfect is a pitfall. Allow yourself to be imperfect.

6. Never let your fear of losing the game—whether in football or in life—keep you from enjoying what you are doing.

7. Remember that mistakes are something to learn from, not something to fear.

8. In times of adversity, hold on to your faith that there is a greater message and wisdom that the adversity will eventually reveal to you.

CHAPTER 30

NFL FORMER PLAYER

DANIEL WILCOX

Magnificent Role Model Inspires Kids to Give Life All They've Got

Daniel Wilcox could have been a statistic. He grew up without a father's guidance in a community filled with violence and drugs. Treated like a criminal by the police, even when he turned to them for help, "I never thought I would make it to see 21," Daniel said. "I thought a cop might kill me."

How this self-described 'ordinary, nothing super special' guy grew into an accomplished NFL athlete dedicated to motivating and inspiring kids is a remarkable story.

He'd be the first to tell you that it started with his mother, Carol Wilcox, a surgical technician at Grady Hospital in Atlanta for over 35 years. She raised Daniel and his sister in single family home in Atlanta, Georgia. "My mom was my difference maker," Daniel remembered. "She made sure I didn't have too much idle time to get into trouble." Carol Wilcox understood that all kids want to feel like they are a part of something. She also wanted her son to be safe. She helped Daniel find games he liked, where he felt like he fit in. This instantly gave him a group of like-minded friends. "My games were football, baseball, basketball and track. Mom taught me how to throw a football and baseball, and she was a little league baseball coach."

Daniel started playing football at age five. His mom made sure he was at practice on time, and that he was always picked up afterwards, even if she couldn't get there herself. "I always had so much respect for my mom," Daniel said. "She worked so hard, and never complained about being a single mom. She never took my father to court for child support. We did struggle at times—I didn't have cool clothes, and sometimes kids would ask me why our phone wasn't on. Mom did everything she could to keep us out of bad environments. She didn't want us to grow up in the projects, and we didn't. She wanted us to live in a house, and we did. We lost that house, though, when I was in high school. That was tough, but we got through it.

"My mom would work extra hours to help me out. She was really tired. She used to ask me to massage her shoulders. I loved doing that for her. They were like bricks—like hard wood. She got really stressed working at the hospital—she would see kids coming in every day, shot and stabbed. This was really hard for her. She made sure I wasn't one of those kids on a stretcher. She was always so there for me. I respected her so much. If I stayed out late I would always call her and let her know where I was and what time I would be home. She trusted me, so she never gave me a curfew."

Early on, Daniel's outstanding athletic talent helped him choose a different path. "I saw kids selling drugs a lot," he recalled. "They had much nicer things than me, but I didn't care. I was patient, and never wanted to live that life. After a while, I was doing so well in sports they wouldn't let me near the stuff! They looked out for me, had respect for me—they thought I would do something with my life. They told me that they had already given up on theirs."

To Daniel, a police officer was far from a role model. "When I was around 12, I was walking home with my two cousins from the boys club, which was right down the street from my house. We had a basketball in our hands. The cops started pointing guns at us and asked us where our guns were. We didn't have any guns; we were having fun walking home from shooting baskets, and they treated us like criminals. It really shook me. Another time I was with my cousin, who is ten years older. His car broke down, and we were on the side of the road. We flagged down the cops for help. They thought we stole the car; they roughed us up, and pulled out their guns. I was traumatized. I ended up not liking cops for a very long time."

Without a father in his life, he looked for older men to fill the void. "There were a lot of things I didn't know, because I didn't have a male figure around," he said. His eighth grade football coach, Freddy Jones, taught him about "football, life, and how to be a man". Daniel has great affection for Freddy, and has stayed in close touch with him over the years.

Daniel didn't meet his father until he was 17, while still in high school. "At first it was shaky—we had our differences, and he apologized. It took 2-3 years to acclimate to each other. He was living in Chicago. He packed everything up and moved to Atlanta. He was around my whole senior year. This really shaped me. I had the father that I'd yearned for my whole life. He did everything he could to help fix my weaknesses to help me grow up and become a man.

"I was raised by my Aunt Lavette and Mom, who were always very gentle. I couldn't handle anyone yelling at me, and this made me hard to handle. Dad helped me get rid of my angry reaction to yelling. The military college I attended helped me out tremendously, too.

When Daniel was in Tampa Bay playing for the Buccaneers, his Aunt Lavette passed away. "I was devastated—she was my second mom—it really crushed me," he said. "My dad took the time to come to Tampa and spend a week with me because he knew how heartbroken I was. From that point forward he became one of my best friends."

Daniel's closest buddy in college was Rufus Leach. "I was fortunate because I had a scholarship," Daniel recalled. "Rufus had to work so hard to pay for his tuition his first year. I was happy when he got a scholarship the second year. He was such a good guy. He planned to build a community center when he graduated. He inspired me so much." Rufus drowned during the summer before their senior year. "I was heartbroken. He had so much inside; he was planning to devote his life to helping others."

Daniel gives Rufus credit for launching his NFL career. He dedicated his senior year in college to his friend, and was motivated to work harder than he ever had before. He pushed himself to perform at a higher level of excellence, which caught the attention of the New York Jets, who signed him as an undrafted free agent in 2001.

Daniel lost another friend when he was in college. "He was one of the most talented athletes I have ever met. People expected a lot from him. He couldn't take the pressure and took his life. This is so tragic. He was a great kid and very gifted. But he didn't have anyone showing him how to build a strong mind."

This tragic death taught Daniel that ability alone isn't enough. "I realized that we need to develop resilience and endurance. Life gives us test and trials. At first glance, we think we can't figure it out, but we always can. It's all about who we are on the inside, and how we address those tests. The trials will make you a better person. You need to stay self-motivated, especially when people say you can't do something and won't help you. You have to fight through those moments, because you will come out on top."

Daniel's strength of character and commitment to excellence has made him the outstanding athlete and remarkable man he is today. "I wanted to be a professional football player, and I understood it was much more than a game," he explained. During his nine years in the NFL, he worked from 6 a.m. to 6 p.m., and had daily homework in addition to watching film. "I have always pushed myself physically, mentally, emotionally. My work ethic is my blessing. It makes me competitive with myself. Competing with yourself pushes you harder and makes you go deeper inside. It helps you develop endurance and resilience and grow in different parts of your life all at once. It makes the sacrifices worth it." Daniel believes that honoring sacrifices is very empowering. It builds your confidence.

These days, it takes him nearly a week to recover from a Sunday game. "Every part of your body is in pain. But we don't take time off. You can never stay home sick. We come into work anyway and see the team doctor. You have to work hard even when you aren't feeling good," he emphasizes. "Some days I can barely walk and feel like I've been hit by a train. I push myself, and I'm always glad I did."

Daniel's passion for the game burns as brightly now as it did in his childhood, and he intends to stay involved in professional football "forever." Although currently a free agent and not playing for a team, he still works out every day, continuing to take great care of his body, mind and soul to prepare for his return to the NFL. Thinking ahead, he has set his sights on becoming a TV and radio analyst when the time comes for him to retire as a player.

Daniel has even learned to appreciate police officers. "It wasn't until I got to the NFL with the Ravens that I began to like cops. We had security guards that were retired cops and we had a lot of cops around too—and they are great."

What Daniel didn't get as a child is the very thing he is giving to kids. He has two beloved sons of his own named Tristan and Julian. He's determined to be the best daddy he can possibly be. He loves giving his son everything he yearned for in a dad when he was a kid.

Daniel launched his Baltimore-based foundation, Empowerment Minds, with his pastor, Jamal Harrison Bryant, because he wants kids to go where they have never been before. "I've been so many places and learned so much. I want every kid to have the same opportunity. It makes such a difference in a young person's life." He recalls the drug dealers his age he knew as a child: "Some kids think there is no hope for them, but there is always hope."

Daniel encourages kids to ask themselves, "Who do I want to be when I grow up? What kind of man or woman do I want to become?" Parents can start asking their children this question at about age four or five. "It's about more than what kind of job you want to do," he explained. "Every kid needs to find an adult role model that they want to be like when they grow up."

A lot of kids use "I am a victim of my environment" as an excuse, Daniel observes. He doesn't let them get away with that. "It doesn't matter where you come from, or who your parents are, or how you were raised, or what environment you're in—it's up to you to become the man or woman you want to be.

You can do just about anything in the world you want," he tells them over and over.

This "no excuses" attitude especially applies to education. "School is practice for real life. It trains you from an early age to become an adult." His challenge: "Go to school every day just like you'll go to work every day; go to school and work hard even when you aren't feeling good. [Of course, if it is serious you stay home.] Lay out your clothes the night before; get to school on time; after school, do your homework first than go out to play.

"Dress clean cut, not like a stud with dreadlocks, t-shirt hanging down to your knees and shorts hanging down to your ankles and hanging off your butt," Daniel advises. "When you dress like a stud, you subject yourself to unnecessary hassles from grownups and cops. This is the description of kids cops look out for. A lot of kids who are in trouble dress like this. The cops won't be able to see the difference between them and you."

Daniel understands how important it is for kids to maintain a certain image in the neighborhood. "Know you can be cool, but you have to be about business as well, and in control your life," he advises. "Be sensible, and you can still be cool with the people you need to be cool with."

Commitment is one of Daniel's biggest themes. "Your drive comes from your passion," he encourages kids. "You have it inside you! People will tell you to give up all the time. Some will scream in your face to quit; they'll tell you that you aren't good enough, fast enough, smart enough, talented enough or creative enough. Don't give up on yourself! You can be anything you want to be in this world. Become head over heels with what that is for you. Never, ever give up."

Daniel explained that this particular message is also essential for adults. "My path to the NFL took 19 years of preparation to become one of the best. I don't care how old you are, it is never too late to go for your dream. Start today. Start right now. Passion will help you tap into your powerful internal drive. You have it inside you; grab hold of it. It will actually put you on a higher road. You'll begin to feel pulled towards your goal, instead of like you're pushing against a huge mountain."

Daniel said that kids take the bad road because their world is so small. "When I was a kid, until football, I hardly got out of my neighborhood. I never saw a college campus until our high school football team visited one. These kids have hardly stepped off their street. We need to get them outside their city and out of their state; to help them see what's out there in the world. "

Daniel's opportunities to travel have expanded his life and helped him grow in ways he never thought he would. His NFL career with the Jets, Bucs and Ravens has taken him all over the world. He's been to Paris, the Berlin Wall and Tokyo, where he played in the Japan Bowl. "It's important for parents to take kids to college campuses," he continued. "Let them see how beautiful campuses are. Introduce them to the college life. Give them reasons to work hard and the encouragement that they can make it."

In addition to his Foundation, Daniel participates in other good causes, such as visiting troops in Afghanistan. He admitted that without his ability to tap into his strong desire and follow through, plus his previous travel experiences, he never would have had the courage to take that trip. "I got to see how they live during war," he related. "When I got off the plane at 2:00 a.m., the temperature was 105 degrees!"

Daniel treasures what, to some, might seem like a bizarre gift. "A soldier sent me home with a huge dead spider in a picture frame. It came into his tent in the middle of the night and he killed it." Why is this unusual memento so meaningful to Daniel? "When I was a kid, I could never even imagine this kind of experience. I would have been too afraid. It is so important for kids to venture out; it expands them so much. If I didn't go to military college, I may not have had enough respect for the soldiers or anyone that lives differently to want to take this trip and help out."

Daniel always tries to be a good role model. "We can take inspiration from a lot of people and things," he said. "What do you admire and respect about others? Anyone who is a great person in my life, I let them influence me; I take their goodness to heart and let that implement positive change in my life. It helps me become a better person. I am always looking for ways to grow."

"My wife Shauna and I are extremely blessed," he continued. "We both love life and respect what it gives us. The older you get, the more you appreciate being alive. It's all about how you can bring joy to someone else and how much joy and happiness you can have. I have grown so much from the good, the bad and the ugly. We get to extract wisdom from the mistakes we make, and when life hits us hard. There is always something good that comes from something bad." Daniel lives his generosity in many ways. Two or three times a year, for instance, he and Shauna go through their closets and give items away to Goodwill and to people they know who are in need. "When we help others," he said, "we get to experience the greatest form of happiness."

Daniel's faith is a large part of the man he is today. He believes in keeping God first and respecting the Bible. "Things are different today from when Jesus walked the earth," he explained. "Keep updating the words in the Bible to relate to you in this day in age. Make sure you have an intimate relationship with God, find the kingdom within. Use the Bible as a backdrop for your life. Keep asking yourself hard questions that drive you inward. What did the Bible mean then, and how does this pertain to my life today? Find your own special and very personal relationship with God. If you can't find the answers keep searching—you will find them. Put this in the center of your life."

Daniel has a special message for kids. "You are the people who are going to make this world better. You're going to take us adults into the rest of our lives. We believe in you, and we are counting on you. Your individual and personal role is very important."

Daniel also has some advice for grown-ups. First, "Be the best mothers and fathers you can be. Make it your very top priority—your children's lives depend on it." Second, "Think of your marriage as the most sacred thing in the world. When times are tough, dig deep and think of ways to grow together and fix the problems. Be a partner that is ten times better than you have ever been before."

Daniel's message touches people and rings true because he has lived it. His drive, values and commitment make him an extraordinary Insightful Player™ team member. He is an inspiring example of just how much one person can enrich the world when he gives it all he's got.

INSTANT REPLAY OF DANIEL'S *GUIDING PRINCIPLES*

1. Find an adult role model that you want to be like when you grow up.

2. Let go of any thoughts of being a victim—you can become anything in the world you want to be.

3. Push yourself to the limit so you can become the best you can be. Be willing to make sacrifices. Honoring the sacrifice is very empowering.

4. Send the right message to the world with your appearance.

5. Develop resilience and endurance. Talent isn't enough.

6. Ask for help—it is a sign of strength and wisdom, NOT weakness. Any successful person that ever lived didn't do it alone. Get support, and find mentors to help you.

7. Find something to be passionate about. Have an unswerving commitment, internal drive, focus and a specific and compelling goal that will catapult you out of bed every day, regardless of your situation. Whatever your goal, do everything you can to make that happen with all you've got!

CHAPTER 31

NFL FORMER PLAYER

BLAISE WINTER

Formidable Hardships Inspired His Mission to Strengthen the Core of Humankind

Blaise Winter was born to set the world on fire. His mission is to justify his birth and glorify his God. He deserves a lot of credit because he had a very tough beginning. If every man, woman, and child read his story they might collectively throw away their self-imposed shackles and actively pursue their dreams.

As a very young boy, Blaise underwent many painful surgeries to correct a cleft lip and palate, as well as surgeries to remove tumors from his ears that resulted in deafness in one ear.

He spent countless hours in speech therapy and was subjected to daily ridicule from unkind children and some cruel adults. His teachers told his parents he was mentally "slow," and went as far as placing him, mistakenly, in a class with intellectually disabled children. His high school coaches told him he had no athletic ability and refused to help him get into college.

Eventually, this child who faced so many challenges would be named MVP of Syracuse University—a school that didn't want him—and drafted into the NFL for a successful 13-year career playing for the Colts, Packers, and Chargers.

In addition to his physical challenges, Blaise's home life was heartbreaking. He said, "My father was abusive and beat the tar out of me emotionally and physically. When I was a kid, I used to think my life was a terrible mistake. In elementary school I planned out how to take my life not once, but twice. Each time I went up to my second floor bedroom and sat on the window ledge. I knew if I jumped out the window and landed a certain way it would kill me. Thank God I was never able to go through with it. I hated who I was but I was clever enough to fool people that I was a happy kid."

One of his favorite stories as a child was *Rudolph the Red-Nosed Reindeer*. Rudolph was a misfit and so were the toys on the Island of Misfits. Blaise could totally relate to the characters in the story. Being able to relate and seeing the story's outcome made a significant difference in helping him begin to believe in himself. Just as the story of Rudolph inspires him, hopefully Blaise's personal story can be a remarkable inspiration to others, young and old.

Blaise had two saving graces in his life: his mother and his great-grandmother. They had a powerful impact on his day-to-day life. His mother was an artist, a gifted poet, and Blaise was always struck by the way she looked at life. He recalls the amazing insights she shared with him on their numerous walks on the streets of New York City. Blaise was fascinated with her genuine ability to be equally awed by things such as the enormity of the skyscrapers, the perfect placement of trees around them, and even her genuine appreciation for the dirt around the trees. He said, "She would tell me moving stories that involved the best of people and the worst of people. She always told me that if I wrapped my arms around adversity I would be blessed. Like most kids, I fought that at first but when I look back on my childhood, I can see how that really gave me courage. My mother showed her unconditional love for me and her unending devotion through her actions."

Even though she taught Blaise to have a positive outlook on life, some of the lessons she taught him were dead wrong. She insisted he and his brother be quiet and not express emotions when his father was home. They never knew what would set him off. As he got older, Blaise hid all his negative emotions from his mother because she was so committed to him and his brother. He knew she deserved so much more. For his own survival, Blaise had to hide all of his emotions at home, and this escalated to hiding them from everyone. Bottling up his emotions created his own private torture and later led to bully behavior and rage. Blaise had to spend a significant amount of time learning how to express himself—a task he is now glad he undertook.

His great grandmother was the only person he had ever met who was a true angel. "I miss her more than I can say," he said. "She had such a beautiful, loving, kind and very gentle nature. She was so simple and so wise. I remember how she would gently put her hands on my chin and tilt it up and say, 'God loves you. '" Blaise's first reaction was to question if this could possibly be true. He would fight it and think, "God doesn't love me," but deep down he wanted desperately for it to be true. Eventually, he did believe it. He continues to be grateful to his great grandmother for that lesson. Through her kind and gentle ways, she taught him to believe in himself much more than anyone else ever has.

Long after Blaise left the house, he had a horrible altercation with his father. Blaise realized he would never be able to reason with his father and decided to stop seeing him. "From that situation, I learned that you don't have to destroy your future or your outlook because of one moment of anger in your present," he said.

Knowing he's not the only one to have a horrible home life, Blaise wants to put forth two crucial messages to other kids. He sums up these two messages as "Stop blaming yourself" and "If you are young and can't get out of your home, find an interest to pursue."

In Blaise's case, the latter message was resolved when he found football. It became his lifeline for developing self esteem and empowerment. Instead of wanting only to run from his father, he was motivated to add value to his life and find something to help him expand his perspective of what's possible. Getting involved with football gave Blaise his first experience of independence and ultimately a sense of freedom.

"When you find that interest that motivates you, develop it and really get involved," Blaise advises kids now. "Look under every rock until you find an activity you really enjoy. Let your emotions flow through your passion. There are many activities out there waiting just for you. You could become a runner or reader, play the flute, dance, sing, act, or do sports of any kind. Disengage yourself from the constant reminder you are living in a very difficult situation."

Blaise also urges kids to stay away from friends who bring new problems. "Misery love company. One of the worst things you can do is to hang out with bad influences or troublemakers. On the football field, no one talks about misery. We learn to focus, grow our skills, and build our self-esteem. Don't let troublemakers who think they have all the answers lure you in. Before you know it, you will be involved with the wrong crowd and participating in risky behavior, in a gang, or part of a hate group."

He points out that he found success by focusing on building a positive momentum with a healthy, fun activity rather than allowing his behavior to land him in prison. "Get around noteworthy human beings who are on a mission," he advises. "Surround yourself with honorable people who allow their passion to flow through something that they truly love and believe in. Find consistently good friends, friends who care about you and themselves in a healthy way. Reach out to noteworthy people of all ages, from every profession, and at those in ministry who care about kids."

Blaise likes to say that his formula for success can be represented by "five I's." "The first I is Influence," he explained. "Find influential people and attach yourself to them. Let them know you admire them. Surround yourself with noteworthy people who are in harmony with your conscience and your inner voice of hope. Take bold steps towards those people. I was lucky my mom was one of these special people. I remember her driving me to football practice. I asked her to pull over so I could throw up. I wanted her to take me home but she wouldn't. My mom told me I made a commitment and once I embraced it, I'd find myself and become much stronger than before."

Blaise discovered she was right. He let her influence him and is glad he did. Because of her strong convictions, Blaise became willing to take risks. In the process of exploring the football field, he found an interest that opened up his world. "Let down your guard and let these people influence you," he said. "Keep things exciting and explore with them. Being ambitious can feel really lonely. Let these influential people guide you through the process."

Blaise's second "I" is Interest. "You've got to have a passion for something that makes you feel like you belong." Blaise found that with football. He was grateful for the challenge and he found it stimulating. Blaise's interest continued to grow and this led him to crave more information to learn more. "Once you grab hold of an interest, you will be internally driven to learn and grow."

The third "I" is for Information. "Gather information about your interest and set specific learning goals," Blaise advises. He started to gather information in middle school when he had decided he wanted to be a professional football player. "The more information I gathered, the more my interest grew. Most of the people in my world, including my fellow players and even my coach, thought I was nuts to have a dream to play in the NFL."

People constantly told Blaise he wasn't strong enough, fast enough, or agile enough. Blaise is grateful he paid attention to his heart and not to all the naysayers. From that experience, he learned to trust his heart… always.

The fourth "I" is for Intention. "Most people have good intentions yet don't honor those intentions," Blaise said. "Become accountable to yourself and to someone else. It is imperative that you consistently feed the fire inside yourself by surrounding yourself with influential people who care about you, embracing your interest, following your passion and gathering information.

The fifth and final "I" of Blaise's theory stands for Interpretation. "Expand your perspective with every setback. You will find a lot of interruptions along the way," he said. "Don't allow any interruption to derail you. Instead, look for the blessings inside all interruptions. Take the time to interpret or understand a setback. Being able to do this will give you a leg up on 99.9% of the human population. Let setbacks teach you and let them expand your perspective so you go through life with a positive outlook."

Blaise used these Five I's on his journey to college at Syracuse University and into the NFL. Many of them were drilled into him by his mother and great-grandmother. If it wasn't for them, he wouldn't be here today. "I know how blessed I am for their amazing support and love," he acknowledged.

When Blaise was a senior in high school, he asked his coach to notify some colleges that he was interested in playing college football. He was stunned by the response he got. "Now is the time to start getting realistic," the coach said. "I can't help you with colleges because they won't have any interest in you. If I reach out to colleges on your behalf, I will look like a fool. I give you credit for trying as hard as you do but you don't have any talent."

Blaise was devastated. He had his heart set on playing college football and then playing in the NFL. "Thank God for my mother," he said, looking back on the experience. "She was really ticked off and reminded me that it isn't over until it is over. She said, 'Come on. Roll up your bags. I am taking you out of school and we are going to travel the country and find a college and football program that appreciates your talent and your character.'"

Blaise and his mother pounded on college door after college door, only to have them all slammed shut. When they traveled through Ohio, his mother took him to Canton to see the NFL Hall of Fame. "I was so inspired and realized I didn't have to be a superstar to make it into a Division I college," he said. "The visit to Canton changed everything."

Blaise took a bold step and went to Syracuse University. At first they didn't want him either. Eventually they recognized his tremendous passion for the game and gave him a resounding "Yes!"

At Syracuse, Blaise met the father he always wished he had, Coach George O'Leary. Coach O'Leary was everything Blaise needed and then some. He saw in Blaise what Blaise couldn't see in himself. "He fought for me, challenged me, and was always on my side. I owe an awful lot to George O'Leary and definitely attribute a lot of my success to him. I can't tell you how much I love that man."

There are other people who have had a tremendous influence and positive impact in Blaise's life. There is his uncle, Gaylord Ingham, a brilliant and well-rounded guy who loved sports; and Bobby Ross, a great coach at San Diego. Greg Bloche, a Packers head defensive coach, was also incredibly important in his life. "Greg Bloche convinced me that if I stopped beating myself up and worrying so much, my playing skills would explode. He also taught me the distinction between being overly desperate to succeed and having the desire to succeed. Once I stopped worrying and created a healthy desire to succeed, I began to really produce on the football field." To this day, Blaise lives by Coach Bloche's words and clearly understands that desire drives you while desperation destroys you.

"Personal development is important. If you make mistakes, don't be afraid to admit you were wrong, learn from the mistake, and then move on," he said. Blaise has worked hard on his personal development. He had to overcome being a bully and a guy with a bad temper. In doing so, he has set some standards that have really helped him along the way. They include becoming keenly aware of his own behavior and learning to evaluate it; admitting to himself and others when he is wrong; and apologizing sincerely for offenses.

This approach has helped Blaise to get back to fundamentals which always expands his perspective. He recognizes he is not perfect and also recognizes he has come a long way from who he was. Blaise knows who he wants to become and his life is all about being relentless in closing the gap from where he is now to where he ultimately wants to be at the end of his life. This has fueled the fire in his soul to be the best human being he can possibly be. In addition, this helps him obliterate guilt and take full responsibility for all his actions—the good, the bad, and the ugly. This process evokes self-forgiveness and continues to encourage him to be a great role model who has a rock solid character and he inspires the same in others.

Blaise feels he was placed on this earth to inspire and challenge people to ferociously grab hold of the champion within and courageously be all they can be… and then some. Blaise is a motivational speaker who is determined to strengthen the core of humankind by teaching people how to believe in themselves, obliterate obstacles, and become unstoppable in pursuit of their dreams. He believes the dreams we have in our hearts have been placed there by God and it is our responsibility to go after them with all our might.

Blaise is eternally grateful for his wife, Angie, and his two boys, Cordell and Donovan. His family is the very center of his universe. He credits Angie for inspiring him to be the best he can be. His love for her is beyond measure, as is his love for his two blessed boys.

Blaise is author of *A Reason to Believe,* an empowering book that gives readers a multitude of reasons to believe in themselves. Blaise's inspiring and content rich live programs are in big demand. He is a genuinely powerful speaker who has a deep rooted passion for his audience and naturally connects with them to elevate their spirits no matter what age, creed, race, or position they have in life. These qualities make him a cornerstone of the Insightful Player™ campaign.

INSTANT REPLAY OF BLAISE'S *GUIDING PRINCIPLES*

1. If you had a rough childhood, don't blame yourself. It's not your fault. We have to deal with the cards we're dealt. Look for an interest that motivates you and fuels your passion for life.

2. Surround yourself with good, honorable people. They will encourage all that is good in you and propel you to be the best you can be. Pay attention and you'll learn so much.

3. When you find an interest, gather all the information you can about it. Doing so will help you develop a growing passion for that interest.

4. You will have setbacks in life. Everyone does. Don't let the setbacks discourage you from pursuing your dream. Be patient, learn from setbacks, and "keep on keeping on."

5. Personal development is imperative. There will be times you make mistakes and have done something wrong. Evaluate your behavior, admit wrongs, learn from mistakes, and keep your eyes on your goals.

6. Dream big. Be willing to learn new things, take risks, and work hard to achieve what you want out of life. If you do this, you'll be successful and you will also inspire others to be the best they can be.

CHAPTER 32

THE CLEVELAND BROWNS'

USAMA YOUNG

PHOTO COURTESY *of Ben Gabbe*

His Radiant Spirit Lights up the World
On and Off the Field

Usama Young is an inspiring ball of energy who leaves a permanent imprint of hopefulness on everyone he meets. His upbeat attitude, genuine concern for others and his unswerving commitment to being the best man he can be will take him far in life—both on and off the field. This hardworking, kindhearted, generous, and bright young man has everything it takes to become an iconic role model for our youth.

In 2007, Usama was selected in the third round (66th overall) of the NFL draft and was signed to a three-year contract with the New Orleans Saints. Usama has been a steadfast asset on special teams since he joined the Saints. He is a quick-footed defensive back and a solid contributor on defense. In 2009, he made the transition from cornerback to safety. That same season, the Saints won Super Bowl XLIV.

In 2008, Usama was selected as one out of many applicants by voters on NFL.com as the winner of the League's "Super Ad" competition, in which players are invited to create and produce advertisements. His father, Leroi, appeared in the Super Bowl ad with him, and spotlighted a young Usama working as a concession vendor at Washington Redskins games. (Eddie Murphy's son Christian portrayed him as a boy.) Winning this competition was a tremendous accomplishment he will never forget, and an experience he and his father will both cherish forever.

Usama feels extremely blessed to be playing professional football for the New Orleans Saints. He attributes his success to his tremendous faith in God and his highly supportive family. God has been quite important to his parents and they always reminded him how blessed he is. His five older brothers always pushed him to work hard and accomplish his goals. Usama said, "I always looked up to my brothers big time and still do. They watched out for me and saved me from making some of the mistakes they made. Being the youngest of six boys had many advantages. My parents always reminded me how much my brothers loved me. Of course we had some fights, but we have been ferociously devoted to each other and always will be. I am very fortunate because my family always believed in me and that has helped me believe more in myself."

Usama recognizes that a lot of kids don't have the tremendous support he had growing up so he reaches out to them every chance he gets. He is on a mission to give every kid he meets as much love as he received from his parents and they take to him instantly because he treats them with respect. His charisma, upbeat attitude, and genuine care for them quickly earns their trust.

Usama is an empowering person who thrives on encouraging kids to believe in themselves. He wholeheartedly believes that every kid has special gifts and talents. He feels frustrated because he believes society has done a terrible job at helping kids recognize and foster their gifts. Because of this, he is devoted to being a champion for kids and especially those in need. He has a special gift of seeing the very best in others and has an unyielding passion to get kids to see it within themselves. Usama learned this from his family and knows how much difference it can make in a kid's life.

When he sees kids on the streets, he'll often ask them, "What's up?" If they tell Usama they are on their way to practice, work, or any activity, he gives them two thumbs up and encourages them to keep it up. If they tell him they are just chilling, he enrolls them into a lively discussion that gets them talking about their interests. If he sees them smoking cigarettes, he says, "Smoking isn't good for you. What positive outcome will come from smoking cigarettes?" He captivates their attention by getting them thinking about how they could spend their time in a more positive way. This always evokes a stimulating conversation that inevitably draws out their interests and desires. For some kids, it is the very first time they get to talk about what interests them most.

Usama loves to watch kids' faces light up when he challenges them to dive head first into their interests. The kids perk up when he reminds them to stay active, persevere, always do their best, and follow their heart. He learned from his parents early on that being idle is not an option because it is a surefire way to get into trouble. Usama is in perpetual motion, has a lot of energy to burn, and has an insatiable appetite to contribute to those in need.

Usama had a modest beginning, growing up in the Washington, DC area as the youngest of six boys with Muslim roots. His mom stayed at home taking care of the kids while his dad drove a taxi. They did have some struggles but were not poor. The most difficult time for Usama was when he was only four or five and his parents split up.

Usama's mom thought it was in the boys' best interest to live with their dad to ensure they would be raised as strong young men. Usama and his brothers lived with their dad during the school year and spent time with their mom during school vacations, holiday weekends, and summer breaks. Even though Usama's mom left the DC area and moved to Ohio to pursue her Ph.D., she remained a strong and loving presence in her children's life.

Usama initially thought it was his fault that his parents got divorced. Most kids in this type of situation feel exactly the same way. He wrestled with feelings of sadness and anger when he had to go back and forth between his parents' houses. Every time he left one of his parents, he was heartbroken to be leaving them. At first, Usama had a hard time understanding why his parents lived separately. His greatest wish at the time was that they would get back together. Usama said, "Every kid wants their parents to be together. It is so sad that most kids think it is their fault that their parents broke up." He wants kids to know it is never their fault, that it will work out in the long run, and that most often it is in the very best interest of everyone. He encourages kids to work through this and get support. Yes, it can be difficult, but their lives will be much more positive for it.

Usama is eternally grateful to both of his parents for maintaining a united front with child-raising and their dedication to teaching him core values. "My father insisted we stay active and made sure we got involved in sports. He kept us busy with house chores and yard work. In addition to sports, I became an avid reader and learned to draw. My mother reinforced keeping active and often said she didn't want to hear me say the "B" word—boredom. My tremendous work ethic came from my parents' encouragement to try new things, and their insistence that I put my heart and soul into every action I take. Every time I feel myself starting to slack off, I hear their voices in my head reminding me to stay dedicated to what it is I need to do."

Usama affectionately recalls how his parents did their very best to keep a smile on their kids' faces. Both his parents remarried, and his mom blessed Usama with a little sister who is eight years his junior. He adores his little sister so much that he couldn't get on the plane fast enough to visit her and his beloved mother for a few days during the Saints' bye week.

Usama's father became a Christian when he remarried. His mother continued her dedication to her Muslim faith, always reminding Usama to pray. His dad took him to church, but as a young teen Usama resisted. One of his brothers told him to listen to his father, so Usama started to pay attention at church. As things began to sink in, his appreciation for his blessings reached new heights.

Usama's faith is now at the center of his world. "God's greatness and blessings are all around us. He created us to strive to be better people. I always strive to be a better person and help everyone I can. God created us to help each other and to be like Him as much as possible even though it is tough to do. My faith in God guides me to be my best. My faith always lifts me up when I'm discouraged and need extra support. What's really cool is that in surrendering to God, I never feel alone in what I'm trying to accomplish in life. The night before every Saints game, I call my father and stepmother and we pray together. This is a ritual I look forward to every week."

When Usama hits bumps in the road, he relies on his faith. "It is easy to be happy when everything is good and everyone is on your side. As soon as things go wrong, we have a natural tendency to put our heads down and complain or even give up. This is when I am motivated to push myself farther and try even harder." He refuses to let life beat him down because he believes the tough times make him stronger and wiser. He looks at the bumps in the road as opportunities for growth that strengthen his character and make him resilient. He is amazed how this approach has expanded his perspective of what is possible.

The person Usama admires most is his dad. "I really listen to my father because he has never steered me wrong. He has always helped me and still does. My father has great qualities. He is attentive and funny. He always has a smile on his face. He stands up for what he believes and will put his foot down if he needs to. I have always respected him and he is such a loving guy."

While Usama was attending Kent State, he received a frightening phone call from his family. His father had been diagnosed with cancer was in intensive care fighting for his life. Usama dropped everything to be by his father's side. He was stunned when he saw his father with eyes shut and hooked up to so many tubes.

Usama was scheduled to play in a college all-star game, and not just any all-star game. This was part of the NFL's pre-draft process. Usama didn't want to play because he couldn't bear to leave his father's side. His family rallied around him and reminded him that his dad would want him to play in the game. With the inspiration from his family, Usama did play, and he played very well. This created an opportunity for him to get drafted later on. His father made a full recovery. For Usama, seeing his father so sick was surreal. It was unimaginable to see his healthy dad in that vulnerable position. This opened Usama's eyes and made him respect and appreciate his father even more.

Usama also highly admires his cousin, whom he loves very much. His cousin was tragically shot and is grateful now to be alive. In spite of being paralyzed from the waist down, he believes there is so much to smile and be happy about in life. This cousin taught Usama that you've got to be strong and build strong character, and this will give you the resilience to endure anything life brings you.

Even though Usama had to go through some tough times in his life, he had, and still has, a very positive upbeat attitude. Going through his parents' split when he was so young, dealing with his father's health, his concern for his cousin, and recovering from numerous sports injuries was frustrating, but Usama learned to work through that. He is grateful for how much these experiences have shaped him in a positive way.

Usama's beliefs are very much in line with the concept behind The Insightful Player™ series. "We should take advantage of the fact that professional athletes can really have a profound influence on kids. It is important we do everything we can to inspire kids," he said.

Usama has a deep-rooted passion to see kids involved with activities. "Surround yourself with people who are successful, who are doing the right things, and have similar goals and interests," he frequently states. From early on, Usama hung around with great kids who became successful and positive people. To this day these childhood friends are very important to Usama. They laugh together and talk about how far they've come and how they got there.

Usama loves reaching out to kids because he knows they need a good influence in their lives. They don't always listen to their parents or perhaps don't have parents who are good role models. Usama remembers how it was when he was young. If a professional athlete had ever talked to him, he would have listened, and if they had taken an interest in him, he would have been blown away. Every chance he gets, Usama hopes to help kids.

Usama's generosity is tremendous. The contributions he makes to others and the volunteer work he does is simply stunning. Not only are kids Usama's passion, but volunteering is something he loves as well. He has done a lot of clean-up work in the New Orleans area. He has worked with Habitat for Humanity and Rebuilding Together. He recently founded the Usama Young Youth Foundation (www.usamayoung28.com/youthfoundation.html), whose mission is to "mobilize youth to work to their potential through hands-on and interactive programming that aim to strengthen youth from single parent homes and underserved communities and youth with learning disabilities through tutoring, leadership development, mentoring and advocacy." This man is so busy it is no wonder that one of his favorite getaways is his cozy bed.

On his one day off each week, Usama makes sure he does something for the community. He talks to kids at schools quite often, since this is one of his biggest passions. He loves to use the blessings he has to bless others. Sometimes the cameras follow him with the other volunteers, but that is not the least bit important to him. Usama doesn't volunteer for the publicity—he does it from his passion and his belief that the greatest level of fulfillment we can experience is in helping others. He recommends, "If you are feeling down, go out and put a smile on someone else's face. Very quickly, you will feel better than ever and have blessed someone in the process."

Usama Young is an Insightful Player™ team member extraordinaire and an iconic role model for our youth.

INSTANT REPLAY OF USAMA'S *GUIDING PRINCIPLES*

1. Bad times will always bring something good, and things will always get better.

2. Say no to boredom by staying active.

3. Find your passion, give it your all, and make sure you have fun.

4. Don't let the bad things get you down. Find something to smile about, regardless of your situation.

5. You can accomplish any goal you have in your heart. Never ever listen to people who tell you that you can't. With commitment, training, and desire, any goal can be accomplished.

6. If you're feeling down, muster up the courage to keep going and put a smile on someone else's face.

7. Being positive is the only way to have a happy life. You can do this and you have it within you.

8. If everything goes wrong, keep in mind it could be much worse. You may have hit a bump in the road, but you are still breathing.

9. You've got to be strong in everything you do. Commit to building your character and you will be amazed at how strong and resilient you become.

10. Surround yourself with people who are doing great things with their lives.

ACKNOWLEDGMENTS

I want to thank God for giving me the desire to work with NFL players to bring many more role models to the forefront of our lives, especially for children. When I first received this insight, I thought of it as illogical and downright ridiculous. But as illogical as it seemed, the more that I ran away from it, the more miserable I became. I am grateful to God for His relentless pursuit to inspire me to take this desire full tilt. Once I surrendered to it, I was blessed with endless signs and attracted the perfect people within and outside of my circle to make Insightful Player™ a reality.

Additionally, I want to thank and acknowledge the following:

My brother, Jimmy Carew, for your tremendous encouragement and always telling me I was already there when I clearly wasn't.

My brother, Dennis Carew, for getting excited every time I added a new player to the roster.

Phyllis McEwen, my mother-in-law, for your enormous support, love, interest, enthusiasm and generosity.

My loving stepchildren, Patrick and Kelly, for your encouragement, interest and support.

My awesome cousins, Frankie and George Coman Lavery Jr. and Dottie MacAveeney, for your encouragement, love and cheerleading.

Marilyn Avakian, my lifelong friend whom I treasure—always there to cheer me along and make me laugh, especially when there was nothing to laugh about.

Dear and beautiful Laura Hess, who gave me endless support with every inch of this journey. You gave me a boatload of encouragement and practical advice, shared all your resources, showered me with love and even took on huge projects.

The late Margie Marsden Duggan for your cheerleading and consistent phone calls.

The late MaryAnn Murphy, my sounding board and confidant, rooting for me hardest before anything clicked.

Ingrid Joy Wolfson for your sound advice, endless encouragement and for celebrating with me every step of the way.

Cornelia Eschborn for your tremendous encouragement, care and support.

Rachel Goldberg for your tender loving care.

Kristin Lozen, my very dear friend.

Barbara Loughlin Yannizze, my very first and forever friend.

Philip Cohen for your constant support, cheerleading and enthusiasm.

Ted Gorski, Get Your Edge LLC, for your enthusiasm, love and tremendous support. Thank you for being such a magnificent role model in the coaching industry.

Dianne Legro, a brilliant coach who helped me strategize when my initial attempts to bring my coaching programs to NFL teams fell short. You gave me profound encouragement and introduced me to the concept of Insightful Player™ and played a significant role in its birth.

Hank Hryniewicz, sports editor of the *Boston Herald*: you shared so many pearls of wisdom, offering tremendous support, perfect advice and ongoing encouragement. You boosted my confidence and fueled my vision, and this led to profound insights that ended up shaping the entire Insightful Player™ campaign.

Nancy Shohet West for your tremendous assistance with the writing and editing of this book and countless editing projects along the way. I was astounded by your tremendous care and your fast turnaround of it all. You are a delight to work with and a top-shelf professional every inch of the way.

Tom Cosentino, my PR guru and President of iMedia Public Relations, for your endless dedication; valuable, constant support; encouragement, insights and generosity. Your magnificent coaching, your brilliant PR campaigns and tremendous belief in my vision enhanced my ability to laser focus and leap forward. I am forever grateful.

Daniella Cuomo, my assistant, for your dedication, patience, graciousness, long hours, and for giving it your all.

Bonnie Andross for your tremendous service and care. You are a very gifted transcriber.

Mark Beal of Taylor for your encouragement, generosity and profound inspiration to get the book completed immediately. Your words of encouragement carried me when I needed it the most.

Vinny Mallozzi of the *New York Times* for your encouragement, cheerleading and for your challenging yet empowering deadline to get my book proposal completed in three weeks. Your belief in Insightful Player™ fueled the book proposal process.

Patrick Hughes for your fabulous care and counsel. You provided me with the most empowering conversations I have ever had in my entire life.

Elizabeth Malia, Personal Assistant to James Brown. I was deeply touched by your uplifting emails and graciousness.

Hugh Mulligan, my computer expert and friend, for coming to my aid at the drop of a hat.

Mike Reiss, *ESPN Boston;* Lou D'Ermilio, Vice President of Communications Fox Sports; Tom King, Sports Writer, *Nashua Telegraph;* Dr. Ron Arndt; Madeleine Homan Blanchard; Patrick and Jill Williams; Jim Vuculo; Pamela Richarde; Sandy Vilas; Robert Alderman; Rachel Goldberg; Sue Cappiello; Rose Alice Hoerst; Jan Gilpin; Robert R. Deleault, Esq.; Diane Bonneau; Andrea Novakowski; Jennifer Anderson; Lynn Gorski; Lyn Allen; Helen Kosinski; Ginny Williams; Daryl Johnson; Karen Callahan; Peggy MacNeil; Jack Marcellus; Ace Cacchiotti; Marlon LeWinter; Anita Grisham; Mercedes Cotchery; Sheila Kelly; Ryan Bird; Ernest, Dawn and Lisa Owens; Marlene Perno; Jack Falvey; Jeff Peters; Stephen Walker; Nancy Gerber; Mitch Meyerson; Doug Gray and the crew at Staples, South Nashua, NH.

Roger Staubach for being the first member on the Insightful Player™ Team.

The Directors of Player Development for all 32 NFL teams.

The Directors of Public Relations for all 32 NFL teams, with an extra special thanks to Stacey James of the Patriots, Mike Corbo of the Bears, Jack Brennan of the Bengals, Neal Gulkis of the Browns, Ryan Robinson of the Jaguars, Jared Winley of the Jets and Artis Twyman of the Rams.

Jeff D'Alessio, Former Editor in Chief, *Sporting News,* for taking the time to read my fist story and for your tremendous feedback and encouragement.

My players' reps: Brittany Gilman, President and Founder BG Sports; Eddie Rhodman Jr., Destined For Success Management, LLC; Ryan C. Scarpa, Esq., Athlete Advocates; Frederick M. DeFinis, Gaslight Management Group LLC; Kristina Nicaj, Starworks; Danita King, PR Noir; Julie Whitney Phillippi, Whitney Communications; Jeremy Snyder, The Factory Agency; YA Teitelbaum, Sue Martin and Glenn Martin, Heath Evans Foundation; Robin M. Caldwell, The J Standard Media Group; Richard Westermayer, Iron Mountain Sports.

My wonderful Corporate Partners who are all contributing so much to our world: Dr. Patrick Williams, Founder, Coaching the Global Village; Stephanie and JD Piche, MingleMEdiaTV. com; Joan Herrmann, Producer, Host and Editor, "Change Your Attitude, Change Your Life" Radio Show and Magazine; Monica Davis, Founder and Editor, *Exceptional People* Magazine; Matt Allinson, Esq., Access Athletes, LLC; John Ballantine, Founder, Trusted Sports, LLC; Dr. Carolyn Breedlove, Ruth Massie and Anita Merina, National Education Association; Dr. Bill Chachkes, Managing Partner/Exec. Editor, *Football Reporters Online/The Pro Football Draft Report;* Media & Public Relations Coordinator -The Beyond Sports Network.

David Hancock, Morgan James Publishing, for your professionalism, flexibility, commitment and tremendous care.

Karla Swatek, Horrow Sports Ventures, for your gung ho spirit, your generosity, and your astounding dedication and encouragement.

Michael Ebeling, Literary Agent, Ebeling & Associates Literary Agency, for sharing your knowledge, your encouragement, and for inviting me to resubmit my proposal even though you graciously declined with round one. Your coaching has been invaluable.

CALL TO ACTION

Please join our bold movement of hope and help us inspire a new generation to overcome any obstacles in their way to achieving success in their lives.

By exposing these inspirational stories to as wide an audience as possible, especially our youth, we can evoke the very best within all of us to make this world a much better and more loving place.

Read these stories with your kids, who will learn that no matter what their circumstances, they are not alone; others have fought the same battles and won. Share them with family and friends. Give them as gifts. Begin discussion groups. But most of all, share them with every young person you know!

Each Insightful Player™ story shows solid evidence of the immense power of the human spirit. We all need to be reminded of this, especially kids and especially now!

Check our website, www.insightfulplayer.com, and our weekly broadcast, www.minglemediatv.com/insightfulplayertv.html, for new content about Insightful Players, including new interviews and opportunities to chat online with athletes, educators and a variety of top professionals in the sports industry.

An Invitation for Corporate & Community Partners

If you or your business or organization would like to get involved in helping Insightful Player™ develop regional, national and worldwide programs to enrich the lives of children, we would love to hear from you. Please feel free to share your "insights" with us by emailing us at programs@insightfulplayer.com.

205

ABOUT THE AUTHOR

CHRISSY CAREW is a Master Certified Personal and Business Coach. This prestigious credential puts her in the top one percent of professional coaches worldwide. She has been inducted into the inaugural Hall of Fame by the International Coach Federation/New England.

She coaches high-integrity professional football players to maximize performance on and off the field. She also works with trailblazers who have an indomitable will and are relentless in their pursuit of elevating the world to awe-inspiring heights. She inspires her clients to reach for the ultimate state of human fulfillment by wholeheartedly embracing their gifts and ferociously sharing them with others.

Insightful Player™ was inspired by Chrissy's role model and beloved late father, Walter R. Carew Sr. He was a dedicated high school coach (in several Halls of Fame as a Head Football and Baseball Coach and athlete). He used sports to help kids build strong character and learn valuable life skills.

Chrissy hosts a weekly Insightful Player™ TV show on minglemediatv.com.

PLAYER
TESTIMONIALS

Insightful Player™ *will make the world a better, more fun and safer place for all. It is so positive and will give kids and adults a lot of hope.* Insightful Player™ *reminds everyone that the right attitude can make us powerful beyond measure and limitless in what we can do in the world. I am thrilled and definitely honored to be an* Insightful Player™.
—Kyle Arrington, New England Patriots

Insightful Player™ *is fabulous and has a great message. We can all help each other out through this and do a great, great thing for our community and for our world. The NFL has such a large stage and it's a part of our culture. What better example for kids than people who have gone through these trials and tribulations that football and life inevitably bring. I am very honored and very happy to be a part of* Insightful Player™.
—Rocky Boiman, NFL Free Agent

Insightful Player™ *is wonderful. I want to thank you for presenting this opportunity to me. Every player should be given the opportunity to share what is truly in their heart. My message is a about love and hope for a brighter tomorrow. If I can touch one child this has been worth it and I thank you.* **—Jason Brown, Saint Louis Rams**

I love Insightful Player™ *and I love the concept. There needs to be more of it. If there is anything you need let me know. I would love to see it grow.* **—Danny Clark, New Orleans Saints**

Insightful Player™ *is great for everyone and everyone needs this. It is important for everybody in the world to see the environment that we grew up in, what we've overcome, how we did it and the benefits we received from facing adversity head on. This is where we got our strength from. The insights shared by each player are valuable. I hope this really inspires people, especially kids to follow their passion no matter what.* Insightful Player™ *is wonderful and I thank you.* **—Jerricho Cotchery, Pittsburgh Steelers**

Insightful Player™ *is a wonderful piece. I appreciate* Insightful Player™ *because it so positive!* Insightful Player™ *is taking a strong stand in showing the world all the positive things NFL players are doing.* **—Rashied Davis, Detroit Lions**

I think Insightful Player™ *is awesome! This will be huge for kids and adults.* **—James Dearth, NFL Free Agent**

Insightful Player™ *is what it's all about! The youth of today will acquire vital lessons from* Insightful Player™ *by learning about the true passion and creativity of the NFL's finest! The platform, that we as NFL players have, is one that I will continue to use for the betterment of the communities in need across the country!* **—Chris Draft, NFL Free Agent**

If the readers would emulate one aspect of each Insightful Player™ *message we could slowly but steadily change the world. Thank you for giving me the opportunity to be an* Insightful Player™. **—Heath Evans, NFL Free Agent**

Insightful Player™ *is an inspiring and informative outlet for everyone. Coach Carew is a vessel giving people the opportunity to engage and learn about players' true words and genuine feelings. I am more insightful about myself because of my conversation with Coach Carew.* Insightful Player™ *reminds people, to stay true to themselves and to fight the fight and make sure that the fight that they're fighting is what they believe in and is in alignment with their morals and ethics.* **—Antonio Garay, San Diego Chargers**

The premise of Insightful Player™ *is caring about others—doing more for others rather than focusing on yourself. This will help the world because everybody feeds off of positive things.* Insightful Player™ *will help people believe more in themselves and this will help change the world.* **—Jarvis Green, Houston Texans**

Insightful Player™ *is a valuable asset to young people and adults too. We all need to conduct ourselves as if there's somebody watching us at all times, because you never know how you might influence kids in a positive way or a negative way. It is great that* Insightful Player™ *is getting these positive stories out there.* **—Steve Grogan, NFL Former Player, New England Patriots**

Insightful Player™ *is awesome! People can see athletes in a different perspective other than that whole big dumb jock thing. We need to start seeing some good stuff about good people who are looking back because there is wisdom in their words. It's an honor to be an* Insightful Player™. **—Ken Harvey, Washington Redskins Hall of Famer**

Insightful Player™ *is very well done. We are on the same team and we have the same mission to create hope where there is none. It is tremendous to partner with* Insightful Player™ *for a common goal. Our partnership is fun and it is the right thing to do.* **—Aaron Kampman, Jacksonville Jaguars**

I appreciate the opportunity to be an Insightful Player™. *A project like this can touch millions! I can't think of anything with this level of uniqueness. I am excited about this and excited about you taking the initiative. My prayer is you stick to it, continue to work hard with it and let God bless it.* **—Reggie Kelly, Atlanta Falcons**

Insightful Player™ *is great! Talking to Coach Carew is motivating.* Insightful Player™ *humanizes the athlete and lets people get to know who we who we are. I am excited to be an* Insightful Player™. **—Devin McCourty, New England Patriots**

Insightful Player™ *will help the world because it will inspire people to realize that whatever they want to do isn't far away if they really focus. It gives people insight into what we have gone through to get where we are today. We are regular people who have gone through some of the same struggles as everyone else. I am excited to be an* Insightful Player™. **—Jason McCourty, Tennessee Titans**

Insightful Player™ *is great! Kids don't have role models and it is great* Insightful Player™ *offers this to them.* **—Karl Mecklenburg, NFL Former Player, Denver Broncos**

Love what Insightful Player™ *stands for, it's awesome! It goes hand in hand with what I really believe—to take the opportunity to use this platform to make a difference in a positive way. To get the voice of the everyday athlete out as well as the super star—that's what I love about* Insightful Player™. **—Billy Miller, NFL Free Agent**

Insightful Player™ *is awesome! What it is doing is critical to our country. We have to look at where we leave this country for our kids and grandkids. That's our responsibility. Something this positive is going to have a positive effect on young people.* **—Steve Nelson, NFL Former Player, New England Patriots**

We need more of what you are doing. You are the first I've ever heard of doing something like this. I have actually had my eyes open and you are the first trying to make a difference on this scale and level. This is incredible! I am overjoyed! **—Montell Owens, Jacksonville Jaguars**

We need role models and Insightful Player™ *is a great campaign! The messages we share will give the readers a sigh of relief because it will remind them they are not alone.* **—Kevin Reilly, NFL Former Player, Philadelphia Eagles**

Insightful Player™ *is a great program; I am very excited about it! Some athletes have a tremendous platform and we should take advantage of it to help others. I believe in your passion and everything you are doing, this will benefit young people. Thank you for allowing me to be included."* **—Tony Richardson, New York Jets**

Insightful Player™ *campaign is novel and a wonderful idea! People need and want to be inspired! Anybody who reads the stories can get some sort of insight into our lives and get some kind of inspiration. They can make themselves better by what we're saying and how you put it together—it can have a positive influence on the world. Professional athletes being able to inspire people is a great combination.* **—Gerome Sapp, NFL Former Player, Baltimore Ravens and Indianapolis Colts**

Insightful Player™ *is a great idea. Influencing others in a positive way and opening up people's minds to see things in a positive way is important.* **—Roger Staubach, Dallas Cowboys Hall of Fame Quarterback**

The Insightful Player™ *campaign is a wonderful tool. We all need to read things, we all need to hear about other people's stories to figure out what's wrong, how to get better or how to get out of a funk.* Insightful Player™ *will give you an ability to cling to someone's story, cling to some idea or cling to some thought that may trigger something and inspire you on to greatness. I cannot wait to see the total package of your project. Thanks for including me.* **—Andre Tippett, New England Patriots Hall of Fame Linebacker**

I believe Insightful Player™ *is laying a foundation of inspiration for many who don't have answers or thoughts on how to approach life and it's many twists and turns. My hope is that, through* Insightful Player™, *readers will be able to find their own truths and stand confident in them while also experiencing special growth within themselves. Thank you,* Insightful Player™. **—Ben Utecht, NFL Former Player, Indianapolis Colts and Cincinnati Bengals**

Insightful Player™ has an incredible vision and this vision is much, much needed. We need more leaders to stand up in the way that Insightful Player™ *has laid out a map for them to do so. I see tremendous potential in* Insightful Player™ *and I think it has a huge, huge, huge value in our culture. It provides a format for athletes to connect in a different way with young kids in such a hugely positive way. I love it!* **—Damian Vaughn, NFL Former Player, Cincinnati Bengals and Tampa Bay Buccaneers**

Insightful Player™ is really needed and it will have a positive impact on the world. The hope is that the impact of the first person who reads the article will spread to a second and third person and each person will become motivated to spread the message to somebody else. Insightful Player™ *will be successful because people will gravitate to it.* **—Benjamin Watson, Cleveland Browns**

Coach Carew is an amazing person. I definitely give Insightful Player™ *two thumbs up. I can't wait to start reading the stories you are writing. Thank you very much. I appreciate the opportunity to be an* Insightful Player™. **—Daniel Wilcox, NFL Former Player, Baltimore Ravens and Tampa Bay Buccaneers**

It is about time that someone takes a stand and highlights noteworthy NFL players and former players. Our kids need role models and Insightful Player™ *is a blessing.* **—Blaise Winter, NFL Former Player, Indianapolis Colts, Green Bay Packers and San Diego Chargers**

Insightful Player™ is major and just what the world needs. So many people overlook how much professional athletes contribute to our youth. It is important to do everything we can to inspire kids. I admire you for what you are doing. **—Usama Young, Cleveland Browns**

BUY A SHARE OF THE FUTURE IN YOUR COMMUNITY

These certificates make great holiday, graduation and birthday gifts that can be personalized with the recipient's name. The cost of one S.H.A.R.E. or one square foot is $54.17. The personalized certificate is suitable for framing and will state the number of shares purchased and the amount of each share, as well as the recipient's name. The home that you participate in "building" will last for many years and will continue to grow in value.

Here is a sample SHARE certificate:

HABITAT FOR HUMANITY

THIS CERTIFIES THAT
YOUR NAME HERE
HAS INVESTED IN A HOME FOR A DESERVING FAMILY

1985-2005
TWENTY YEARS OF BUILDING FUTURES IN OUR
COMMUNITY ONE HOME AT A TIME

1200 SQUARE FOOT HOUSE @ $65,000 = $54.17 PER SQUARE FOOT
This certificate represents a tax deductible donation. It has no cash value.

YES, I WOULD LIKE TO HELP!

I support the work that Habitat for Humanity does and I want to be part of the excitement! As a donor, I will receive periodic updates on your construction activities but, more importantly, I know my gift will help a family in our community realize the dream of homeownership. **I would like to SHARE in your efforts against substandard housing in my community!** *(Please print below)*

PLEASE SEND ME _____ SHARES at $54.17 EACH = $ $_____

In Honor Of: _____

Occasion: (Circle One)   HOLIDAY   BIRTHDAY   ANNIVERSARY

      OTHER: _____

Address of Recipient: _____

Gift From: _____ *Donor Address:* _____

Donor Email: _____

I AM ENCLOSING A CHECK FOR $ $_____ PAYABLE TO HABITAT FOR HUMANITY <u>OR</u> PLEASE CHARGE MY VISA OR MASTERCARD *(CIRCLE ONE)*

Card Number _____ Expiration Date: _____

Name as it appears on Credit Card _____ Charge Amount $ _____

Signature _____

Billing Address _____

Telephone # Day _____ Eve _____

PLEASE NOTE: Your contribution is tax-deductible to the fullest extent allowed by law.
Habitat for Humanity • P.O. Box 1443 • Newport News, VA 23601 • 757-596-5553
www.HelpHabitatforHumanity.org

Printed in the USA
CPSIA information can be obtained
at www.ICGtesting.com
JSHW052016140824
68134JS00027B/2501

9 781614 480549